F.W. Harvey
SOLDIER, POET

ANTHONY BODEN

For Mr Wood
With Best Wishes and
many thanks!
Anthony Boden
4 July 91

ALAN SUTTON
1988

For Eileen and Patrick

ALAN SUTTON PUBLISHING
BRUNSWICK ROAD · GLOUCESTER

First published 1988

Copyright © Text Anthony Boden 1988
Copyright © Extracts from F.W. Harvey's work,
Patrick Harvey 1988

All rights reserved. No part of this publication may be reproduced,
stored in a retrieval system, or transmitted in any form or by any
means, electronic, mechanical, photocopying or otherwise, without
prior permission of the publishers and copyright holder.

British Library Cataloguing in Publication Data

Boden, Anthony
F.W. Harvey : soldier, poet.
1.   Poetry in English. Harvey, F.W.
(Frederick William), 1888–1957
I.   Title
821'.912

ISBN 0–86299–553–1

Typesetting and origination by
Alan Sutton Publishing Limited
Printed in Great Britain

Contents

If We Return
(Rondeau)

If we return, will England be
Just England still to you and me?
The place where we must earn our bread?
We, who have walked among the dead,
And watched the smile of agony.
And seen the price of Liberty
Which we have taken carelessly
From other hands. Nay, we shall dread,
     If we return.

Dread lest we behold blood-guiltily
The things that men have died to free.
Oh, English fields shall blossom red
For all the blood that has been shed
By men whose guardians are we,
     If we return.

Introduction

Frederick William Harvey was born on 26 March 1888 at Murrell's End in the Gloucestershire village of Hartpury. He was one of that generation whose lives were caught up in the splintering experience of the First World War, who 'walked amongst the dead' but were spared only to see their dreams of lasting peace cast aside in a second conflict. Will Harvey viewed humour as an act of courage with which to overcome adversity, and he possessed both humour and courage in large measure. Although a solicitor by profession, he was a gifted poet by inclination, as well as a tough soldier, sportsman, broadcaster and good companion.

Soon after war broke out in 1914 Harvey joined the 5th Battalion of the Gloucestershire Regiment and was amongst the first volunteers to land in France early in 1915. As a corporal he was decorated for gallantry, but, soon after being commissioned as a lieutenant, he was captured and spent the rest of the war as a prisoner.

Much of Harvey's best-known work was written during the war, both in the trenches and later whilst he was in captivity. Some of these poems first appeared in the *5th Gloucester Gazette* and were published shortly afterwards by Sidgwick & Jackson in two collections of his verse: *A Gloucestershire Lad at Home and Abroad* (1916) and *Gloucestershire Friends: Poems from a German Prison Camp* (1917). It was whilst he was a prisoner of war that he wrote his most popular and enduring poem 'Ducks', which gave him his title for the third collection: *Ducks and Other Verses* (1919). 'Ducks' travelled the world, has been included in many

Introduction

anthologies and is still one of the poems most frequently requested on radio poetry programmes.

After the war Sidgwick & Jackson published two more collections of Harvey's verse: *Farewell* (1921) and his work of greatest maturity, *September* (1925). In addition, they published his only book of prose, *Comrades in Captivity* (1919), an account of his years in German prisoner-of-war camps. In 1926 Harvey was honoured by the inclusion of a volume of thirty-one of his poems in the prestigious Augustan Books series, and in that same year a further collection, *In Pillowell Woods*, was published by Frank H. Harris. This was a time in which Harvey's Gloucestershire idylls matched the nostalgic mood of people yearning for a return to the apparent quiet prosperity of pre-war days. The mood did not last. One by one the books went out of print.

Although Harvey's poems continued to appear in anthologies, as they still do, no new work was published until 1947 when Oliver & Boyd produced a selection in a five-shilling Saltire edition under the title: *Gloucestershire*. By then the public, barely recovered from the Second World War and living through one of the coldest winters in memory under conditions of extreme austerity, failed to listen to Harvey's song. His war had not been their war.

Now, seventy years after the ending of the Great War and with the benefit of a long perspective, there is renewed public awareness of the suffering of those many thousands of young men who crossed the Channel bravely to face unspeakable horrors and to fight and die in muddy holes. Equally, there is a revival of interest in that infinitely smaller number who earned the title 'War Poet' and through whose words we can relive the hopes, fears, doubts, sorrows, humour and courage of the many. Will Harvey was one of these, a contemporary of Thomas, Owen, Sassoon, Brooke, Graves, and of his dear friend Ivor Gurney.

. . . . .

On the 29 March 1980, a service of dedication was held in the south transept of Gloucester Cathedral at which Lieutenant-Colonel H.L.T. Radice of the Gloucestershire Regiment unveiled a tablet to the memory of Will Harvey; it bears the following inscription, which includes a quotation from the poet's own work, his 'F.W.H., a Portrait':

> Frederick William Harvey D.C.M.
> Soldier and Poet of Gloucestershire
> 1888–1957
> He loved the vision of this world and found it good

All the music chosen for the service was by Gloucestershire composers: Basil Harwood, Tony Hewitt-Jones, Sebastian Wesley, Hubert Parry, and Harvey's friend Herbert Howells. Harvey's poem 'Beauty', dedicated to Sir Edward Elgar, was read by another Gloucestershire friend and fellow poet, Leonard Clark. All this was exactly as Will Harvey would have wished it. His purpose in life had been to celebrate the glory of Gloucestershire and now, after many years of neglect, his county was returning his selfless salute.

Harvey's work was introduced to a new generation in a recent, inexpensive and welcome volume of poems, including many not previously published (*F.W. Harvey – Collected Poems 1912–1957*, D. McLean 1983). We can now discover afresh and by turns the lyrical beauty, sorrow, humour and wisdom in lines which so often fulfil A.E. Housman's maxim that poetry must be felt in the throat, in the solar plexus, or down the spine.

Will Harvey never forgot the comrades who marched with him to war; who fought, wept, laughed and prayed by his side. This centenary tribute to him must also be, at least in part, a tribute to all the men of the 5th Battalion of the Gloucestershire Regiment in the Great War, as well as to one who was their voice. He would have wanted it so.

MINSTERWORTH

26. 3. 1888

March winds bugled that morn
In ear of a babe unborn:
'Up, child! March!'
Lord, I have heeded Thy horn.

Song of Minsterworth

Air: 'The Vicar of Bray'

In olden, olden centuries
  On Gloucester's holy ground, sir,
The monks did pray and chant all day,
  And grow exceeding round, sir;
And here's the reason that they throve
  To praise their pleasant fortune,
'We keep our beasts' – thus quoth the priests,
  'In Minsterworth – that's Mortune!'*

*So this is the chorus we will sing,
  And this is the spot we'll drink to,
While blossom blows and Severn flows,
  And Earth has mugs to clink to.*

Oh! there in sleepy Summer sounds
  The drowsy drone of bees, sir,
And there in Winter paints the sun
  His patterns 'neath the trees, sir;
And there with merry song doth run
  A river full of fish, sir,
That Thursday sees upon the flood
  And Friday on the dish, sir.

*So this is the chorus we will sing,
  And this is the spot we'll drink to,
While blossom blows and Severn flows,
  And Earth has mugs to clink to.*

The jovial priests to dust are gone.
  We cannot hear their singing;
But still their merry chorus-song
  From newer lips runs ringing.
And we who drink the sunny air
  And see the blossoms drifting,
Will sit and sing the self-same thing
  Until the roof we're lifting.

*So this is the chorus we will sing,
  And this is the spot we'll drink to,
While blossom blows and Severn flows,
  And Earth has mugs to clink to.*

---

* The ancient name of the parish was Mortune – that is, the village in the mere; and the name was changed to Minsterworth early in the fourteenth century because it belonged to the Minster or Abbey of Gloucester, and was the Minster's 'Worth' or farm where the cattle were kept. – F.W.H.

I

The Redlands

A few miles to the west of the old city of Gloucester is a land of
water-meadows and orchards entwined in the green curls of the
River Severn. Clinging shyly to the northern bank of the river,
almost hidden from the view of motorists speeding by to Chepstow
and to Wales, is the village which to Will Harvey was 'the queen of
riverside places', the place where he spent his youth, his first and
most lasting love: Minsterworth.

Howard and Matilda Harvey had moved to Minsterworth in
1890 from the quiet village of Hartpury, a few miles to the north,
when their son Will was two years old. His earliest memory was of
seeing, as a tiny child, a hunt galloping over the Hartpury meadows: bright flashes in the sunlight, 'view halloos' and the raucous
yelping of the pack.

The Harveys were of yeoman stock. Both Will's father and
grandfather were farmers and the land which Howard Harvey
bought at Minsterworth was ideally suited to the traditional farm
so rarely seen today. There were pigs and poultry, dairy cattle,
orchards of pear, apple and plum, and crops in the cultivated fields.
But Howard Harvey introduced another enterprise; he bred the
great shire horses which in those days pulled the plough and the
haywain. The property had once been known as Parlour's Farm,
but now, befitting the red earth of Minsterworth, it was called The
Redlands.

The large Georgian farmhouse at The Redlands still stands, well
back from the main road and opposite what is now the Apple Tree
Inn. The massive brick-built barn is still there too, but the

The Redlands.

The duck-pond at The Redlands.

cattle-sheds, dairy and stables are silent. The solitary house is approached along a driveway bordered on one side by laurel bushes and on the other by a lawn, upon which the Harveys played croquet under the impassive gaze of a pair of stone lions. Behind the house was Will's own wonderland: the big garden where he could play alone whilst Matilda kept watch from the house. Will occupied that special place in his mother's heart reserved for a first-born son; extra-special as an earlier pregnancy had ended in a painful miscarriage.

To the little Will the lawn must have seemed like a prairie in which he could run and jump. But, better still, there was a small pond surrounded by trees where squirrels played; a square, rustic summer-house with a pointed roof; in the spring a crocus ring in the grass, dotted about with primroses. Beyond the garden was a paddock with a duck-pond for his delight. On either side of the paddock were fields with ancient names: Stony Barton and Barn Ground. Here Will grew to love the natural marvels of his surroundings through all the changing seasons. And nature rewarded him with a voice to tell of his love.

The Round Pool

When high flies the swallow
Fine weather will follow
And to this green hollow
    Will little boys come,

All heedless of mothers
And grim elder brothers,
Schoolmasters and others
    Who sit stern and glum,

To play round the water
With shout and shrill laughter
Till sunset and after,
    Forgetful of all;

While I never heeding
Time's growth and rank seeding,
Mouse-like do sit feeding
   On joys past recall,

And hark to a singing
Of hours fleetly winging
To nowhere, yet bringing
   For ever new joy,

When earth was a chalice
Of wonder, not malice,
And time but a palace
   Built for a boy.

Howard Harvey was a popular man. He worked the land with his brother Ernest and the two of them were familiar figures as horse-dealers in Gloucester, where they traded from an enclosure shaded by plane trees in the old cattle market. Howard was well known for his generosity and open, trusting nature; never short of friends who sought the warmth of his company, knowing that a visit to The Redlands would not end without a gift of vegetables, eggs or poultry. Tramps too knew that The Redlands was a 'good house' and left tell-tale chalk marks on the brick wall by the gate for the benefit of hungry fellow-travellers.

Will's father was attentive and kind in the care of his horses. Shortly after moving into The Redlands he bought a massive stallion which had been ill-treated and was, in consequence, of uncertain temperament and apt to kick out. One day, Matilda, looking out of the window, was alarmed to see that little Will was no longer in the garden where he had been playing. She rushed down to the pond, fearing what she might find and calling out 'Where's Willy?' Howard and the farm boys came rushing in to the garden. The child was not in the pond and so an anxious search began. At last, they found him in the stables. Will was standing with the new horse, embracing one of its hind legs and resting his

Howard Harvey (*c.* 1900).

head against the animal, which remained absolutely still and docile, gazing round in curiosity at the child.[1]

In the six years from 1890, Matilda Harvey gave birth to four more children: first Eric, then Gladys in 1892, Fitzroy (Roy) in 1893 and lastly, in 1896, Bernard. Will now shared his games as an elder brother, but never a 'grim' one. The Harvey children all inherited that most splendid quality of the Gloucestershire farmer: a sense of humour. Friends and cousins came often and The Redlands was filled with life and laughter.

As the five children grew together their energetic games developed in them the speed and co-ordination of hand, foot and eye from which good sportsmen are made. Will became an enthusiastic and effective cricketer, footballer and hockey player, much in demand by local village teams. Later, he went on to play cricket and hockey for the Gloucester City teams and ultimately cricket for Lydney. Will even invented a particularly fast and unpredictable form of cricket which was played at The Redlands. This hilarious game was later to be described by Will's friend and fellow Gloucestershire poet Leonard Clark: 'You played Harvey's cricket in a long, narrow court, no more than four feet wide, at the back of the house. There were no wickets but only a high wall behind you. The courtyard also had a roof which covered it for half its length. The ball was a hard one, something in size between a cricket and a fives ball. You hit this, or at least tried to hit it, with a shortened hockey stick. You were out if the ball hit the wall three times. Every visitor to that house who had any interest in cricket was pressed to play that version of the game, whatever the season of the year. It had a long list of distinguished casualties, including two cathedral organists (bumps on the head), four county batsmen (broken knuckles), and many of the local farmers (normally, black eyes). I begin to ache again when I think of my wild efforts at that savage game.'[2]

Howard and the farm boys taught Will to ride even before he could read, not letting him cut lessons short in spite of his complaints when his little legs were stiff and sore from sitting astride the broad spread of the big horses' backs. 'The cure for that', Howard would say, 'is to get right up again!' In time, Will was given a pony of his own and the world grew from the confines of garden and farmyard to the fascination of exploring the Severn meadows.

Opposite The Redlands, Watery Lane leads through orchards and fields to Minsterworth village and Corn Ham, a broad tract of open land held in a restless, uncertain crook of the river. This was a good place to ride, even if sometimes the Severn asserted its sovereignty and flooded the ground such that Will, quite unafraid, turned for home with the water rising to touch the pony's belly.

Eric, Roy and Bernard grew to be tall and good-looking, characteristics inherited from their mother. Will, however, remained short and was always, unjustifiably, ashamed of his appearance, later describing himself as: 'A thick-set, dark-haired, dreamy little man, uncouth to see'. In his features and olive skin was a hint of the Jewish blood inherited from Tillie's great-grandmother, Catherine Levi. Perhaps to compensate for his lack of height and handsome looks, Will determined to develop his physical power. He became a keen weight-lifter, delighting himself and others with displays of strength. The gardener at The Redlands, Joe Free-man, himself no lightweight, was astonished when young Will suddenly came up and lifted him bodily off the ground, a trick often repeated for the amusement of friends.[3] Mrs Harvey protested in vain that the effect of straining under such heavy weights would surely retard Will's growth. And only rarely did he ignore her advice.

Matilda Harvey, always 'Tillie' to her husband, was the insepar-able heart of Will's Minsterworth world. To him she was more than a much-loved mother, the symbol of constancy and reassurance. Her tall, stately beauty, sensitive mouth, russet eyes and quiet-spoken dignity dazzled his imagination. In his mind she held the authority and grace of a Roman patrician lady, whose guidance and comfort he sought to the end of her life.   Matilda, both home-loving and talented, ran The Redlands household with an ideal blend of domestic order and perceptive good taste. In this she was helped by a cook, washerwoman and live-in kitchen maid. Her unmarried sister, Kate Waters, also lived at The Redlands and shared in the chores as well as the privileges of so comfortable a home. Kate was a fine cook and extremely popular with Will, especially so when she made the delicious damson cheese which was his particular favourite.

Matilda Harvey (1902).

The Redlands

The table at The Redlands boasted the best from the farm. And from the river nearby came a yield of silver treasure harvested by moonlight in traditional Severn putcheons.[4] There is salmon-fishing by Minsterworth no longer, but men still wade out with lantern and net to catch the elusive local delicacy which Will loved to eat, fried with egg, for his breakfast: elvers!

> Up the Severn River from Lent to Eastertide
> Millions and millions of slithy elvers glide,
> Millions, billions of glassy bright
>   Little wormy fish,
>   Chewed-string fish,
>   Slithery dithery fish,
> In the dead of night.

Matilda's joy was to make a good home for her family. But more than that alone, she was a cultured though simple woman who loved the arts, whose most proud possession was her grand piano, which she played well, and who entertained herself and her guests with a pleasant singing voice. She was ambitious for her children and insisted that they should have the very best education the family's means would allow.

Will was to be brought up as a gentleman.

My Village

> I love old Minsterworth. I love the trees:
> And when I shut my eyes they are most clear,
> Those leafy homes of wren and red-breast dear,
> Those winter traceries so black and light.
> I love the tangled orchards blowing bright
> With clouds of apple blossom, and the red
> Ripe fruit that hangs a-shining in blue air
> Like rubies hanging in the orchard's hair.

F.W. *Harvey* SOLDIER, POET

I love old Minsterworth. I love the river
Where elver fishers bend with twinkling lights
And salmon catchers spend their fruitful nights.
I love the sleek brown skin, the mighty rush,
The angry head upreared, the splendid hush
When the Great Bore (grown breathless) 'ere he turns
Catches his wind; and nothing on the thick
Tide moves; and you can hear your watch's tick.

I love old Minsterworth. I love the men:
The fishers and the cider-makers and
All who laugh and labour on that land
With humour and long patience loved of God.
I love the harmless gossips all a-nod,
The children bird-like, and the women old
Like wrinkled crab-apples: and I will pray –
God save old Minsterworth, and such, for aye.

II

Day-Boys and Choristers

Standing only a few feet away from the river bank at Minsterworth is the Parish Church of St Peter, opened in 1870 and aptly-named in a place where once village fishermen gave part of their catch to an earlier church. The Severn, dissatisfied with this proxy tribute, had often washed over the graveyard, forced its unwelcome way under the doors and rippled up the nave to kiss the chancel steps. This watery intrusion was solved with Victorian thoroughness. The old church was demolished and its proud, decorated successor raised up by four feet and protected from the river by an earthen bank. Twenty years after its consecration the new village church became a regular place of worship for the Harvey family.

Will's attendance at St Peter's was no mere obedience to middle-class convention. The liturgy of the church, the familiar, insistent metre of the Psalms and the rich language of the Authorised Version of the Bible gave the child his first knowledge of the power of words.

In 1906 the Revd C.O. Bartlett was appointed vicar at Minsterworth. The families at The Vicarage and The Redlands enjoyed each others' company and the Bartletts' son, Nigel, who was the same age as Bernard, became a good friend of the Harvey boys. In his teenage years Nigel often visited the farm to play tennis or cricket with the brothers, or set off on walks over the Severn meadows with one or more of them, the Harvey family pet spaniel, Nelson, chasing on ahead.

Will was a committed and lifelong Christian and, in his youth, took an active part in the life of St Peter's Church, serving as both

Minsterworth Church.

churchwarden and choirmaster for a time. Later he would write: 'My love for certain men and women is the all-compelling personal argument for another life than this. Earth is too small.'

In one of the charming little poems for children which he wrote during the war, Will captures the wonder of a small boy from Minsterworth village going to church for the first time; in a subscript to the poem he tells us that it is 'a true tale':

Little Abel goes to Church

And this is what he heard
And saw at church:
Oh, a great yellow bird
Upon a perch –
Quite still upon a perch.

And then a man in white
Got up and walked to it,
And talked to it

Day-Boys and Choristers

For a long while (he said);
But the yellow bird
(Although it must have heard!)
Never turned its head,
Or did anything at all
But look straight at the wall!

School was not for Will Harvey until he was nine years old. Until then, his education was placed in the care of a governess, Miss Whitehead, the erudite daughter of a local vicar. She introduced Will to the world of literature, including the work of her favourite poets, Shelley and Browning amongst them. She was soon to discover that her young pupil not only shared her enthusiasm for verse, but that he had the ability to memorise lengthy poems with apparent ease. By the time Will was seven years old he could recite Shelley's 'To a Skylark' and the Twenty-third Psalm by heart. During the following year much more was committed to his memory, including Macauley's 'Lays of Ancient Rome' and, a particular favourite, Browning's 'The Pied Piper of Hamelin', that delightful children's story in verse of no less than three hundred and three lines.[1]

Miss Whitehead was not Will's only teacher at The Redlands. Tillie happily shared her musical talent with her first-born, patiently sitting by his side at the piano and guiding him along the uneven, stony road of scales, arpeggios and broken chords. Will was an eager pupil and became a competent pianist, but always complained that his fingers were only fit to hold a cricket bat and not quite long enough for the piano.

It was soon found that he had a good singing voice and so his first school was probably an automatic choice for Howard and Tillie. In 1897 they sent him as a day-boy to The King's School in Gloucester, which since the days of Henry VIII had provided choristers for the cathedral.

Early each morning Will set out on his pony from Minsterworth along the road into Gloucester. These were the days before motor cars and lorries spoilt the peaceful scene with noise and fumes, or even electric street lamps illuminated the way. His journey took him

The King's School ('The College'), Gloucester.

past Highnam Court, country home of the composer Hubert Parry, and across the river at Over Bridge. All the while he would see the city set in its valley, dominated by the magnificent tower of the Cathedral Church of St Peter and the Holy and Indivisible Trinity, an inescapable landmark and his daily goal. Riding down the gently sloping road, he would enter Gloucester by the Westgate Bridge and come into the city which breathed history from its Roman shape, its ancient buildings and evocative street names. Here King William ordered the Domesday Book to be compiled; Bishop Hooper was burned at the stake by Queen Mary's command; and Colonel Massey's Roundheads withstood a Royalist siege.

The King's School stood, as it still does, in the shadow of the cathedral. But unfortunately the education which it offered was a far cry from that of today's fine school. The headmaster was notorious for his drunkenness and the standard of discipline was abysmal. It seems that the Dean and Chapter of the cathedral at that time were interested in the school only as a source of choristers.

School began at 8.45 a.m., but was interrupted by morning service from 10.15 to 11.30. Before lunch there was music practice between 12 noon and 1 p.m. with lessons resuming at 2 p.m. Evensong was from 4 to 4.45 p.m.,[2] after which Will climbed back on his pony, patiently waiting in the schoolyard, to clop back to Minsterworth and tea.

Will settled into the rigorous routine of cathedral school life. He excelled at cricket and football, and even became a serious amateur weight-lifter for a while. In spite of the low standard of tuition, he was happy to claim in later years that he had, at The King's School, 'learned to love music and the Cathedral and to learn how to learn'.[3]

In the autumn term of 1900 a new boy, two years younger than himself, entered The King's School. Will barely noticed this boy with whom, eight years later, he would forge strong links of friendship. He was Ivor Gurney.

· · · · ·

In 1902 Howard and Tillie decided that Will should have a change of school. This may well have been because of the poor academic reputation of King's at that time or simply because his voice had broken. However, unlike Eric, Roy and Bernard who were all sent as boarders to Abingdon, for Will they selected Rossall School. Certainly the standards at Rossall were high, but there is another plausible reason for their choice. Will had begun to be troubled by a small glandular swelling in his neck and, at a time when tuberculosis was a pernicious scourge, they feared that their son had an infected gland. No treatment with drugs was available and, short of surgery, plenty of fresh sea air was a recommended treatment. Rossall School is situated on the breezy Lancashire coast close to Fleetwood. However, in addition to the suspicion of a developing medical problem, Will was beginning to display that characteristic sometimes found in the creative spirit; he was, they said, 'highly strung'.[4]

It can well be imagined that Will was reluctant to leave his beloved Gloucestershire and all his friends. On his first day at Rossall, Tillie took him up to Lancashire in a taxi. Arriving in Fleetwood early, mother and son walked together by the sea for a while, wrapped up against a chilly autumn day. Then, like so many before him and since, a rather anxious boy was kissed goodbye at his new school and left with his trunk and his thoughts.

The first flavour of Rossall life which Will had to taste was the initiation ceremony. The custom then was for newcomers to be made to stand on a table in the refectory during the evening meal and to give some sort of performance, probably of saucy verses, in front of the whole school gathered there. Perhaps this nervous lad was expected to dissolve into tears; but not so. Up climbed Will, amid jeering, laughter and the banging of table-tops. Quite un-deterred he began to speak in an unfaltering voice:

> Hamelin Town's in Brunswick,
> By famous Hanover city;
> The river Weser, deep and wide,
> Washes its wall on the southern side. . .

The noise stopped. Every boy in the room began to listen in amazed silence and admiration as, on and on, through hundreds of perfectly-remembered lines, Will recited Browning's 'Pied Piper of Hamelin', coming at length to the last of its fifteen stanzas:

> So, Willy, let me and you be wipers
> Of scores out with all men, especially pipers!
> And, whether they pipe us free from rats or from mice,
> If we've promised them aught, let us keep our promise!

The Chapel, Rossall School.

When Will sat down it was to cheers, respect and acceptance. In the following weeks and months the respect was consolidated as he went on to gain places in both the football and hockey First XIs.[5]

By the time Will was sixteen his voice had settled into a pleasant baritone and, although he did not consider himself a musician, he was persuaded to enter for the singing prize at Rossall. The scene in the crowded school chapel as Will made his way to the chancel steps past pupils and staff to sing his solo can well be imagined. He had chosen John Hatton's setting of Herrick's poem 'To Anthea', which had been recorded in 1904 by Sir Charles Santley. The pianist played the opening bar, but Will, suddenly gripped by nerves, missed his entry. Without hesitating the pianist repeated the introduction as though by design, stressing the prompt notes a little more forcefully, and this time all went well. Will sang from the heart:

> Bid me to live, and I will live
> Thy Protestant to be,
> Or bid me love, and I will give
> A loving heart to thee.

The singing prize was his.[6]

Will left Rossall School in 1905. Back at The Redlands the months passed by pleasantly, but by the time he reached his eighteenth birthday in the following year he still had no clear idea of what he should do to earn a living. He had begun to express his love for Gloucestershire in verse and most probably cherished a wish even then to become a poet. But Tillie, ever practical, wanted a firmly-based profession for her eldest son.

Taking the initiative as always, she hauled Will off to a phrenologist. Will sat in puzzled silence whilst fingers probed the mysteries of his cranial 'bumps'. After a while, the examination concluded, the phrenologist pronounced that Will would be suited to the musical or legal profession.[7] That was good enough for Tillie: a lawyer he would be!

III

Dreams

On 21 July 1906, Will embarked upon the study of laws common, civil and criminal, articled to Mr Frank Treasure, a Gloucester solicitor. Treasure's office was then, as it is now, situated in St John's Lane, a narrow byway forming the hypotenuse to the right angle of Northgate and Westgate.

Along these two Roman streets, and their sisters Southgate and Eastgate, folk from the Gloucestershire countryside came to trade in the city with produce from the fields, fish and elvers from the Severn, sheep and wool from the Cotswolds, cattle from the meadows, timber and coal from the Forest of Dean, and heavy horses from Minsterworth. Hard by in Gloucester's ancient docks tall-masted ships unloaded cargo from far away and sailed out again laden with wool and flour. The market, the streets and the inns were filled with men and women in whose faces was recorded a proud and ancient rural English heritage.

These sights, sounds and smells were in sharp and tantalising contrast to the shaded precision of a solicitor's desk. Lifting his eyes from dry documents, Will could gaze out of the windows at the back of Treasure's office and see, almost close enough to touch, the beckoning tower of Gloucester Cathedral.

Try as he might, Will could not prevent daydreams of Cotswold ways and Severn meadows from leading his mind away from the essentials of tort, contract and conveyance. Time and again he would wander out of the office to find a quiet place by the river, in the woodlands or on the hilly slopes around the city to sit and study nature's stirrings and harmony.

One day, in 1908, Will had boarded a tram in Gloucester when a young man whose face was vaguely familiar came and sat beside him. A few words quickly established that both had attended King's School, although in different classes. The young man was Ivor Gurney, now an articled pupil of Dr Brewer, the cathedral organist.[1] The conversation of the two turned to music and poetry; and so began a lifelong friendship.

Sometimes, if Ivor Gurney could get away from the cathedral, the two friends would go off together, sharing their discoveries and talking endlessly of music and books. A favourite place was Chosen Hill, close enough to the city to be reached easily, but far enough away to be blissfully tranquil. From the top of the little hill the view stretches away across the Severn Vale to the Malverns, the Cotswolds and Bredon; there are traces of an encampment from which the Romans kept watch over Gloucester, and a little church marks a place of worship older than Christianity. Will and Ivor felt themselves to be possessed by Gloucestershire. For them the life-giving air carried the essential balm of Gloucestershire's earth.

Whenever possible the pair would escape together to the welcoming farm at Minsterworth to help in the fields, to walk in the Severn meadows, to pick fruit in the orchard, to play 'ping-pong' on the long dining-room table or cricket with Will's brothers and friends, to set off with guns to bag rabbits for the pot, to make music, and always to talk. They bought a little boat, the *Dorothy*, and found in her the strenuous pleasure of sailing wide stretches of the Severn to favourite riverside places: Framilode and Bollopool. In later, less innocent years, both men celebrated the *Dorothy* in verse. Here is Will Harvey's poem:

Ballade of River Sailing

The *Dorothy* was very small: a boat
  Scarce any bigger than the sort one rows
With oars! We got her for a five-pound note
  At second-hand. Yet when the river flows

Dreams

Strong to the sea, and the wind lightly blows,
    Then see her dancing on the tide, and you'll
Swear she's the prettiest little craft that goes
    Up-stream from Framilode to Bollopool.

Bare-footed, push her from the bank afloat,
    (The soft warm mud comes squelching through
        your toes!)
Scramble aboard: then find an antidote
    For every care a jaded spirit knows:
    While round the boat the broken water crows
With laughter, casting pretty ridicule
    On human life and all its little woes,
Up-stream from Framilode to Bollopool.

How shall I tell you what the sunset wrote
    Upon the outspread waters – gold and rose:
Or how the white sail of our little boat
    Looks on a summer sky? The hills enclose
    With blue solemnity: each white scar shows
Clear on the quarried Cotteswolds high and cool.
    And high and cool a fevered spirit grows
Up-stream from Framilode to Bollopool.

Envoi

Prince, you have horses; motors, I suppose,
    As well! At finding pleasure you're no fool.
But have you got a little boat that blows
    Up-stream from Framilode to Bollopool?

. . . . .

The City of Gloucester is more than the commercial focus of a largely agricultural community. For over two and a half centuries it

---

23

has played host in every third year, alternating with Hereford and Worcester, to the annual celebration of music known throughout the world as the Three Choirs Festival. The music is centred around the cathedrals of the three cities and the programme each year includes one or more large-scale choral works. Whilst a boy at King's School, Will Harvey would undoubtedly have attended some of these concerts and become familiar with oratorios such as Handel's *Messiah*, Mendelssohn's *Elijah* and the great choral works of J.S. Bach. However, in those days a number of less worthy pieces were also performed and a glance at the programmes of the time shows that the festival was treading a rather unadventurous path. Then, in 1900, a new work was heard in Birmingham which was destined to blow open the long-closed windows of English choral tradition.

Edward Elgar, a devout Roman Catholic and pillar of the Three Choirs Festival, composed his oratorio *The Dream of Gerontius* in exultant mood. He knew the worth of his creation and inscribed the finished score in quotation from Ruskin: 'This is the best of me . . . this, if anything of mine, is worth your memory'. Cardinal Newman had written his visionary poem, set by Elgar, in 1865 in response to emotions felt at the death of a dear friend. His words and Elgar's magisterial music combine in a devout expression of Catholic Christianity: an affirmation of unshakeable faith.

The only difficulty for the Establishment was that this faith was not that of right-thinking Protestants. No matter how God-given was Elgar's inspiration, his masterpiece was at first deemed unsuitable for performances in Anglican cathedrals. Even Sir Charles Villiers Stanford, the respected composer and professor of music, is said to have told Elgar: 'My boy, it stinks of incense'.

It has to be remembered that the Church of England had, in the previous seventy years, been buffetted by the arguments which had surrounded the Oxford Movement: the activities of that group of clergy which had exerted pressure for the Church to move towards Anglo-Catholicity. Add to this the fact that John Henry Newman had been a pivotal figure in the group; that he had taken his beliefs to their ultimate conclusion and become a convert to Roman Catholicism; that he had risen in the hierarchy of the Church of

Rome to become Cardinal Primate of England, and a hostile reaction from the Anglican Church was hardly surprising.

None the less, if the doors of Gloucester Cathedral were to be, for the time being, closed against Elgar's finest work, the members of Gloucester Choral Society would sing it in any case. In the Shire Hall, on the evening of 3 December 1906, *The Dream of Gerontius* was performed in Gloucester for the first time. Gervase Elwes, the original Gerontius and himself a staunch Catholic, sang the name part; Percy Underwood sang the parts of The Priest and The Angel of the Agony; the name of the contralto soloist is lost. Eighteen-year-old Will Harvey was in the audience. The impact of the work upon him was immediate, lasting, and in his own words, 'white hot'.

Writing to his great friend Jaeger, Elgar had said that he imagined Gerontius a sinner, a worldly man, and so he did not fill 'his part with Church tunes and rubbish but a good, healthy full-blooded romantic, remembered worldliness'.[2] This vision of death and the journey of the soul after death exactly matched Will's instinctive beliefs and hopes: that it was perfectly reasonable and proper to enjoy life to the full in this world, and yet not be denied atonement and the chance to see God 'in the truth of everlasting day'.[3]

The first flagstone of the path which would eventually lead Will Harvey to Rome had been cemented into place.

. . . . .

Credit for the first Gloucester performance of *The Dream of Gerontius* must go to the conductor of the Gloucester Choral Society and founder of the Gloucestershire Orchestral Society, the largest amateur orchestra in the country, Dr Herbert Brewer, also the cathedral organist and Ivor Gurney's teacher. In 1907 another pupil came to Dr Brewer, a young man from Lydney, a small town in the Forest of Dean. His name was Herbert Howells.

Howells' father was a tradesman whose business had failed, but Herbert's musical talent had already been noticed and he was fortunate enough to attract the patronage of the wealthy Bathurst family who funded his private lessons with Dr Brewer. Later Howells became an articled pupil alongside Ivor Gurney.[4]

Howells and Gurney were very contrasting characters: Howells short, good-looking, carefully dressed and precise in manner; Gurney bespectacled, often untidy, disorganised and fun-loving. Even so, they had much in common: an ambition to achieve something worthwhile in music and to find fame, an appreciation of poetry and, not least, a deep love for Gloucestershire. Their lasting friendship was assured and, when Gurney introduced Howells to Harvey, three like minds met in harmony. A triumvirate of remarkable creativity was born.

In the following years the three friends developed artistically together and Will continued to strive with the law. Through professional contacts in Gloucester he met another lifelong friend: the solicitor John (Jack) Haines, himself a published poet and friend of poets. Ivor Gurney and Will Harvey were regular callers at Haines' office in King Street[5] and one can imagine that very little of the conversation was concerned with legal matters.

Haines was a fine hockey player, eventual chairman of the Gloucester City Club and a member of the England Hockey Selection Committee. Will played regularly for the Gloucester City Thursday XI and therefore his contacts with Haines – business, literary and sporting – were frequent. In addition, he was often invited to visit the Haines' family home: 'Midhurst' in Green Lane, Hucclecote, just outside Gloucester.[6]

It is remarkable that four young men of like-mind, like-age and inspirationally supportive of each other should come together in the same place and at the same time as if so pre-ordained.

Equally firm in friendship and in support of Will's poetry was William (Pat) Kerr, civil servant and published poet: a literary talker, and writer of style and wit, who was to become leader-writer for the *Yorkshire Post* and literary critic of the *Gloucester Journal*. Kerr held strong Catholic beliefs and undoubtedly influenced Will in the direction which his spiritual path was to take.

At about this time Will wrote in his notebook: 'Only a muscular Catholicism can save England'.

IV

Renaissance

On the morning of 26 March 1909, The Redlands was a scene of bustling activity. Tillie supervised the preparation of a huge picnic; Howard and the farm-hands groomed one of the shire horses and made the haywain ready for passengers; and all the household looked forward with excitement to a very special outing. When all was ready, the horse, with head-brass gleaming, harnessed between the shafts, and picnic baskets, stone jars of cider and ginger-beer fetched outside, everyone – family and servants – climbed into the cart. Howard took the reins and off they set for May Hill to celebrate Will's twenty-first birthday.[1]

May Hill is a popular beauty spot which floats high over the Severn Vale, wearing a small coronet of trees on its broad forehead, unmistakable from any point in the valley. From atop May Hill, the silver arm of the Severn can be seen in all its meandering length, passing narrowly by up-river villages, wearing jewelled bracelets at Tewkesbury and Gloucester, spreading into tidal flats, and reaching out its wide palm to the Bristol Channel.

It is easy to imagine the enjoyment and simple pleasure of that fine, but cool, spring day in 1909 when Will came of age surrounded by a loving family and friends. It was to be the last of the rare occasions when Howard Harvey could relax away from the farm with his wife and children.

Howard's life was one of hard, unremitting work: out in the fields from early morning until darkness in all seasons tending horses, cattle and crops, or driving his team in the cold and wet to customers as far away as Birmingham. Inevitably this exertion took a toll on his health and he suffered greatly from phlebitis in his legs. Perhaps even at Will's birthday picnic he had been in pain, but none present could have guessed just how fragile was his grip on life. On 5 December 1909, at the age of 56, Howard Harvey died.

At about this time Will began to write down some of his thoughts in a notebook, along with quotations from books which he had read and random lines of verse which came into his head. Later, pages from the notebook which he wished to keep would be pasted into his scrapbook, and this scrapbook has come to rest in the County Records Office, Gloucester.

After his father's death Will wrote:

Dec. 5th 1909 Father died (Burial on Dec. 9th)
Dec. 14th 1909 Nothing is so hopelessly, awfully, wearying as grief. Now I understand how the disciples were 'sleeping for sorrow'.

Will realised just how very much he had owed to his father and came to regret that he had never thanked him for his love, the comfort of his home or for all the money spent on his education – money earned at such cost to his father's health. As he grew older Will would say: 'I never properly knew my father'.[2]

The Horses

My father bred great horses,
　　Chestnut, grey, and brown.
They grazed about the meadows,
　　And trampled into town.

They left the homely meadows
　　And trampled far away,
The great shining horses,
　　Chestnut, and brown, and grey.

Renaissance

Gone are the horses
  That my father bred.
And who knows whither? . . .
  Or whether starved or fed? . . .
Gone are the horses,
  And my father's dead.

Friends who had been regular callers at The Redlands during Howard's lifetime, and whom he had never sent home empty-handed, now began to fall away one by one.

Will, entering the fourth year of his law studies and anxious about his progress, found himself of age, the eldest brother and *in loco parentis*. To a young dreamer, often haunted by self-doubt, the sudden responsibility was awesome and perhaps a little frightening. Younger brothers and sisters would look to him to take the lead and, although he had friends to encourage him, the closest of these, Ivor Gurney, was himself plagued by fits of depression and uncertainty. Fortunately for Will, he had by his side one whose strength of character and resilience made up for any weaknesses in those around her. Inevitably, Will's attachment to his mother, always strong, became indissoluble.

Tillie must have known very well that Will was deeply unhappy, not only because of the loss of his father but also because he, a free spirit at heart, was feeling caged-in by the life she had chosen for him. He was unable to cope with routine, seeing no purpose in conformity for the sake of advancing the cause of a materialism which he despised. Throughout his life this was his personal battle, bravely admitted in verse.

Unstable

A hill in steadfast loveliness
Wears the morning's misty dress,
Puts on the sunlight's golden crown,

Dons a starry or purple gown;
But keeps against all weather-fate
Its own form inviolate;
And such is the happy destiny
Of some men. But alas for me,
I would be steadfast as the hill,
But am as water running still
The path it must. I would be frozen
In ecstasy of some shape chosen –
Whether of joy, whether of pain,
Matters little. I would remain
Finely myself, but consecrate
To beauty be it love or hate.

But when by any known device
Was water fixed unless in ice?
I dimple into good. I eddy
Back into evil, bravely ready
To change again, reflecting ever
My mood: but my desire, never.
O sooner shall the honey bees
Forsake Spring-blossom, than I freeze,
And sooner shall a playing fountain
Turn to rock, than I to mountain.

On 4 April 1910, Will wrote in his notebook: 'For some time it has been born in upon me that I am not yet *Awake!* – that somewhere down beneath this garment of flesh is the *Real me* – with the *Real Eyes*. Is it possible that I may one day wake and "see things as they are"? or can *Death* alone awake the soul now walking in its sleep?'

Maybe Tillie simply felt that he needed a holiday or perhaps she thought that a few weeks far away from both Treasure's office and the 'distractions' of Ivor Gurney and Gloucestershire would refresh his spirit and give him renewed vigour for study. Whatever the reason, in 1910 she sent Will and Eric off on a European tour,

The Harvey family at The Redlands, 1910. Standing: Roy, Eric,
Gladys & Bernard. Seated: Kate Waters, Georgina Harvey (cousin),
Tillie and Will.

travelling through Switzerland and northern Italy, with Florence as
their destination.

By this time Eric, feeling a strong sense of vocation, was already
determined to work towards ordination in the Church of England.
Will, on the other hand, committed Christian though he was, knew
that for him attendance at Minsterworth Parish Church was
becoming little more than habit.

He well understood that the wonders of nature which so inspired
him were dependent upon a God-given, eternal discipline. In the
sphere of human creativity he had greatly admired the ancient
Romans since his childhood, and he realised that their achievements, fused permanently into Western civilisation, could not have
been accomplished without the imposition of discipline on others
and, particularly, of self-discipline, sometimes harsh. Will was
beginning to sense that he too must impose a discipline upon

himself if he was to hope for success in his application to studies or in his literary ambitions. But the key to the secret of self-control and fulfilment which was offered by the Anglican Church somehow, for Will, refused to fit the lock.

In this mood Will set off with Eric for the continent; a mood captured in one poem, the genesis of which came to him on the southward train journey.[3]

Gloucestershire from the Train

The golden fields wheel round –
  Their spokes, green hedges;
And at the galloping sound
  Of the train, from watery sedges
    Arise familiar birds.

Pools brown, and blue, and green,
  Criss-crossed with shadows,
Flash by, and in between
  Gloucestershire meadows
    Lie speckled red with herds.

A little flying farm,
  With humped grey back
Against the rays that warm
  To gold a last-year stack,
    Like a friendly cat appears;

And so through gloom and gleam
  Continues dwindling,
While in my heart a dream
  Of home awakes to kindling
    Fire, and falling tears.

. . . . .

What were Will's impressions of Florence? Here, above all others, was the place which proclaimed that feeling of hope and confidence heralded by the birth of the Italian Renaissance. Here in the first decades of the fifteenth century individual men had drawn aside the dark, Gothic veil of the Middle Ages to discover a new way of living, in which the human personality showed its versatility by expression in many forms: advancement of the mind, perfection of the body, cultivation of the social graces and appreciation of creativity in the arts. Surely Will was able to relate to these men who, having cast off the medieval yoke of confining rules and prohibitions, found freedom to enjoy beauty and to savour the opportunities of this world. Like him, the artists of the Renaissance found inspiration in antiquity and their works reflected a renewed interest in classical mythology and in the beauties of the human body. He would have seen around him the results of their increased interest in secular subjects, but also he would have known that Renaissance artists still looked to the Church as their greatest single patron. At every turn was a masterpiece created in response not only to patronage but also to divine inspiration – that very inspiration which he so ardently desired.

In Florence, art and liturgy combined in a unifying act of worship, and it seems probable that the experience of both fired Will's imagination, beckoning him further towards a new faith and firmness of purpose.

That I may be Taught the Gesture of Heaven

God of the steadfast line,
Who laid the curving Cotswolds on the sky:
God of the hills,
And of the lonely hollows in the hills,
And of the cloudy nipples of the mountains:
Teach me thy passionate austerity!
God of elm twigs

And of all winter trees
Etched ebony on sunset, or bright silver
  Upon hard morning heavens;
  Cunning shaper of ferns,
And ferns which whitely gleam on frosty windows
  And snow-flakes:
God of the naked body beautifully snatched
To some swift-gestured loveliness of Heaven:
  Master
  Of stars,
And all beneath most passionately curbed
In Form: catch up my sprawling soul and fix it
  In gesture of its lost divinity!

On 17 December 1910, Will wrote in his notebook:[4]

There is no halfway mark for me. It is one thing or the
other. I have done strange sins because they seemed lovely to
me. But I swear I would be as bold the other way could I
see the beauty of being so (– – – or must a man sometimes
live by rule? – shutting his eyes?)
    Could I but once fully realise the Beauty of Christ! No
Man was ever turned from his desires by the dread of Hell.
    The utmost effect of that is to turn out respectable cowards.
    I am not a coward.
    The reward of the Christian is to be Christlike.

The year 1911 brought cruel disappointment. Will failed his law
examinations and was plunged into despair. In the autumn, Ivor
Gurney had enrolled as a student at the Royal College of Music and
moved into lodgings in Fulham. Will too went up to London, but
for him there was none of the satisfaction or fulfilment which
awaited his friend. His lot was to spend six miserable months
working through a crammer course in Lincoln's Inn Fields. Four
things sustained him at this time: his mother, his friendship with
Gurney, his faith, and his humour.

Throughout his life, even at the bleakest times, Will Harvey was always able to smile inwardly at himself. Now, beset by failure, he retyped an essay written five years previously when he had first entered Frank Treasure's office:

HUMOUR

The humorous man is not the shallow individual who looks on 'the bright side' of life: he is the hero who can look on both sides and yet smile.

All absence of sensation is immoral. The laughter of the man who looks only on the bright side is silly and wicked. So meaningless is the cynicism of the man who looks only on the dark. To be humorous one must recognise both. For the only humour worth possessing is a product of both.

There is a strange idea that humour cannot be cultivated: that it is a gift! But is not every other faculty that we possess a gift? The flowers in the garden, and the dirt you grow them in and the water you pour on them, – Are they not all gifts? Yet gardeners cultivate carnations.

The position is that of a fully supplied housekeeper, who has eggs and rice and milk and fire and a basin and an oven, complaining that she has not been gifted with a rice pudding.

There are, of course, persons not so well off, who have no eggs or rice: and in that case I admit we must be content to eat bread and milk when we dine with them. But humour is a dish of which most of us possess the ingredients, though few of us are not too lazy or morbid to mix them.

Gladness is an essential portion of the wheel of life. But humour is light everlasting upon the turning spokes. Nor is it possible for anyone to point out as cut and dried joys the things which brighten his life on earth. Take them away. The spirit of joy will find other garments. This is a law of nature. Not the most determined of the gloom throwers but must accept such gifts. The worst, while we live, that can be done is to accept them sulkily, and question the spirit in which they are offered. It is a mean notion, but common. Yet most of us are not intentionally sulky.

Only sulky, or otherwise, we are all apt to allow ourselves to be overshadowed by sorrow. This is not because we feel sorrows too much (that is impossible) but because we allow our souls to be dominated. It is against such domination humour fights. Against the spear of Goliath he brings but pebbles. Yet he prevails. He fights the uneven battle with a smile contemptuous of defeat – contemptuous of victory. 'Kill me,' he shouts, 'and I shall still laugh, *for ever*'.

It is a glorious arrogance of the soul which cries out upon circumstance. And it is as divorced from pride as anything in the world. Humour, like love, 'endureth all things', even though it hopeth not for all things. Its faith is greater than hope being unconscious and unsuspected. Courage has many lovely shapes, but of all, humour is most lovely to look upon. The very sight of it is a wine to raise the heart. . . .

But I have a confession to make. This very essay, written in adolescence, was an attempt to stimulate such courage. It was written in sadness and disillusion. And it is not a bit humorous. That is what makes me laugh!

1911.

. . . . .

Whilst in London, although still an Anglican, Will began to attend the Brompton Oratory, at that time the premier Roman Catholic church in England. He even joined the singers in the choir and they very much wanted him to become one of their number.[5]

He had already encountered the severe displeasure of the Revd Bartlett in Minsterworth and Tillie's views on the matter, although unknown, may be guessed. It seems likely that at about this time he began to receive formal instruction in the Roman Catholic faith, and certainly there was to be no turning back after this point.

Renaissance

On the fly-leaf to his copy of *Ecce Homo* Will wrote: 'From a boy (when in Rossall Chapel I dreamed *seriously* of crucifying myself to make men realise what Christ did – as if that were all!) I had felt the vital impatience of *Realising, Believing* (as I put it later – for he who once truly believes cannot but do –) as Fact and as Truth what Christ did.'[6]

He detested the study of law as much as ever, but he *was* working and imposing discipline upon himself. He had no choice. Of course, he was homesick.

Lincoln's Inn Fields

In Lincoln's Inn Fields where you chiefly find
Law students, tramps, and babies, comes the wind
Out of the west: and straightway brings to me
Large visions of my dear, my own country.

Dear city of mine I see you like a dream
Below blue hills which shadow you and seem
Sentinels of the peace which comes to me
When I am in my dear, my own country.

High Lassington I see your woods again
Blown all about and wet with falling rain,
What Druid spell have you cast over me
Sweet woodlands of my dear, my own country.

And you dear home of mine that in my dreams
I visit. And all you my pretty streams
That dream and shine by many a shivering tree
In the dim meadows of my dear, my own country.

The great farm horses splashing in the pool
Shrill with delight of birds, the coppice cool;
These things the friendly wind brings here to me
For tokens of my dear, my own country . . .

In the summer of 1912 he was back at The Redlands, preparing to sit his examinations once more and, apparently, unsuccessfully seeking publication for his early attempts at verse. In his scrapbook there is a draft of a letter to Lascelles Abercrombie ('Mr A') who, with Rupert Brooke, John Drinkwater and Wilfred Gibson, formed a group of poets associated with the Gloucestershire village of Dymock. John Haines knew Abercrombie and introduced Will Harvey and Ivor Gurney to him.

> Dear Mr. A,
> I feel very despondent about my work. Friends tell me it is good (usually picking out the wrong things to praise). Editors do not agree with them – or me. It is not yet a question of living by writing. If it were I should starve. But (since I can't help writing) why in God's name cannot I get published – sometimes? Of what absurdity am I guilty which Editors see and I do not? What is Nature up to anyway. If I am no good why must I keep on? It is because I am now thoroughly miserable and *ill* through pondering this problem that I send these things for your judgement.[7]

What that judgement was, or even if the letter was sent, we do not know. However, letters of encouragement certainly came from Ivor Gurney who, by then, had been joined at the RCM by Herbert Howells. Gurney, studying under Sir Charles Villiers Stanford, had found his voice and wanted nothing more than for his best friend to realise his potential. In July 1912 he wrote:

> Dear Willy,
> . . . How do you get on? Have you written much? Doesn't this sacred hunger for Spring nourish that fire in you? If it does not yet, get, as I have just got, Davies *Farewell to Poesy, Foliage* (his latest book) and *Songs of Joy* – the finest lyric poetry in English. God bless the day when Haines recommended that last book to the Gloucester Library. What a Treasury of divine simplicity!
> Willy, dear, your photograph is on the piano not far from

me as I write in bed. Have your confounded family given it their august approval yet? How does the daily round, the common task go? More slippily than formerly I hope.

Don't think that your poetic gift will not develop because you have to be at office most of the day. I do not believe it. There are too many examples to the contrary.

Remember – 'Daily Telegraph' on Wed and Fri, and 'Academy' every week, and 'Bookman' every month.

Yours ever,
I.B.G.[8]

In December 1912 Will Harvey qualified as a solicitor and the following month was in court dealing with his first case: a collision between two horses and carts.

. . . . .

In spite of everything, Will continued to feel ill and to be gloomy and despondent about his lack of acceptance as a writer. In the spring of 1913 he went to spend a few days in Droitwich, Worcestershire, in the hope that the famous spa waters there would improve his health. During and since his years at Rossall School there had been no improvement in the swollen gland in his neck. In fact it had slowly continued to worsen. Now, in Droitwich, a doctor taking his medical history noted the swelling and advised Will that the infected gland was the cause of his illness and depression. Will wrote in his notebook:[9]

Droitwich. I am so glad to know that I am physically ill.
Pessimism which can be taken out with a knife is tolerable.

He accepted medical advice that the gland should be removed surgically. In July 1913 he was admitted to the Gloucester Royal Infirmary for an operation.

Drowsily recovering from the anaesthetic, he heard the soft voice of an Irish girl calling him back to reality. He awoke to find a

Will Harvey, December 1912.

charming face with blue-green dancing eyes smiling down at him, rich auburn hair tucked into a nurse's veil. This was Sarah Anne Kane. In the following days she and Will discovered that they shared many interests, ideals and a common religious conviction. Almost inevitably, they fell in love.

Anne, one of three children, was a farmer's daughter from close by Tubbercurry in County Sligo on the Atlantic coast of Ireland. When she was only two years old, her father, during haymaking on a hot June day, went for a swim in the sea and was drowned.

Anne's mother was left to run the farm and to bring up her three children alone. Life must have been a great struggle and Anne could remember days when the only meal for the family had been a single goose-egg. However, Mrs Kane reduced her farm to a smallholding and used some of the capital to give Anne that greatest gift of any parent: a good education. Anne was sent to a convent school in northern France. Presumably much cheaper than a similar establishment in the British Isles, the school was run by nuns and the regime was harsh.

Returning to Ireland, Anne's days were filled with housework, peeling potatoes and digging. Eventually she made up her mind that she would take up nursing as a career and so, even though her mother had wanted her to stay and help on the smallholding, she left home, travelled to England and gained a place at the Gloucester Royal Infirmary's school of nursing.[10]

Will, at last, was happy. He was in love, in Gloucestershire, in better health, in legal practice, and the cricket season was under way. He still did not relish the enclosed office life of a solicitor, but he found that he enjoyed advocacy in the magistrate's court very much, especially when defending a client. In this role his mastery of the English language and his easy wit came into their own. Unfortunately, the terms of his Articles of Indenture prohibited his practising law within thirty miles of Gloucester for a period of ten years.

Late in 1913, with much reluctance, he accepted a post in Chesterfield, Derbyshire, and resigned himself to separation from Anne, from his mother and from Gloucestershire once more. But before he went he jotted down the following enigmatic note, now in his scrapbook:[11]

Fri Dec 5th 1913

Could this be decoded to read: 'Fri Dec 5th 1913, Proposed to Sarah Anne Kane'?

Ivor Gurney wrote to Will in Chesterfield after a visit home from the RCM:[12]

> You don't know what Portway was today – you don't
> know! I could only sing for joy, and cry in my heart with
> pure happiness. Great black shadows, white violets, intensely
> blue sky, and a sun like wine to the soul.
>   Damn London!

And Will could equally have answered: 'Damn Chesterfield!' But he had little time in which to contemplate his homesickness. This was 1914, and on 28 June a fateful starting-pistol was fired in a far-away Bosnian town called Sarajevo.

V

Drum Taps

At the outbreak of the First World War the Gloucestershire Regiment consisted of six battalions, the 1st and 2nd Regular, 3rd (Royal South Gloucestershire Militia) and three Territorial battalions: the 4th, 5th and 6th, two of which were based in Bristol and one, the 5th, which had its headquarters at the Barracks, Gloucester.[1]

On the 3 August 1914, the day before Britain declared war on Germany, the 5th Battalion was on its way to Marlow-on-Thames for a fortnight's camp. To many of the men this was the only chance that they would get of an annual 'holiday' and, in the beautiful weather of that summer, they were looking forward with light-hearted expectation to soldiering with friends.

No sooner had the battalion arrived in Marlow than word of hostilities began to spread. In the late afternoon rain began to fall and rumour became reality. Camp was struck immediately and the men returned to Gloucester that night. But now they were on active service.

On Sunday 4 August Germany declared war on Belgium and invaded her. The following day the men of the 5th Battalion mobilized for war and paraded through the city to a civic reception in their honour. As they marched along, the people of Gloucester ran from offices and shops to cheer and wave.

> Oh, it's Tommy this, an' Tommy that, an' 'Tommy, go away';
> But it's 'Thank you Mister Atkins' when, the band begins to play.'

Past the Corn Exchange they marched and on to the Shire Hall where the mayor greeted them on the steps and led them in to a farewell tea. As Gloucester was saying a proud goodbye to its sons, Austria-Hungary was declaring war on Russia, and Montenegro was declaring war on Austria-Hungary.

After the civic reception the men were cheered on their way to the railway station where a troop train was waiting to take them to the battalion's war station: the Isle of Wight. Time for last kisses, brave words, 'home by Christmas' reassurances and not a few tears; at 7.20 p.m. the train pulled away from Gloucester and home. After the remarkable speed of their preparations for battle readiness the men of the 5th Battalion were now to experience, not for the last time, the frustration which results from uncoordinated planning.

The troop train from Gloucester arrived in Portsmouth at 11.30 p.m., long after the last ferry had sailed for the island. One man remembered the scene: 'Portsmouth was bathed in brilliant moonlight. Warships at anchor swept the sea with the beams of their fierce searchlights. Spent night in Clarence Pier Pavilion and slept on chairs. Some of the fellows threw their kit off before "retiring", while others preferred to slumber in their full war regalia. Our friend Archie could not sleep, so at about 2 a.m. he got up, wormed his way through a multitude of chairs, mounted the platform, and commenced to play a serenade on the piano. The musical interlude woke almost everyone up, and the cursing of the recumbent troops was entirely out of keeping with the time and place.'

Before first light the cold, grubby and tired men boarded a steam packet which ferried them over to Ryde where a weary old train was waiting to take them on to Newport. This worn-out antique of the railways may have been adequate to carry local passengers and holiday-makers laden with no more than suitcases, buckets and spades. It was certainly not up to carrying a whole battalion of troops, each man burdened with a heavy pack and other equipment. Slowly the engine wheezed its way out of the station and set off on its painfully slow journey punctuated by frequent tedious halts. At last the strain proved too much and the locomotive coupling came apart, to the great amusement of the troops, some of whom offered the flustered driver a piece of string to recouple his engine! This poor man's patience must have been sorely tried and, later on, some of his charges jokingly alleged that he had taken a walk back down the line to pick up a lump of coal which had fallen off the tender, so slow was their progress.

At last Newport was reached, but no transport was available and the men had to face a long weary march in the rain to Albany Barracks, Parkhurst. When they arrived, rations were very scarce and lunch for the battalion was no more than weak tea and very thin stew.

On the 9 August, after only three nights on the Isle of Wight, the Glosters were promptly moved to Swindon for intensive training, just thirty-five miles from their home city.[2]

Meanwhile recruiting had begun in earnest and men throughout Gloucestershire, as elsewhere, rushed to join the Territorials, their trades and professions a litany of town and country life. They came from the fields: farmers, farm labourers, cowmen and dairymen;

Newly-enlisted volunteers for the Glosters Territorials, at the Cross, Gloucester, 1914.

from the ironworks: strikers, drillers, fitters and foundry-men; from the great estates: grooms, gardeners, stablemen and page-boys. There were grocers, bakers, butchers, bricklayers, pawnbrokers, clockmakers, dentists and solicitors.[3] Almost the whole of the Gloucester Rugby Football team enlisted, ensuring that the 5th Battalion was unbeatable at the game. And Will Harvey's cricket team drew stumps and went off to war.

Ivor Gurney came home from the Royal College of Music and volunteered to join the Glosters, clearly wishing both to serve his country and to do so at the side of his best friend, Will Harvey. Equally, he saw in the Army his chance to impose a discipline upon himself from which he hoped would come mental stability and strength. In August 1914 the Army could afford to reject less than fully-fit recruits and Ivor was turned away. The situation was very different by February 1915 when he tried again; this time he was promptly accepted. Herbert Howells' health, however, was never up to the standard required for service and he remained at the RCM throughout the war.

Eric Harvey, second left, at Oxford, 1914.

Drum Taps

Three of the four Harvey boys enlisted in the army on the same day, 8 August. Will, back from Chesterfield, and Eric, who had been up at Oxford reading theology at Brasenose College, both joined the 1/5th Battalion Glosters. Roy, an engineer at the railway works in Swindon, Wiltshire, joined the Royal Wiltshire Yeomanry. Only Bernard, too young to serve, was left behind at The Redlands to cope with running the farm. On their last morning at home together the three elder boys were photographed sitting with their kitbags on the steps at The Redlands. Then Will, alone for a while before they set off for the station, wandered out of the garden gate to say a silent goodbye to Minsterworth and to kiss each of the trees on either side of the little lane by the house.[4]

A Prayer

O Lord, within my heart for ever
Set this sweet shape of land and winding river,
That I may taste their comfort till I die
And feed upon them in Eternity.

Roy, Will and Eric Harvey at The Redlands before joining their
battalions, 1914.

VI

Bernard

In the days following the departure of Will, Eric and Roy, responsibility pressed in on Bernard. Tillie depended upon him to manage the farm with little assistance now that the younger hands had answered Lord Kitchener's call for volunteers. Although untrained, Gladys too offered her services as a Voluntary Aid Detachment nurse and was to be at home far less than before. Bernard's comparatively carefree life, enjoying youthful pleasures with Nigel Bartlett, was now hardly possible.

One minor pleasure which he did keep up, however, was completing the weekly competition page in the *John Bull* magazine. Bernard had a quick brain and easily found solutions to these puzzles. He regularly sent in his entry to the magazine, but to date, in spite of many correct answers, he had never won a prize. Now that he was the man of the house and no doubt feeling very adult, he wrote to the editor of *John Bull* asking how it could be that his envelope had never been amongst those lucky first few winning entries to be opened. He received no reply but, perhaps by coincidence, within a few weeks he did indeed win and received a handsome cheque. So handsome that he could now afford to realise one of his cherished ambitions.

Roy was the proud owner of a splendid Zenith motor cycle. Earlier in 1914 he had ridden down to the Isle of Wight and returned with photographs and an account of the exhilaration of his touring holiday. Not surprisingly, Bernard longed to have a motor bike of his own – and now he could afford to buy one.

On 20 September 1914, Bernard pushed his new machine out of

Bernard and Eric Harvey with Nigel Bartlett.

Roy Harvey on the Zenith motorbike, Isle of Wight, 1914.

the gate at The Redlands and set off to try it out on the road to Gloucester. Picking up speed he was suddenly aware of a servant girl riding her bicycle towards Minsterworth on the wrong side of the road. Bernard swerved to avoid her and, at the same moment, she swerved too. Now Bernard was on the wrong side of the road. In his attempt to get back across the road, the motor bike skidded out of control. Bernard was pitched into the roadside; his unprotected head took the full impact of the crash.[1]

By a dreadful irony, Tillie's only son to be spared the perils of war died before his elder brothers had even arrived in Flanders. Under the heading 'The Late Mr Bernard Harvey', the following account of Bernard's funeral appeared in the Gloucester *Citizen* newspaper:

The funeral of Mr Bernard Harvey of The Redlands, Minsterworth, whose death occurred at the Royal Infirmary, Gloucester, on Sunday as the result of a motor cycle accident, already reported, took place on Wednesday afternoon at St Peter's Church, Minsterworth. The deceased, who was only 18 years of age, was one of the most popular young men of the village, and his passing away so early in life and the sad circumstances surrounding his death together created a feeling of sincere sorrow and regret amongst the inhabitants, who, as showing the affection and regard entertained for the deceased, attended his funeral en masse. The scholars from Minsterworth School, with their Headmistress, were also present, and paid their last tribute of respect by lining the road at the entrance to the churchyard. Here the cortege was met by the Vicar (the Rev. C.O. Bartlett), the Rev. Canon Park, the Rev. Minor Canon A.E. Fleming, and the choir. The church was crowded to its utmost capacity and during the service the hymn 'There is a land of pure delight' was feelingly sung. The opening sentences were read by Minor Canon Fleming, and the special lesson was read by Canon Park, while the Vicar pronounced the committal rites and prayers at the graveside, where the huge concourse of people gathered around joined in the hymn 'On the resurrection morning'.

The coffin was of unpolished English oak. On the lid was a full-length Calvary cross, and at the foot the plate bore the inscription: 'Bernard Harvey; Died September 20th, 1914; Aged 18 years.'

The demands of farm work do not cease, even in the face of death, and Tillie's grief was overlaid with anxiety about the management of The Redlands.

Of the three elder brothers, Eric had the most practical ability on the farm. When he was still a boy his father had sent him to market to learn how to sell horses and had been delighted when Eric made a good sale. It was to Eric that Tillie now turned for help. An application was made for his compassionate discharge from the Army. In October, Private E.H. Harvey was released from active service for one year and returned to The Redlands to work the land until a tenant farmer could be found. This done, and Tillie provided with an income from the rent, Eric resumed his studies at Oxford. When, in October 1915, he was recalled to the 1/5th Battalion, the

Private Eric Harvey temporarily discharged from the Army, October 1914.

Bernard

Gloucestershire Regiment, it was as a commissioned officer. A few days before returning to active service Eric and his cousin Gwen were married.[2]

Home in Gloucester for a last leave before his own departure for the front in May 1916, Ivor Gurney visited Tillie at Minsterworth. In his poem 'The Farm', dedicated to 'Mrs Harvey and Those Others', he captures the desolation of the now melancholy house and contrasts it with the warmth of The Redlands past, a symbol of constancy and hope in a world gone mad.

The Farm

A creeper-covered house, an orchard near;
A farmyard with tall ricks upstanding clear
In golden sunlight of a late September. –
How little of a whole world to remember!
How slight a thing to keep a spirit free!
Within the house were books,
A piano, dear to me,
And around the house the rooks
Haunted each tall elm tree;
Each sunset crying, calling, clamouring aloud.

And friends lived there of whom the house was proud,
Sheltering with content from wind and storm,
Them loving gathered at the hearthside warm,
(O friendly, happy crowd!)
Caress of firelight gave them, touching hair
And cheeks and hands with sombre gleams of love.
(When day died out behind the lovely bare
Network of twigs, orchard and elms apart;
When rooks lay still in round dark nests above,
And Peace like cool dew comforted the heart.)

The house all strangers welcomed, but as strangers kept
For ever them apart

From its deep heart,
That hidden sanctuary of love close guarded;
Having too great a honey-heap uphoarded
Of children's play, men's work, lightly to let
Strangers therein;
Who knew its stubborn pride, and loved the more
The place from webbed slate roof to cellar floor –
Hens clucking, ducks, all casual farmyard din.
How empty the place seemed when Duty called
To harder service its three sons than tending
Brown fruitful good earth there! But all's God's sending.
Above the low barn where the oxen were stalled
The old house watched for weeks the road, to see
Nothing but common traffic; nothing its own.
It had grown to them so used, so long had known
Their presences; sheltered and shared sorrow and glee,
No wonder it felt desolate and left alone . . .
That must remember, nothing at all forget.

My mind (how often!) turned and returned to it,
When in queer holes of chance, bedraggled, wet,
Lousy I lay; to think how by Severn-side
A house of steadfastness and quiet pride
Kept faith to friends (when hope of mine had died
Almost to ash). And never twilight came
With mystery and peace and points of flame –
Save it must bring sounds of my Severn flowing
Steadily seawards, orange windows glowing
Bright in the dusk, and many a well-known name.

ANOTHER
SOUND

The Orchard, The Sea
and The Guns

Of sounds which haunt me, these
  Until I die
Shall live. First the trees,
  Swaying and singing in the moonless night.
(The wind being wild)
  And I
A wakeful child,
That lay and shivered with a strange delight.

Second – less sweet but thrilling as the first –
  The midnight roar
Of waves upon the shore
Of Rossall dear:
The rhythmic surge and burst
(The gusty rain
Flung on the pane!)
I loved to hear.

And now another sound
Wilder than wind or sea,
When on the silent night
  I hear resound
  In mad delight
  The guns. . .
They bark the whole night through;
  And though I fear,
  Knowing what work they do,
I somehow thrill to hear.

VII

Reveille

The three Territorial battalions of the Gloucestershire Regiment, the 1/4th, 1/5th and 1/6th, were part of the South Midland Division, which subsequently became the 48th Division. Along with the 7th and 8th Worcesters, the 1/4th and 1/6th formed the Gloucester and Worcester Brigade, later the 144th Brigade. The 1/5th was combined with the 4th Oxford and Bucks, the Bucks Battalion of the Oxford and Bucks Light Infantry and the 4th Berkshires, to form the South Midland Infantry Brigade, which was to become the 145th Brigade.[1]

In the second week of August the South Midland Division was concentrating in Swindon, Wiltshire. The 1/5th Glosters arrived there on 9 August whilst, on the other side of the Channel, the British Expeditionary Force was landing in northern France.

The men of the 1/5th Battalion pitched camp in Swindon Park and set about training. Early each morning the troops and nearby residents of Swindon were awakened by the battalion band playing rousing but unwelcome airs. Then followed days of physical exercise, rifle and foot drill. But this earnest business was not without amusing incident as military endeavour encountered sub-urban life. One morning a particularly tall NCO, Sergeant Durrett, was standing rigidly to attention as chief marker on parade. A small dog strolling through the park assumed that the sergeant was an extra lamppost provided for his convenience and made full use of the facility!

On 15 August the battalion was paraded for the last time in

F.W. Harvey, August 1914.

Swindon Park and a call made for volunteers for foreign service, to which all the officers and 90 per cent of the men responded. Each volunteer received a £5 gratuity, much of which was spent that evening making merry in the Cricketers Arms.

The next morning, the battalion was taken to Hockliffe in Bedfordshire en route to Chelmsford. The men were billeted in barns and stables.[2]

At Hockliffe a jaunty figure wearing a straw boater joined the battalion. This was the Reverend G.F. Helm, the newly-appointed Anglican chaplain, a man whose great personal courage and genuine concern for the troops were often demonstrated in the cruel days of war which lay ahead. He was also a man of foresight whose meeting with Private Will Harvey was one of those happy coincidences which lead to lasting treasure. It was Canon Helm who conceived the idea of a regular battalion journal as a means of keeping men at war amused, informed and in good heart. He started the *5th Gloucester Gazette*, which was the first of the regimental trench magazines to be published in France. This modest paper gave Will an opportunity to reach out to eager readers and to see his verse in print for the first time.

Canon Helm became a much-loved and admired padre, always close to the men, bringing cheer and comfort, heedless of his own personal safety. One recorded incident will serve to epitomise his character. In June 1917 the battalion was in the line at Hermies on the Bapaume–Cambrai road. Following a day of fierce action, in which several of the Glosters were killed and wounded, a lone figure was observed walking up the main road with a walking stick: it was Canon Helm. He enquired about the dead and immediately arranged for their burial in the moonlight and in full view of the enemy. No shot was fired either during the taking down of the wounded or during the burial service. The next evening a shell dropped right on the spot where the burial had taken place.

Canon Helm served throughout the war and then held livings in various parts of Gloucestershire, including Stroud, Berkeley and Dursley. He was a founder-member of the 1/5th Battalion Old Comrades Association and maintained an active interest in its affairs. In 1938 he was appointed Chaplain to the King. He died in

1958 and is buried in the churchyard of St Peter's, Bournemouth, where he was a curate for some time after his retirement.[3]

. . . . .

On 19 August 1914, the battalion left Hockliffe on what the men would always remember as 'the long march': a march of eighty miles to Chelmsford, spread over five heavy-laden days of hot sun, aching limbs but high spirits. The footsore soldiers arrived in Chelmsford at 11 a.m. on 24 August and lay down to rest under the cool shade of trees in Admirals Park before settling in to their billets – private houses in the town.

The battalion was stationed in Chelmsford for the double purpose of guarding the east coast and for training. Day after day new recruits from Gloucestershire arrived in Chelmsford and were to be seen in the streets in an odd assortment of uniform and civilian clothes: some in khaki tunics, odd trousers, cloth caps or trilby hats; others in khaki trousers and blazers or sports jackets. These willing volunteers were slowly transformed into trained, disciplined troops; the battalion was organised into a four-company system and brought up to full strength. Will Harvey wrote in his notebook:

> *1914.* I am a man looking out for something worth buying – ready to spend all to get it. And I had almost given up hope.[4]

Whilst at Chelmsford he was received into the communion of the Roman Catholic Church.

In September 1914 the 2/5th Battalion of the Gloucestershire Regiment was formed to act as a second line to the 1/5th and, after a short time in Gloucester and Northampton, this new battalion also was moved to Chelmsford.

Training was rigorous, but not without comic relief. Writing to a friend during his own time in Chelmsford in 1915, Ivor Gurney

Men of the 1/5th Battalion Glosters training at Chelmsford.

described the daily timetable: 'Reveille 5, Breakfast 6.30, Dinner 1.30, Tea 4.30–5 , and on all the time between those hours!'[5] The days were made up of foot drill, rifle drill, physical training, firing and bayonet practice, long route marches and inspections. Field operations were often conducted in a 'cowboys and Indians' spirit. One such exercise was remembered many years later:

> We were on Field Operations at a place called Felstead. During the 'battle' Sergeant Richards and his merry men were taken prisoner and locked in a barn. Trying to summon help, Sergeant Richards managed to push a few tiles off the roof and shine an electric torch. His antics were discovered and a bucket of water pitched into the hole; muffled shouts were heard from the sodden 'prisoners'. They eventually got free, and the Sergeant picked up a couple of fowls by their legs and flung them at Captain Hague. Then he made a desperate dash for liberty but was tripped up and bound hand and foot. The captors were naturally highly delighted with their achievement![6]

At this time, the threat of attack from the air was a new and disturbing possibility. Zeppelins had been sighted, huge and ominous, looming out of the night sky. There was a theory that these airships were guided to their targets by the headlights of motor cars being used as flashlight signals. Men of the battalion were armed with Japanese rifles, organised into aeroplane picquets and sent out on the main roads around Chelmsford to watch for Zeppelins and to search passing cars for secret signalling equipment. They went out at 7 p.m. each evening and returned at 6 a.m.[7] Innocent motorists must have been terrified to be stopped at gunpoint whilst their vehicles were searched. Needless to say, nothing suspicious was ever discovered, but by the summer of 1915 Zeppelin attacks on England were frequent and on two occasions bombs were dropped on Chelmsford.

On 14 October 1914 the South Midland Division was inspected by King George V at Hylands Park. Fifteen thousand men were on parade. By February 1915 the 1/5th Battalion was fully trained and judged to be ready for action.

During the time that the battalion had been training, the web of international conflict had become irreversibly entangled. All hope was lost of a short, decisive campaign. Soldiers and civilians alike had been stunned by the full horror of news from the first Battle of Ypres: the British Army smashed in an heroic effort to defend a narrow salient. Casualty figures were appalling, and all for no gain whatsoever. For the first time, men were digging trenches. War's hunger now awaited the arrival of the Territorials and Kitchener's volunteers.

At 5.30 p.m. on 29 March, under the command of Lt.-Col. J.H. Collett, the 1/5th Battalion left for the front. This time there were no cheering crowds. The people of Chelmsford watched in thoughtful silence as the men, cheerful nonetheless, marched to the railway station.

Their troop train arrived in Folkstone at 9 p.m. and, under a brilliant moon, the battalion embarked in RMS *Invicta* for the crossing to France.[8] On board there were 29 officers and 1,020 men.

Ivor Gurney arrived in Chelmsford with the 2/5th Battalion in April, missing Will Harvey by just a few days.

The 1/5th Battalion Glosters before leaving for Flanders (Will Harvey arrowed).

To Days of Battle

Here's to the days of danger, and fine daring,
   And fellowship so free:
Those days when stout of heart 'the Fifth' went faring
   Over the sea!

Hardship was something: *fellowship was all*
   In that grim strife.
So may it prove with us, whate'er befall
   Till the end of life!

VIII

Plug Street

The RMS *Invicta* landed in Boulogne at 11.10 p.m. on 30 March. If Chelmsford had given the battalion a subdued farewell, Boulogne's welcome was utterly silent. The men formed up on the quayside, adjusted their heavy packs and set off to march over difficult, cobbled streets, out of the town and up a seemingly endless hill to camp at St Martin.

Sleep that night was impossible as a bitterly cold north wind cut through the French tents in which the shivering troops were bivouacked. The next morning they marched to a nearby railway station and entrained in cattle trucks, 32 men to each truck, to be taken to Cassel.

From Cassel the 1/5th Battalion marched five kilometres to Steenvorde in Belgium where the lofts and barns of farms were taken over as billets. During the next two days the 1/4th and 1/6th Battalions of the Gloucestershire Regiment crossed the Channel, made the railway journey from Boulogne to Cassel and marched to Winnezeele and Oudezeele respectively. By Good Friday, on 2 April, the whole of the 48th (South Midland) Division had assembled in Belgium and was reviewed by General Sir Horace Smith-Dorrien.

In the afternoon of 4 April the 1/5th Battalion marched the ten kilometres to Meteren and were again billetted in lofts and barns. The men were allowed to rest for two days and for the first time received a free issue of 'Studio Brand' cigarettes, with the flavour, as one man put it, of a 'cross between Arf a Mo' and dried beech leaves'. Nonetheless, in anxious times these small comforts were a

Harvey's France, March 1915–August 1916.

THE PLUG STREET EMPIRE.

6-50   TWICE NIGHTLY   9

SPLENDID PROGRAMME
Fresh Bill each Week.

1. Overture—" A." Company Orchestra.
    Conductor—Drummer LAPPINTON.

    Instruments :
    First Mouth Organ ... Pte. WALKER.
    Second   „   „ ... Pte. BUNDY.
    First Biscuit Tin ... C.S.M.WAGSTAFF.
    Mandoline ... ... Pte. SPIERS.
    Massed Triangles and
    Concertinas under the
    direction of ... ... Drm. CARPENTER

2. Screaming Farce—" *Brigade Time* "
            Watches by Ingersoll.

3. The Three Alkalis in their Smoke Swallowing Act
        Thyo, Hypo, and By Carb.

4. Great Wire Walking Act
        by Slip Over, Trip Up, and Dammit,
        who will put their foot in it twice nightly.

5. Little Willie in his Lightning Act, entitled
        " *Pop off,*" *or* " *Phiz Bang.*"

6. Cresol and Chloride will appear in their realistic
        Fly-catching Act.

7. Great Fight for the Championship of the World
        Special engagement of Jack Johnson and White
        Hope. 15-inch gloves, 17 yards ring.
        Referee—President WILSON—if not too proud.
        Time-keeper—A. FUSE.

8. Great Looping the Loop-hole Scene
        by Telly, Scopic and Snipem.

9. Song—Frosti's Good-bye
        " *When Little Willie comes.*"

10. Thrilling Yarn, entitled : " *The Ship that*
        foundered," or " *The Smack that reached the*
        Bottom," by U. 19.

11. The famous Cross-talk Comedians in their patter
    Song—
            " *Kay & Kayenne.*"

Wigs and Beards by N. O. CLIPPER.

NEXT WEEK : Special arrangements have been
    made by our patrols for a visit from the Famous
    Saxon Troupe of Wire Walkers.

POPULAR PRICES ; Sandbags . . . frs. 1.50
                        Dug-outs 50
                        Parapets . . . Free.
        Admission by identity disc only.

Respirators are damped each evening instead of
fire-proof curtain being lowered—by arrangement with
the Lord Chamberlain.

From the *5th Gloucester Gazette*, No. 3, 15 June 1915.

great morale booster. For two days the Glosters sat thoughtfully smoking their cigarettes whilst trying not to hear the sound of guns pounding very quietly in the distance.[1]

Canon Helm, too, was attempting to boost morale as he worked on the first issue of the *5th Gloucester Gazette*. The paper did not appear until 12 April, by which time the battalion was in action, but the editorial and Will Harvey's first contribution were written in the first few days of the month; both are light-hearted, confident and comic. The editorial ends:

> We have no cause for anxiety. The national character has reasserted itself, in spite of false prophets. We never stood better in the eyes of the world than we stand today, and with that spirit our Regiment is instinct.

Harvey's piece is not so much a poem as a topical rhyming joke:

A.   is the Adjutant's horse, who foretells
    Our real destination to be Dardanelles.
B.   is the beer over which 'twas discussed
    To edify Germany's agents we trust.
C.   stands for Chelmsford, the town of our training,
    And where it is almost continually raining.
D.   is the word which all of us said
    When the billets were changed and we hadn't a bed.
E.   is for England, now distant and dear,
    When we see her white cliffs again, how we will cheer.
F.   is the Frenchman who answered 'quite so'
    To our 'S'il vous plaît Monsieur, donnez-moi l'eau'.
G.   is the Glo'sters – those grim gory fighters
    Who've cleared all the trenches from Bailleul to Ypres.
H.   is for Hell, the place where the Hun
    Sings 'Wacht am der Styx' when his fighting is done.

F. W. Harvey SOLDIER, POET

I.   is the Indian who cries 'Souvenir'
     With a Teutonic head on the end of his spear.

J.   is for Joffre – we haven't yet met him
     But thousands of Germans will never forget him.

K.   is for Kitchener – humorous bloke
     Who conceals all his flippancy under a cloak.

L.   is the letter he wrote to the trenches –
     Beware of the wine, and keep clear of the
        wenches.

M.   is our money – exactly eight bob –
     Paid us on Fridays to finish this 'job'.

N.   is the nominal labouring man
     Who strikes for more wages whenever he can.

O.   is the output on which we depend
     To bring this detestable war to an end.

P.   is the pack and the pick that we carry
     With hurdle and sandbag the foeman to harry.

Q.   is the query 'What will he do,
     Should he also pick up a comrade or two?'

R.   is the French road well studded with cobbles
     O'er which the perspiring warrior hobbles.

S.   is the Sergeant, familiarly 'Serg',
     Whose temper is short, his vocabulary large.

T.   is the trench where they safely abide,
     Glad that it's deep, and sufficiently wide.

U.   is for Uhlan who's scarcer by far
     To-day than he was at the start of the war.

V.   is Vin Rouge which 'tis foolish to buy
     On a route march in front of the Officer's eye.

W.   is the water which no one should drink
     In spite of what rabid teetotallers think.

X.   is last Xmas.

Y.   is next year.

Z.   is the end of this alphabet 'ere.

. . . . .

Plug Street

Of the three Territorial battalions the 1/5th was the first to go into the front-line trenches. On 7 April the men marched away from Meteren to Ploegsteert, a distance of fourteen kilometres, and reported to their headquarters, a deserted brewery at the edge of a large wood. The brewery itself had suffered bomb damage and shells constantly whistled over its roof to explode in fields nearby.

Ploegsteert, popularly known to the British as 'Plug Street', had seen heavy fighting in 1914. Throughout the winter the trenches had been held by men of the 4th (Regular) Division. Now they were to be relieved by the 48th (Territorial) Division.

The war for which the men of Gloucestershire had trained so long was upon them with sudden shock.

On the nights of 8 and 9 April, led by men of the 4th Division, relief columns picked their way through the vast, water-logged wood; underfoot was a rocking, tortuous track of duck-boards over which mud oozed at each unsteady step. On and on by devious

Ploegsteert Wood.

A lookout using a periscope, Ploegsteert.

ways they advanced towards the trenches; suddenly halting, motionless, as enemy Very lights turned the night sky to shining brilliance and the wood was swept from end to end by machine-gun and rifle fire. Past their heads whizzed bullets which snapped into the surrounding trees. In clearings they passed makeshift shallow graves, centres of an all-prevading and nauseous smell of death.

Thus they came to the edge of the wood to find that there were no communication trenches in this section of the line. Out into open fields they stepped, completely at the mercy of enemy fire. Dodging, crawling, running, in panic to miss the spray of bullets, and jumping at last into the trenches, only 70 to 200 yards away from the German front line.[2]

On the morning of 9 April the 1/5th Battalion suffered its first casualties: Sergeant Lloyd was wounded by a sniper and young Private Lee was shot in the left eye whilst trying to use a periscope. Ten days later Lieutenant Barnett was observing enemy lines through a telescope when he was killed by a sniper's bullet – the first member of the battalion to die in action.[3]

This was trench warfare in which there was neither advance nor retreat, only holding the line. For the next three months the north-western section of Ploegsteert Wood was home for the 1/5th Glosters. Days and nights under fire in the stench and squalor of the trenches; April rains turning the earth to muddy caramel; summer heat filling the air with swarming flies; rats for companions and always the ceaseless din and death's cold stare.

Every few days those going back to rest at Steenverck or to baths at Nieppe, and those taking their places in the line, faced the perils of the journey through the wood and the dash over open ground. But in spite of all, humour and friendship overcame fear. Typical of the humour were the spontaneous contributions to the *5th Gloucester Gazette*. The second edition appeared on 5 May and the following extracts illustrate its style. The hand of Will Harvey ('F.W.H.') was frequently to be found in its pages:

The Route March

(With apologies to Dr Browne)

This route march is a blighted thing – God wot.
The sun –
How hot!
No breeze!
No pewter pot!
He is a blooming pool
Of grease –
'The Sarge',
And yet the fool
(He's large)
Pretends that he is not.
Not wet!
Foot-slogging over Belgian ways –
In summer blaze!
Ah! but I have a sign;
The sweat
Keeps dripping off this blessed nose of mine.

F.W.H.

. . . . .

NATURE NOTES

Birds sometimes select queer nesting places. A lark built a nest and laid three eggs therein at the top of a trench parapet. One day our sapper section indulged in a little trench mortar practice over the nest, and, immediately after a bomb had been fired, it was found that one of the eggs had hatched out. Evidently the young bird was anxious to know what was the matter.

It seemed strange, while heavy shell fire was in progress recently, to hear the bursts of shell fire punctuated by the homely call of the cuckoo.

" When you're all dressed up "

From the *5th Gloucester Gazette.*

F.W. Harvey SOLDIER, POET

We hear that one of our Company Commanders dislikes the rats which have quartered themselves in his dug-out, but it affords a fine opportunity for the acquisition of a Company Mascot. They are rumoured to be as large as rabbits.

Did a certain officer enjoy the boiled blackbird's egg with which he regaled himself at breakfast?

Quite a feast of song is afforded by the nightingales in the vicinity of our trenches.

. . . . .

To the Editor of the *5th Gloucester Gazette*

Sir,

I beg to enclose (with Alice's permission) the following letter received by her from the front, and I venture to believe that you and your readers will be astonished at the dangers our brave boys face – and survive.

Faithfully yours,
F.W.H.

Somewhere in France.
(Date censored)

Dearest Alice,

Well, we are here at last – less than a dozen yards from the Germans – shells bursting all round. Bang! Bang! – there go two more. (Oh, Alice, where art thou?). It is night, dark and stormy. Standing at my post I can hear the Huns gnashing their teeth and turning over the leaves of their books prior to singing the 'Hymn of Hate'. How terrible for our listening patrols who are now standing with their ears resting on the enemy's parapet. I've ''ad some'.

Besides that, these devils have taken to exuding blue gases – directly against the advice of the Bishop of Zanzibar.

I must now chuck it.

Upon my vigilance depends the lives of my comrades, and the enemy is advancing by short rushes.

Percy.

PS I forgot to say how proud we are of our officers.

PPS Am expecting a stripe.

And Will Harvey got his stripe too! As did another soldier in his company with whom he formed a close friendship, Raymond E. Knight, always just 'Knight' or 'R.E.' to Will. Knight, a graduate and running blue, was, like Will, a good singer and the two delighted in singing choruses from the Gilbert and Sullivan operettas, particularly *HMS Pinafore*. Both men had a keen and similar sense of humour, matching tastes and temperaments. Both were keen sportmen and prepared to face danger. Both had probably shown qualities of leadership, and were now both lance-corporals.

Out of the line there was the chance for pals to visit Armentières, although that town had been bombarded, to drink coffee in *estaminets* and perhaps to find a good farmhouse meal. After days in the trenches the greatest luxury would have been a hot bath, but this was hardly possible. A member of the battalion described the scene at Nieppe:[4]

> The Battalion marched to Nieppe for baths. The 'place de bath' was inside a large brewery. It was a very funny sight to watch clusters of men bathing in the numerous ex-beer vats. About twenty men were allotted to each vat, half filled with water, to which was added a solitary lump of soap. The time I spent in the vat was chiefly wasted looking for the wherewithal to make a lather. The water became so thick that I gave up the search and jumped out when the Sergeant Major's bell tolled, feeling as grubby as ever.

On returning to the Ploegsteert trenches after one march from 'rest' some members of the battalion noticed, not for the first time in similar circumstances, that the damaged sails of a nearby windmill began to revolve as they approached. It was later reported that the owner of the windmill had been shot as a spy.

At the end of April news reached Will Harvey of the death of Rupert Brooke on the 23rd of the month. For the first time Will revealed the serious aspect of his nature to the readers of the *5th Gloucester Gazette* in his sorrow for beauty lost.

To Rupert Brooke

Dead in the Defence of Beauty
(Sub-Lieutenant in the Hood Battalion of
the Royal Naval Division, died of disease
in the Dardanelles.)

Sweet singer of this latter day
Whom Death unkindly takes away,
Yet in the Spring-time of thy power,
Take thou in this most mournful hour
The thanks of one whom often thou
Hast helped to rapture. Take the praise
Of all who in these sordid days
Have needed liveliness. Though now
Thy songs are ceased, and though their wine
Of Beauty that is all divine
No more brings holy drunkenness
Into the Soul; yet ne'er the less
Thy end's sheer glory. Evermore
Joy diadems thy death to all
Who loving thee – love beauty more,
Since in thy death thou showest plain
Though Songs must cease and Life must fall
The things that made the songs remain.

                F.W.H. 30/4/15

MILLS PILLS

WORTH
A "MINNIE"
A BOX.

GUARANTEED TO
CLEAR ANYONE OUT

From the *5th Gloucester Gazette*.

In the same issue, the third, one small article under the title 'The Private's Litany' shows the wry humour of the unknown writer in summarising the thoughts of all soldiers in that trench, which to them was 'Rotten Row':

From 3 days of fatigue under the name of rest; from parcels on the last day; from fog till 8 a.m. (or after); and from all things that prolong stand-to; from flies; from sentimental songs and from 'Tipperary'; from trench-inspection by staff officers and the Colonel; from French beer; from people that refuse to lend, and from people that borrow; from Sergeant Peter Huggins; from listening patrols and from dead Germans; from the lady who takes your money and says 'no compris', Deliver me!

Even to Will, careless as he was for his own comfort, there was one thing about which he raged in verse: the price of dry spring days in the trenches – flies!

Ballade of Beelzebub – God of Flies

Some men there are will not abide a rat
   Within their bivvy. If one chance to peep
At them through little beady eyes, then pat
   They throw a boot, and rouse a mate from sleep
To hunt the thing, and on its head they heap
   Curses quite inappropriate to its size.
I care for none of these, but broad and deep
   I curse Beelzebub – the God of Flies.

Others may hunt the mouse with bayonet bright,
   And beard the glittering beetle in his lair,
And fill the arches of the ancient night
   With clamour if a stolid toad should stare

Sleepily forth from the snug corner where
   They fain would rest. But I will sympathise
With beetle, rat and toad. I have no care.
   I curse Beelzebub – God of Flies.

The tiny gnats they swarm in many a cloud
   To tangle their small limbs within my hair
And sting. The blood-flies dart; and buzzing loud
   Blue bottles draw mad patterns on the air.
The house flies creep, and what is hard to bear,
   Feed on the poison papers advertised,
And rub their hands with relish of such fare!
   I curse Beelzebub – God of Flies.

Envoi

Prince – Clown of Europe – other shall make haste
   To call damnation on your limbs and eyes.
Spending good oaths upon you were a waste,
   I curse Beelzebub – the God of Flies.

. . . . .

Until the end of May the battalion received no supplies of Mills bombs. The Germans were using 'Little Willies' and 'Coalboxes' to bombard the British trenches, in comparison with which the 'jam tin' bombs used by the Glosters were crude and unreliable, consisting of no more than a little gun cotton unside an old jam tin which was thrown by hand. In the afternoon of 6 May, Lieutenant Guise was explaining to his men the working of one of these weapons when it exploded in his hand, killing the lieutenant and Private Bates. The rest of the men were badly wounded, some of them blinded.

The next day the German guns were turned upon the village of Ploegsteert itself. Many civilians were killed. The bombardment continued for three days. Men of the 1/5th Battalion returning to the trenches passed crowds of old men, women and children standing in the fields just outside the village clutching bundles of their possessions, gazing pitifully towards homes which were being reduced to rubble.[5]

At the end of May the Germans began to dig mines towards the British trenches and a new dimension of destruction began as exploding mines gouged great craters out of the earth. On 6 June at 10.23 a.m. the British blew up a mine under the enemy's front line. Again, a description by one who was there:[6]

> At the moment of the explosion, the trench in which we stood swayed very slightly backward and forward, a dull thud was heard, and the German trench and its occupants were blown up into the air some 200 feet. The huge black mass seemed to suspend itself for a second or so, and then spread out to twice the size as it fell to earth. The effect was very weird. The Warwick artillery immediately shelled the crater with salvoes of high explosive shells. Sergeant Morris and his machine-gunners took up commanding positions and peppered hot and strong, while rapid fire rang all up the line. Despite the heavy fire, the enemy manned the crater time and again with machine-gunners, who no doubt made the most of their job – while they lived.

In the evening of 24 June the 1/5th Battalion marched away from 'Rotten Row' to Bailleul. They left behind sixteen more graves in Ploegsteert Wood.

With amazing understatement an officer of the battalion wrote: 'The three months here (Ploegsteert) were more or less uneventful.'[7]

IX

Conspicuous Gallantry

Entering Bailleul in the early morning light of 25 June 1915 the men of the battalion encountered a dispiriting sight. Outside a casualty clearing station were lined row upon row of stretchers upon which lay hollow-eyed men, coughing, choking and gulping the air. They were all Canadians who had fought in the Battle of Hill 60 and fallen victim of the first attack in which the Germans had used a new and horrifying weapon of hate: gas.[1]

For two days the battalion remained at rest in Bailleul and then, in night marches, began their progress south to be held in reserve for the Battle of Loos. Their route took them through Vieux Berquin and Gonnehem, and on 28 June they reached Allouagne, twenty kilometres from Bailleul, where they remained until 12 July. These two weeks, in spite of field operations and route marches, came as an interval of sunny delight away from the roar of the guns.

It is probable that the battalion camped somewhere between Gonnehem and Allouagne, which are only five kilometres apart. Two accounts of their stay describe the place as being Allouagne, where especially remembered were cherry trees loaded with fruit for their picking on warm summer days.[2] Certainly the camp was in the barns and stables of a farm close to a chateau which was occupied by a kindly banker. To Will Harvey this haven was 'Gonnehem'.

Gonnehem

> Of Gonnehem, it will be said,
> That we arrived there late and worn

With marching, and were given a bed
Of lovely straw. And then at morn
On rising from deep sleep saw dangle –
Shining in the sun to spangle
The all-blue heaven – branch loads of red
Bright cherries which we bought to eat,
Dew-wet, dawn-cool, and sunny sweet.
There was a tiny court-yard, too,
Wherein one shady walnut grew.
Unruffled peace the farm encloses.
I wonder if beneath that tree
The meditating hens still be.
Are the white walls now gay with roses?
Does the small fountain yet run free?
I wonder if that dog still dozes . . .
Some day we must go back to see.

Leaving Allouagne, again by night, the battalion marched to
Noeux-les-Mines and, on arrival, bivouacked in open fields. As if
by a signal, a thunderstorm broke in the warm summer's night,
drenching the encamped men. The days of comfort were over. Will
Harvey certainly spoke for the whole battalion in his description of
that night:

Noeux-Les-Mines

There stands a town named Noeux-les-Mines
Raised by no mortal hand I ween.

There did we stay a live-long night;
And sad and evil was our plight.

Like water from a water butt
The rain poured down. And doors were shut.

Therefore we built us bivvies in
A bank – but Ah! the roofs were thin.

And soon the rain through all the cracks
Dripped in and trickled down our backs.

Each weary soldier robbed of sleep,
Frighted the night with curses deep.

Or strove with loud and hideous song
To make the darkness seem less long.

One, like unto Diogenes,
Betook him to a tub – and fleas.

His name I cannot quite recall,
But what *he* said was best of all.

With Satan and his powers in league,
A sergeant then did cry 'Fatigue'.

And out into the lashing rain,
We all must tumble once again.

To dig in trenches and to wish
We were not human men, but fish.

When we returned outworn – chill,
No rum was there our cares to kill.

And so until this very day,
Talking of town, our soldiers say:

'Of all the towns that we have seen,
Vilest by far is Noeux-les-Mines.'

. . . . .

(The 'One, like unto Diogenes' was Private Lee-Williams, who turned a dog out of its kennel and got in!)[3]

Now followed one of those changes of plan which seemed calculated to sap the energy of men and to undermine their faith in the competence of their own High Command. The long march south from Bailleul had brought the 1/5th Glosters to within ten kilometres of Loos, circling to the west and south of Bethune. At 9 p.m. on 16 July the order to 'fall in' was given and the battalion was instructed to march to Ames: thirty-four kilometres from Noeux-les-Mines and back to the north-west, passing Allouagne once more.

All night they marched through drizzling rain until, at 4 a.m. the next morning, exhausted, they topped a ridge and saw the spire of Ames church piercing the dawn light.

After resting at Ames on 17 July, the men set off for the railhead at Bergette at 7 a.m. the next day to be rattled down to Doullens in closed cattle-trucks. Doullens was the station serving the sprawling battlefield south of Arras. Here were Thiepval, Ovillers, Bapaume and Albert. To the south flowed the Somme. Into this crucible the Glosters now tramped, passing Sarton and Bayencourt on the way. Their destination was to be the front-line trenches at Hebuterne.

The war was almost one year old and, although they could not know it then, another year was to pass before the men of the Gloucestershire Territorial battalions left the Hebuterne sector.

At dusk on 20 July the battalion relieved the 1st Battalion, 93rd Regiment of the French Army in the front-line trenches. What a welcome they received! The grateful French troops had decorated the trenches with flowers and paper streamers; more flowers surrounded a large declaration of 'Bienvenue!' The French commander even presented the battalion with the gift of a cow which was greatly prized.[4] And there is no wonder that the French were overjoyed to see the men of Gloucestershire; a modest description of those early days at Hebuterne was given by a battalion signaller: 'Here was restricted routine varied by sudden raids to be made or to be fought off, with constant casualties from shell, mortar and bomb; perilous wiring parties, spells of duty at listening posts out in "No-Man's-Land", made bearable only by the rather grim humour and the cheerfulness of all ranks, and by chance of seven days' leave.'[5]

Out of the trenches for periods 'at rest' in Sailly-au-Bois or Bus-les-Artois, the men did their best to recreate a semblance of civilised life. Sporting competitions, concert parties – the officers bought a piano for the men – visits to *estaminets* and walks in the still unruined countryside helped to counterbalance the lunacy of life and death in the line. An article from the *5th Gloucester Gazette* illustrates the remarkable spirit of the times.

WHIST DRIVE

On Monday, July 26th, No. 12 Platoon held a Whist Drive. Entrance fee 2d.

Thirty-two players, including distinguished visitors in Sergt. Finch and Corpl. Watkins, sat down to the tables, or rather the waterproof sheets, the ladies being members without hats.

As usual at whist drives there was quite a merry buzz of conversation, but as soon as Lance-Corporal Robertson arrived with a continuous string of prizes and it began to be whispered round that the booby prizes were eminently desirable and numbered three, the play became very tense and keen.

Lance-Corpl. Harvey was ever casting a wistful eye on the bottle of champagne, while Pte. Draper was not unobservant of the pot of jam.

The programme was varied with 'Klondyke', 'Misere' and 'Kimberley'.

As the lights failed Lance-Corpl. Robertson supplied each set with candles, an action which pleased all until they found at bedtime that it was their own candles which had been burnt.

The prize-winners were as follows:

First prize for top score		
(Ladies or Gentlemen)	L-Corpl. Harvey	Champagne
1st Lady	Corpl. Watkins	Tin of Apricots
2nd Lady	Pte. Parr	Tin of tête de porc
1st Gentleman	Sergt. Young	Tin of peaches
2nd Gentleman	Pte. A.G. Davis	2 tins of sardines
1st Booby	Pte. Draper	Pot of Stephens' jam
2nd Booby	Pte. Elliott	1 biscuit
3rd Booby	L-Corpl. Brien	1 Rough Rider cigarette

Sergt. Finch was graciously asked by Sergt. Young to present the prizes, and proceeded to do so with all his well-known esprit and bonhomie. He so praised up the skilful play of Corpls. Harvey and Watkins, expatiated on their generous natures and fondled their prizes so lovingly, that these two winners felt very relieved when at length they did hold the prizes in their own hands.

Other prizes were likewise handed over with small sermons on the evil of greed, and each winner was called upon for a speech.

One joke of Corpl. Harvey's kept the room rocking for five minutes. But the sardine winner was somewhat stage-struck, for he thrice could get no further than the middle of his opening sentence – and then Sergt. Finch struck in 'The gentleman wishes to say how pleased he is to be the fortunate recipient of this beautiful prize, whose magnificence has overcome his utterance'; etc., etc., etc.

'Those were the sentiments you wished to express my lad, weren't they? Very good, to your seat. "Quick March"!'

Sergt. Finch ended by congratulating all and sundry upon the most enjoyable evening they had spent, and hoped another drive would take place shortly.

R.E.K.

Raymond Knight and Will Harvey.

'R.E.K.' was, of course, Corporal Knight, the great comrade of Will Harvey who, by now, was known affectionately to all as 'The Little Man'. In the same issue of the *Gazette*, Will's own contribution was a poem in which he delineated beautifully between his scorn for material discomfort or danger and the treasures stored in his mind.

Ballade of the Rich Heart

What thief is he can rob this treasury,
  Which hath not gold but dreams within its gates?
What power can enter in to take from me
  My treasure, while upon the threshold waits
  'Courage', my watch-dog, keeping back the fates
Which follow close until I do depart
  In safety from their little loves and hates?
Singing of all I carry in my heart.

Guarded of dreams against all evil chance,
  With young Adventure arm in arm I go
To laugh at Luck and silly Circumstance.
  And, counting naught that comes to me my foe,
  I change, if 'tis my whim, the winter snow
To blowing blossom: and by that same art
  I fashion as I will Life's weal and woe:
Singing of all I carry in my heart.

Let me go lame and lousy like a tramp
  But feel the wind and know the moonlit sky!
What matter if the falling dew be damp –
  Still is it dew! And well contented I
  Among my dreams (in seeming poverty)
Far from the cities and the noisy mart, –
  With Life and Death – my dearest friends – to lie,
Singing of all I carry in my heart.

Conspicuous Gallantry

Envoi

Prince of this world, high monarch of all those
Who deem Reality life's better part,
Herewith I tweak thy crooked royal nose —
Singing of all I carry in my heart.

For one who in childhood and youth had been considered 'highly strung' and who had often been beset by melancholy, this bravery born of reverie may seem surprising. When 'at rest' Will wanted nothing more than to be left alone to write verses. He was separated from Gloucestershire, Anne and all that he held dear. Even so, the discipline of Army life, his humour and, above all, the comradeship of good men sustained him at so awful a time, and somehow he found a strange tranquillity in the trenches. Now that he was staring into the eyes of fate, as opposed to facing self-induced fears, he was given the necessary courage. Within days of writing 'Ballade of the Rich Heart' that courage was put to the test.

On the night of 3 August a patrol commanded by Corporal Knight, assisted by Will Harvey and six other men, was sent out to reconnoitre in No Man's Land. A few, last whispered instructions and one by one they crawled to the top of the parapet, paused, scrambled over and darted for the cover of scrub or shell-hole. Knight and four men were armed with rifles and bayonets; two others with revolvers and Mills bombs. Will carried a revolver and a heavy bludgeon. When the men had regathered around their two NCOs, the patrol moved slowly and silently over the wasteland of wreckage and death towards a clump of bushes suspected of being an enemy listening-post. Having reached about 350 yards from the safety of their own trenches they heard coughing on their right.

Creeping towards the noise they found themselves within a few paces of an enemy listening-post, put out to cover a working party which was deployed 400 yards away. Several armed Germans were clearly visible. One of the enemy, hearing the patrol, came towards them in the darkness, rifle cocked. Knight shot him.

A cutting from an illustrated war paper showing Lance-Corporal Will Harvey shooting one of the men of a German listening post at Hebuterne.

Knight and Will rushed the post, shooting two others. The rest of the patrol then came up, but, meanwhile, Will had chased after a German who was running back to enemy lines. He caught him up, and felled him with his bludgeon. The seemingly stunned man then made signs of surrendering, but as Will seized him the man tried to grab the revolver from his hand. Will pulled the trigger, but all his rounds were spent.

By now the enemy, fully alert, were opening fire from their trenches. Knight, seeing Will's danger, shouted to him to get back. The prisoner wrenched himself free and ran off.

With bullets whizzing, the patrol dashed back, reaching Allied lines at 11.15 p.m.

. . . . .

On 13 September 1915 the 1/5th Battalion was 'at rest' at Bus-les-Artois. Before setting off for a route march, the men formed up in a field just outside the village. The Commanding Officer presented the ribbon of the Distinguished Conduct Medal to the newly-promoted Sergeant R.E. Knight and to Lance-Corporal F.W. Harvey. The following citations were read out:

The Distinguished Conduct Medal has been awarded to:

2382 Corpl. R.E. KNIGHT, 1/5th Gloucestershire R. (T.F.)
    For conspicuous gallantry on the night of Aug. 3–4, 1915, near Hebuterne, when, in command of a patrol, he went out to reconnoitre in the direction of a suspected listening-post. In advancing he encountered the hostile post evidently covering a working party in the rear. Corpl. Knight at once shot one of the enemy, and with Lance-Corpl. Harvey rushed the post shooting two others, and, assistance arriving, the enemy fled. Three Germans were killed and their rifles and a Mauser pistol were brought in. The patrol had no loss.

2371 Lance-Corpl. F.W. HARVEY, 1/5th Gloucestershire R. (T.F.)
    For conspicuous gallantry on the night of Aug. 3–4, 1915, near Hebuterne, when, with a patrol, he and another non-commissioned officer went out to reconnoitre in the direction of a suspected listening-post. In advancing they encountered the hostile post, evidently covering a working party in the rear. Corporal Knight at once shot one of the enemy, and, with Lance-Corporal Harvey, rushed the post, shooting two others, and, assistance arriving, the enemy fled. Lance-Corporal Harvey pursued, felling one of the retreating Germans with a bludgeon. He seized him, but, finding his revolver empty and the enemy having opened fire, he was called back by Corporal Knight, and the prisoner escaped. Three Germans were killed, and their rifles and a Mauser pistol were brought in. The patrol had no loss.

Before leaving for the front Will had written in his notebook:[6]

I will not fear to take *ALL* LIFE. For God and not the devil rules the world. And he knows what experience we stand most in need of. Here is the key to all the gilt and iron doors.

Even so, the actual taking of human life could not be expected to leave unaffected so sensitive a soul. The only clue to Will's mental state at this time is in a letter to friends from Ivor Gurney, himself now in training with the 2/5th Battalion Glosters in Chelmsford: 'My best friend has just got a DSM (sic) . . . but his nerves are pretty shaky.'[7]

Gurney had received with admiration the news of Will's medal and he was even more enthusiastic about an exquisite poem which he had seen in the *5th Gloucester Gazette*. In a letter to another friend he wrote: 'My best friend has just got the DCM. Also he has written this:

In Flanders

I'm homesick for my hills again –
  My hills again!
To see above the Severn plain
Unscabbarded against the sky
The blue high blade of Cotswold lie;
The giant clouds go royally
By jagged Malvern with a train
Of shadows. Where the land is low
Like a huge imprisoning O
I hear a heart that's sound and high,
I hear the heart within me cry:
"I'm homesick for my hills again –
My hills again!
Cotswold or Malvern, sun or rain!
My hills again!"

That will be in anthologies hundreds of years hence, surely.'[8]

X

'The Bird Stuffer'

In the weeks following Will's daring patrol with Raymond Knight, and narrow escape from death, the Germans stepped up the intensity of their offensive in the Hebuterne sector. Enemy artillery, machine-gun and rifle fire were all increased, as was bombardment by *minenwerfers*: rifle grenades known less than affectionately by the Allied troops as 'Minnies'. Night patrols by the Glosters were continued, but now the enemy was more vigilant in No Man's Land. One patrol was surrounded by Germans near the enemy barbed wire. All but two, Lieutenant Moore and Lance-Corporal Rodway, managed to get away. These brave men, trapped, fought to the end. In the morning light their bodies were seen lying near the enemy wire; around them were at least four German dead.[1]

Now came the rain and with it that most demoralising aspect of the trench soldier's life – mud. Throughout the autumn the rain poured down, transforming the front line into a series of boggy canals. Leaking dug-outs were soon ankle-deep and the sides of trenches began to collapse. Standing for hours on end in water and mud resulted in many men suffering from trench foot. At night, movement in the trenches was even more difficult than by daylight. In such conditions it could take half an hour to cover 200 yards, dragging out one foot, embedded in mud to the knee, uncertain that the next step would find a hold beneath the quagmire.

An entry in the diary of the 1/4th Glosters for 7 December 1915 illustrates the Hebuterne trench conditions which prevailed throughout the autumn and winter.

Pumping out a trench, Hebuterne.

'The Bird Stuffer'

Battalion in the trenches. Night 6th/7th December rather
finer and very quiet. Men hard at work baling and pumping
and removing fallen side of trenches, pumping out sumps
and repairing same. The shelters for officers and men are
untenable as most have fallen in owing to the wet and are
half full of mud and water. The communication trenches are
especially bad. 'Biron' [*the trenches all had French names,
having been recently held by French troops*] for the last
hundred yards towards the firing lines is practically
impassable and 'Montrallier' in same condition from
'Haddon' to firing line. 'Napier' could not be used, also
'Sercouf'. The right company's post in 'Hoche' could only
be relieved at dusk and had to remain for twenty-four hours
at a time, and the listening post for thirteen hours: and the
left company's post in 'Bataille' could only be relieved by
night along the parapet. Continuous baling and pumping is
being kept up and sumping. 'Haddon' trench was kept free
but very bad by barricade and 'Remand' is impassable too.

Again, turning the impossible to humour, a waggish entry in the
5th Gloucester Gazette:

X.....t 4.9.15.
. . . Only men with a very well developed and powerful side
stroke can get along our communication trenches. Others
have to walk outside and risk being hit by the (?) maxim
which fires at 5 minutes past and 25 minutes to every hour.

SUN RISE ⎫ Suspended until further notice,
MOON RISE ⎭ or for duration of war.

and elsewhere in the same issue:

Nth CORPS SUMMARY

Right Division. – A noise resembling a trench pump or a
   German consuming soup was heard at 9.30 p.m.

95

Our Artillery opened fire on the GORGE in X, and
about half an hour later the noise ceased.
Rainfall for last 24 hours – 4.3836 metres.
High tide – 6.40 p.m.

Centre Division. – A prearranged provocative scheme was
successfully carried out by our Artillery in conjunction
with our Infantry.
A German opposite the STUNTED OAK fired a shot at
10.23 p.m. This breach of promise was preceded by
a salvo of variegated lights from the enemy's third
line.
An excellent system of shower baths has installed itself
in all dugouts.
Weather – Showery.
Rainfall. – (We regret that the graduated mess tin was
inadvertently buried in one of innumerable land slides.)

Left Division. – An Officer's patrol *Again* penetrated the
enemy's system of artificial lakes. Whilst the enemy's
attention was distracted by an (Unpaid) Lance-Corpl.
imitating a flight of wild geese rejoicing over an unopened
egg, the officer rammed and sank four ration punts lying
alongside the Company (?) headquarters.
The stewards were drowned in their sleep, so know
nothing about the matter at present. The Officer reports
the punts to have been in a bad state of repair. In addition
two Unteroffiziers were snared with caviare sandwiches
and brought into our lines.
All remaining trenches in this sector are supported by
telephone wire revetment only.

Washed out of their homes by the floods, thousands of rats
infested the dug-outs. As if this wet squalor was not misery enough,
another pest assailed the men which even periods 'at rest' did not
relieve:

It was just at this period of our trench life that one noticed at various times of the day certain of one's comrades acting in a very odd manner, and when they thought they were being observed, became embarrassed or affected an air of unconcern. This extraordinary behaviour soon became more general – in fact the General himself may have caught on the craze – i.e. the scratching of the uniform with short intervals between each operation. The truth leaked out eventually. Lice, the most obnoxious of all minute wanderers of the night, had begun to make themselves felt. A good bath coupled with a change of strongly disinfected garments, did not prevent the wretched things from becoming more familiar with one's attire. An hour after the bath and change, one would be the disgusting possessor of just as many families of 'chats' as were innocently lodged in the garments handed over to the Sprinkler Bath Attendant to be boiled and baked. Repeated efforts were made to exterminate them by means of the special powder sent out from England, but the little devils simply dug their heels in, and eating it wholesale, waxed fat.[2]

Whilst 'at rest' at Bus-les-Artois on 9 October the officers played the sergeants at football: result, nil–nil. In the evening a concert was given by the Motor Transport Troupe. The programme was only half-way through when the alarm sounded for all the men to return to their billets immediately and pack up for inspection by the CO. In a nearby field, Lt.-Col. Collett kept the battalion standing for an hour whilst he carried out a minute inspection of each man, paying particular attention to their water bottles. To his chagrin no 'gargle', the object of his search, was found.[3]

This small incident shows that, in spite of trench conditions, there was no let-up in the maintenance of military descipline in or out of the line. But nor was there any resentment at its enforcement, which is the more surprising. To his credit, Lt.-Col. Collett showed no resentment either when Will Harvey submitted a poem about him to the *5th Gloucester Gazette*. In fact, it appeared on the front page of the September 1915 edition in large print and in solitary isolation.

The C. O.

(*With apologies to Herrick.*[4])

A sweet disorder in the dress
Kindles in him small kindliness.
My slack puttees him oft have thrown
Into a fine distraction.
An erring lace he cannot bear
Nor the neglected flowing hair.
Did he command that splendid force –
The W.V.T.C. – of course
He'd see they dressed with careful art,
Very precise in every part.
And would, I'm certain, never dote
On the tempestuous petticoat.

But, in any case, the CO had already recommended Will and Raymond Knight for commissions, and on 15 October these came through. The *Gazette* gave the battalion advanced notice of the good news.

Most of our readers are by this time aware that 'F.W.H.', who has contributed so much to this *Gazette* is none other than Lce.-Corpl. F.W. Harvey, DCM. We are very glad to think that although he will shortly be in 'another place' – i.e. forsaking the Lower for the Upper House – he will still help to make this *Gazette* just what is has always claimed to be: 'A record, serious and humorous, of the Fifth Gloucestershire Regiment'. While we congratulate him and Lce.-Sergt. Knight on being awarded the medals they have so thoroughly deserved we wish them, and Lce.-Corpl. Robertson, every success in their new rôle.

A few weeks earlier Will had been granted a few days' leave at home. The Redlands again and the stunning contrast of Tillie's care, quiet comfort and Anne's love, set against the unspoken pain of trench life. By now Eric was engaged and soon to be married before taking up his commission with the 1/5th Battalion Glosters, and Roy had transferred from the Royal Wilts Yeomanry on being appointed to a commission in the Royal Engineers in June 1915. How proud Tillie must have been that all three of her soldier sons were to be officers, although trembling inwardly perhaps.

Whilst at home Will completed three poems for the *Gazette* under the combined heading 'Leave'. They are: 'The Soldier Speaks', 'The Awakening' and 'Land of Heart's Delight'. Here is the second of them:

The Awakening

At night, in dream,
I saw those fields round home
    Agleam.
Drenched all with dew
Beneath day's newest dome
    Of gold and blue.
All night –
All night they shone for me, and then
    Came light.
And suddenly I woke, and lovely joy!
I was at home, with the fields gold as when
    I was a boy.

. . . . .

Thus shall men rise up at last to see,
Their dearest dreams golden reality.

F.W. Harvey SOLDIER, POET

His return to France was marked in the *Gazette* for October by three pieces, including two humorous poems, one in honour of the sergeant-major and the other a triolet 'The Crossing':

> I'm not feeling well,
> And the waves won't be quiet,
> My companions can tell
> I'm not feeling well.
>
> And I'm going to – Oh hell!
> Supply fishes their diet.
> I'm not feeling well,
> And the waves won't be quiet.

. . . . .

The Church at Hebuterne.

'The Bird Stuffer'

In mid-November 1915 Will was again home from France, this time for a few weeks of officer training. Leaving the mud temporarily, and the life of a junior NCO permanently, he came away from the front line burdened down by his full kit, the books which had been his trench companions and a small statuette of the Sacred Heart salvaged from the ruins of Hebuterne's shattered church.[5] It is probable that he also carried in his pack the manuscripts of the many poems written at the front and which, with additions published in the *5th Gloucester Gazette* up to July 1916, were to comprise his first and most successful collection of verse: *A Gloucestershire Lad.*

One reader of that collection, writing to a friend who had given it to him as a gift, remembered meeting Will on his way back to England:

> I have looked through *A Gloucestershire Lad*, and find to
> my surprise that I know the author. I was in the same
> division in my lance-corporal days. I met Harvey when I was
> going home on promotion. Someone pointed him out to me
> as a DCM. I never saw anyone less like a hero in my life.
> Imagine a small, dirty, nearly middle-aged man, wearing
> glasses and an apologetic air, trudging along the *pavé* under
> a huge pack (he looked more like a learned tortoise than
> anything else I can think of), grasping a huge hard wood
> bludgeon – the bludgeon he did the deed with. I remember
> saying to a Gloucestershire private, 'Your DCM looks as if
> he stuffed birds in civil life', and we called him 'the bird-
> stuffer' all the way to Blighty.
>
> He was, I think, taking the bludgeon home to his mother,
> and was most apologetic about his medal when I
> congratulated him. So he is a poet into the bargain! This is
> a wonderful army of ours![6]

XI

A Gloucestershire Lad

'After all, Harvey could not get leave, and so every part of my plan miscarried, and we never met. Well, well; so wags the world . . . . This is chiefly to let you know that we are nearly certain to be off on Saturday to Tidworth that haunt of devils.'[1] So wrote Ivor Gurney in February 1916, informing friends that the 2/5th Battalion Glosters were leaving Chelmsford. Will Harvey had returned to France in the previous month to rejoin the 1/5th at Hebuterne.

The pip on his sleeve brought, of course, new burdens. The leadership and therefore the lives of his men, rather than his own life alone, were now his responsibility. He would also have a greater insight into the conduct of the war and perhaps a glimpse of the reality, the awful reality, of the shortcomings of the High Command. The winter was bitterly cold, but not until 23 February were the soldiers issued with warm coats; even then, the coats became a refuge for lice. Standing in half-frozen mud Will would have watched the suffering of his men knowing that his role was to ask them to suffer more.

His time in England would have stunned him with another reality: the ignorance of people at home about conditions at the front. Sandwiched between two of Will's poems in the March 1916 edition of the *5th Gloucester Gazette*, we find the following article:

ON LEAVE

It was delightful to be home, of course. First time too. So I sallied forth at 11.30 a.m. on the first morning to spread

Second Lieutenant F.W. Harvey.

myself a bit – after all we had been in front line trenches for seven long months. I had a few good original jokes too.

The morning was fine, and everything surprisingly as I had left it. The same ancient dog was parading in the sun at the house at the corner. The same ancient man, who always came on Thursdays, was making the day hideous with 'Tom Bowling' on the same impossible cornet. The same ancient road man was performing mystic rites with a juicy-looking pat of mud. I remembered in my childhood wondering why it wasn't good to eat. I couldn't see any sign of the dashing damsel (the owner, I believe, of the ancient dog) but an earnest young woman in nurse's kit on a bicycle who nearly knocked me down at the crossing may have been she. It was just as I was wondering about this and looking back that I collided with Mrs Vic. Mrs V. is a remarkably good talker. She got off the mark at once. 'So glad to see you, Arthur. How well you look! What, on leave? How nice! And when do you expect to go abroad? Soon, I suppose. I'm afraid you won't look so well after you have been in those dreadful trenches. Really, I can't think how those poor dears stand it. Fancy shells bursting all round them day and night, and no pyjamas to sleep in! Well, good-bye, I hope you'll get out soon. I expect you're looking forward to it' – and off she went. I took a deep breath, and went on somewhat stunned, but then, I reflected, Mrs Vic. was not a genius anyhow.

Eventually I laughed and was hailed at the same time by the Vicar. 'Hullo, Brown,' quoth he, 'What are you doing here?' I replied that I was 'back on leave'. He paused and I could see that he was wondering how to conceal the fact that he hadn't the foggiest notion whether I had been out of England, or not. 'Oh!' he began, 'Let me see. What Regiment are you in? Oh, yes, the Gloucesters, of course' (making a plunge) 'they're abroad aren't they?' I told him they were, and had been for seven months. He looked doubtful. 'I suppose you haven't been in the – er' – firing line yet?' he queried. 'You have? Really! I had no idea. I suppose the trenches are very warm spots. Continual

fighting, eh? Well, well, and when is the war going to end?
You fellows out there must know much more about it than
we do.' I told him I didn't know, and he seemed
disappointed. 'One of our wounded tells me the Germans
can't last another month. Such an interesting man with
wonderful experiences – an Irishman. He tells me the stories
of German atrocities are perfectly true. He says himself that
he found in a village captured from the Germans during the
retreat from Mons, a large case addressed to the Crown
Prince and marked immediate and perishable. When they
opened it, it was full of children's hands.' He looked at me
obviously expecting me to play up, but I felt that Pte.
O'Callaghan (that was the wounded man's name) was
probably uncappable, and the Vicar hastened on obviously
suspecting me of prevarication. I felt puzzled, and several
sizes smaller.

Still pondering, I spied James. James is a bachelor, and
unfit for service, but leads an active life during the war
doing a variety of amazing jobs. He was in a hurry, but
crossed the road, and shook me warmly by the hand. 'Heard
you'd gone out, old man. How are you? I suppose you
haven't been in the front line yet?' I explained, somewhat
hopelessly. 'Well, well. When's the war going to end? You
ought to know. Heard the story of that trench at Wipers?
They were so close to the Boches, – so the chap who told
me said – that they had one parapet, and took turns at the
loop holes. So long, I must hurry on now.'

And so on. Things went from bad to worse. I talked to 18
people, of whom 3 asked me when I was going to the front,
9 asked me when we were going into the firing line, and all
asked me when the war was going to end. Finally I met
Smith. 'Tell me,' he said, 'all about the trenches.' 'Well, of
course,' I replied, 'we haven't really been in the firing line
yet. There is such a demand to be sent into the front line,
that there is a long waiting list at GHQ of Battalions
waiting their turn. Every month there is a ballot for the
privilege, though no Regiment who has not been out at least

twelve months can enter. It is wonderful to see the joy when the news comes that a regiment has succeeded. They march up with bands playing, and colours flying – you must have seen the pictures. Bayonets are fixed, and all the fuses of the bombs lighted. Often the bombers, out of sheer light-heartedness throw bombs at each other, and other less fortunate regiments on the road. Soon they pass through the 10th, 9th, 8th, 7th, 6th, 5th, 4th, 3rd and 2nd lines and reach the goal of their march – the firing line. They are of course shelled on the way. If they are not shelled it is pathetic to see their disappointment. Often they refuse to proceed until a proper baptism of fire is theirs. (Oh yes, I like shelling. It is a glorious and exhilarating sensation. Any of the London Daily Papers will tell you so.) Finally they reach the front line. Often there is a struggle with the Regiment already there, who are of course reluctant to move out. However, fighting begins at once. Every rifle bursts into rapid fire, every bomb is hurled at the hated enemy. The roar of rifles, bombs, shells and *minenwerfers* is continuous by day and night. Hardly can the men be persuaded to eat, or take a sip of rum. From time to time an attack is made on the German trenches, when the uproar is double. By night the sky is lit up from sea to sea with star shells. Any of the papers will tell you what a star shell is. So the war goes on day and night. That is what the Official Communiqués mean when they say 'On the Western Front all is quiet'. Then you should see the dug-outs. Wonderful places they are. The walls are hung with pictures by the most famous artists, and carefully papered. The ceilings are in many cases beautifully frescoed. Baths with hot and cold water are provided. The floor of the trenches themselves are always covered with oil-cloth – provided by the RE.'

Smith was openly interested, but puzzled about something. 'I thought the Gloucesters had had some casualties,' he remarked. 'One lad I heard of, was, I know, shot through the head. I don't understand —.'

'Oh, yes,' I replied, 'we have had casualties. Not from

German bullets, of course – mostly from falling down stairs.
The man you heard of may have been one of those who
committed suicide because he couldn't live always in the
firing line.'

Smith pondered. I could see his last doubt was removed.
'Most interesting,' he murmured; 'what you tell me all
agrees with those splendid accounts in the *Daily Hum*. And
when will the war end?' 'February 29th, 1917,' I answered,
and left him pondering.

I was not kind to Smith but I felt better as I walked back
home to enjoy a civilised meal and people who did
understand.

The poem in this issue and that which precedes it take on a
mantle of sharp bitterness for perhaps the first time. There is none
of the vacuous jingoism here which just then was flowing from the
pens of men such as Herbert Asquith ('Above the clouds what lights
are gleaming?/God's batteries are those,/Or souls of soldiers,
homeward streaming,/To banquet with their foes?'). Nor is there
any self-pity in these lines. The first poem printed in the *Gazette*
opens in the style of one of F.W.H.'s light-hearted ballads, but at
line six the fumes rise from the unstoppered acid bottle.

To The Kaiser – Confidentially

I met a man – a refugee
  And he was blind in both his eyes, Sir,
And in his pate
A silver plate
('Twas rather comical to see!)
  Shone where the bone skull used to be
Before your shrapnel struck him, Kaiser,
  Shattering in the self same blast
(Blind as a tyrant in his dotage)
  The foolish wife
Who risked her life,

As peasants will do till the last,
Clinging to one small Belgian cottage.

That was their home. The whining child
  Beside him in the railway carriage
Was born there, and
  The little land
Around it (now untilled and wild)
  Was brought him by his wife on marriage.
The child was whining for its mother,
  And interrupting half he said, Sir,
I'll never see the pair again
  Nor they the mother that lies dead, Sir.

That's all – a foolish tale, nor worth
  The ear of noble lord or Kaiser,
A man un-named
  By shrapnel maimed,
Wife slain, home levelled to the earth
  That's all. You see no point? nor I, Sir,
Yet on the day you come to die, Sir,
  When all your war dreams cease to be
Perchance will rise
  Before your eyes
(Piercing your hollow heart, Sir Kaiser!)
  The picture that I chanced to see
Riding (we'll say) from A to B.

In 'A Present from Flanders', printed in the ninth edition of the
Gazette, the mood is of pastoral serenity until the last two lines
snatch us by the lapels.

A Present from Flanders

Where dewfall and the moon
Make precious things

A Gloucestershire Lad

On every small festoon
A spider slings:

Treading – like dead leaves, under
All drifted days
Happy the lovers wander
In Winter ways.

No thought of pain perplexes
The peace they hold.
No worldly sorrow vexes
The lovers. Gold –

All golden gleams the way,
How strange such riches
Drawn from rough men should be,
Seven or eight worlds away
Fighting, and carelessly
Dying in ditches!

It is not that the men who are forced to fight 'seven or eight worlds away' die because of their own carelessness of course. The poet's anger is directed at the Establishment of seven or eight worlds removed which apparently does not care greatly about them.

By April, preparations were under way for the 'Big Push': the Somme offensive. Perhaps Will sensed the slaughter ahead. Perhaps, too, the death of Nigel Bartlett, aged 22, on another front set the very real possibility of his own death churning over in his mind. Whatever the cause, the poems now became shrouded in foreboding. Of three which were printed in the *Gazette* under the collective title 'A Gloucestershire Lad', only the latter two appeared when the book bearing the same title was published in September 1916.

Nigel Bartlett.

A Gloucestershire Lad

The Day

In thunder and thick hail
　Of Death's on-driving storm
The day of battle breaks.

Now earth beneath us shakes
　Threshed with a hellish flail
For granary of the worm.

Lo, here at last the hour
　Wherefore our prayers were said
Whereto my fate has moved . . .

God of the living and dead
　O gird us now with power
For all that we have loved!

To his Maid

Since above Time, upon Eternity
　The lovely essence of true loving's set,
Time shall not triumph over you and me,
　Nor – though we pay his debt –
　Shall Death hold mastery.
Your eyes are bright for ever, your dark hair
　Hold an eternal shade. Like a bright sword
Shall flame the vision of your strange sweet ways,
　Cleaving the years; and even your smallest word
Lying, forgotten with the things that were,
　Shall glow and kindle, burning up the days.

The Return

The unimaginable hour
   That folds away our joys and pain,
Holds not the spirit in its power.
   Therefore I shall come home again –
(Where ever my poor body lies) –
   And whisper in the Summer trees
Upon a lazy fall and rise
   Of wind: and in day's red decline
Walk with the sun those roads of mine
   Then rosy with my memories.
Though you may see me not, yet hear
   My laughter in the laughing streams –
My footsteps in the running rain . . .
   For sake of all I counted dear
And visit still within my dreams
   I shall at last come home again.

By now Eric, commissioned in the Gloucestershire Territorials, had rejoined the battalion and was serving in France. The *Gazette* records that another Lieutenant Harvey, Roy of course, of the Motor Machine Gun Corps, paid a short visit to the 1/5th Glosters one afternoon, and so it is possible that the three brothers were able to meet together for one last time.

Roy's visit may well have caused a stir because he would have arrived in one of the first armoured cars to be used in warfare. This was literally a motor car; a massive automobile covered in armour-plating with a machine-gun mounted in a turret on top of the body. Such was the vehicle of the Motor Machine Gun Corps. Not until July 1916 did the first tanks appear: two wheels at the back and marked 'HMLS' – 'His Majesty's Land Ship'.

At this time Edith Harvey, a cousin, was in London contributing to the war effort by driving ambulances and lorries. Will sent his poetry to Edith who typed it and prepared it for publication. She suggested submission of the first collection, *A Gloucestershire Lad*,

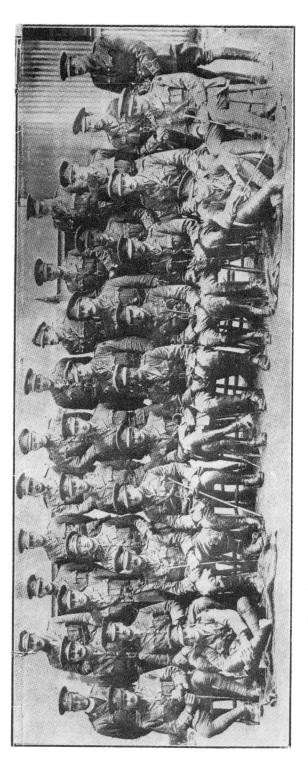

The Officers of the 2/5th Gloucesters photographed on Salisbury Plain before embarkation for France.

Back row: Lt. B. C. Bernard, Lt. J. Hunter, Lt. J. Hunter, Lt. Naldrett, Lt. Vaughan, Capt. L. Dudbridge, 2nd Lt. Knight, 2nd Lt. Harvey, 2nd Lt. Foster, 2nd Lt. Blyth.

2nd row: Rev. P. Milum, Capt. Worthington, Lt. E. H. Harvey, Capt. C. S. Cole, Lt. C. Cole, Capt. M. F. Badcock, Lt. Pyke-Nott, Lt. O. Harrison, Lt. Miles, Capt. R. B. Sinclair, Lt. Curtois, Capt. Bickwell.

3rd row: Capt. J. K. E. Rickerby, Capt. Wise, Capt. A. F. Barnes, Major Wales, Major G. C. Beloe, Lt.-Col. P. Balfour, Major the Right Hon. C. P. Allen, Major G. Davies, M.P., Capt. J. E. Hollington, Capt. S. B. Tubbs.

Front row: 2nd Lt. Wallick, 2nd Lt. Neal.

Roy Harvey sitting on an armoured car.

to Rupert Brooke's publisher, Sidgwick & Jackson. The head of the firm, Frank Sidgwick, readily accepted Harvey's work on its merit.[2]

Some time later Marion Scott, Registrar at the Royal College of Music and Ivor Gurney's mentor, wrote to Harvey's mother asking how she might achieve a similar success for Gurney's poetry, which was being sent to her from the trenches. Mrs Harvey's advice and assistance were clearly successful; Sidgwick & Jackson accepted Ivor Gurney's first volume of poems, *Severn and Somme*.

At the end of April, Will and Eric were summoned back to England, transferred from the 1/5th to the new support battalion, the 2/5th, and billeted at Park House Camp on Salisbury Plain awaiting orders for France. On 5 May the 2/5th Glosters were present at a huge parade inspected by King George V.

> It was a most impressive sight. Twenty thousand men, hundreds of horses and wagons all moving together in an endless line, under the command of a single man -- all very fine, fixed bayonets, drawn swords, and bands playing. One does not wish to be a pessimist, but I could not help wondering how many would come back alive from France. The whole mass rolling forward looks irresistible. I have

never before taken part in a review on this scale. As we went by, there were scores of pretty girls and smart motors. I wonder if they realised how much extra work this show meant to us – how we had been up and about since 4.30 a.m., had marched nine miles carrying 70lbs. on our backs – and did they realise that we should get nothing to eat except hard biscuits until 4.30 p.m. . . .[3]

Nor could the pretty girls have realised that only seven weeks later an equal number of men to those marching proudly in endless line past their King would lie dead at the end of a single day of battle.

On 25 May 1916 the 2/5th Glosters sailed to Le Havre and on 15 June they were in the trenches at Laventie; Pte. Ivor Gurney was with them. At last Will and Ivor could meet, albeit infrequently. Gurney was not in Will's platoon and in the heat of battle the opportunities to talk together were sadly few.

The first day of July came and with it the Somme offensive. The 5th Glosters were spared the carnage of that first day of squandered lives, but in the weeks that followed they were to pay the price demanded by a faceless High Command.

The *5th Gloucester Gazette* of September 1916 proudly records the three Military Crosses, two Distinguished Conduct Medals and seven Military Medals awarded to officers and men of the battalion; one of the Military Crosses to Second Lieutenant Eric Harvey.

In the same issue of the *Gazette* appears the official statement on the effectiveness of the offensive, which leaves unsaid far more than it claims:

THE BATTLE OF THE SOMME

No matter what test you take, the offensive on the Somme has shewn itself in every single point superior to the German effort upon the Verdun sector last February and early March. It struck against a wider front; captured more ground more quickly, took far more prisoners and far more guns – it was at once the greater and the better of the two operations.

Laventie.

This is followed by the journal's own, modest editorial:

> The part which a single Division is called upon to play in
> such a Battle is not great, if measured by the actual frontage
> upon which it operates. Nevertheless the 48th Division, our
> own Brigade, this Battalion, have done their bit in the Big
> Push. In years to come, their record, in common with that of
> other Divisions which operated on the La Boisselle, Ovillers
> and Pozieres sectors, will be famous. The men of the 48th
> helped to make history.

Of the bloodstained miscalculation which was the Somme what
remains to be said? Of the five days and nights of heavy artillery
bombardment which was to have destroyed the enemy front line
and wire, but did neither; of the obedient infantrymen who went
over the top and walked forward to be cut down by unremitting
machine-gun fire; of the 60,000 British casualties on the first day of
the battle, 20,000 of them dead?

In the third week of July, the 1/4th, 1/5th and 1/6th Battalions of

The Somme, 1916.

the Glosters Territorials were in the front line north-east of
Ovillers. The Commanding Officer of the 1/6th Battalion, Lt.-Col.
Micklem, gave the following account of his men in action on
22 July:[4]

'Party of RE, under Lieutenant Briggs, with a covering party,
moved off ahead of the Battalion to place a tape on a due
east line from Point 47 to the railway. Lieutenant Briggs
worked rapidly and well and the tape was fixed just before
the head of the Battalion reached the railway end of the
tape.'
    Three companies were attacking with one in reserve.
'The Battalion moved through Ovillers along the road and
emerged at Point 78. They proceeded in single file along the
left of the railway and formed up on the tape behind the
covering party. The area over which they had to move was
being steadily shelled with 5.9s, but the men behaved well
and the companies moved into their assembly positions
without a hitch.
    'At about 12.15 a.m., they started moving forward, and
though the shelling continued there were few casualties.
Shortly before zero the leading waves were roughly 70 yards
from their objective and still moving steadily. At this period
machine-gun fire was opened from the front and fell about
39 and 40 on the right. The fire was very accurate and the
leading waves were cut down. The subsequent waves moved
on but very few got through the zone of the machine-guns.
    'As far as I can gather from statements of the few NCOs
and men who returned, a party of about six men entered the
enemy trenches just north-west of Point 40 and engaged the
enemy with bombs. One of this party has returned. He
states that he was captured and his equipment and bomb
bag taken from him. However, in the excitement he
managed to get a bomb out of his pocket, which he threw
among his guard, and in the confusion escaped. All the
officers but one who started are casualties and information
is difficult to obtain, but it seems that the last waves of the

consolidating company did not get into the zone of machine-gun fire. They state that they saw the whole of the unit on their right retire and retired after them. The following numbers have been reported unwounded up to the present: A Company (left assault) 42; C Company (right assault) 29; D Company (consolidating company) 71.

'Casualties were difficult to collect as gas shells were fired on roads 78–39 and gas helmets had to be worn, but at 6.15 a.m. bearers and volunteers were working in the open quite unmolested up to a line about east and west through 47.

'One of C Company's Lewis guns, with three of the team, is reported to be dug in about 40 yards west of Point 40.

'Casualties among officers were very heavy, C and D Companies losing all theirs and only one coming in from A Company. As far as I can gather they are as follows: 3 killed, 2 probably killed, 4 wounded and brought in, 1 suffering from gas. The RE officer whose section went forward is also missing.

'The cause of the failure was, in my opinion, the lack of artillery preparation. None of the machine-guns previously reported had been knocked out and the enemy line had hardly been shelled at all. The barrage which I understood was to keep the enemy's heads down while the assaulting troops advanced was quite useless as there were long intervals when not a single shell burst on the front to be attacked. The result of this was that the enemy's machine-guns, having nothing to worry them, were able to fire on the assaulting troops as they pleased.

'From all accounts the men behaved very well and moved steadily through a heavy shell-fire, but the zone of the machine-gun fire seems to have been quite impassable. The commanders of the leading companies were killed and the men who have returned state that their behaviour was magnificent, particularly Lieutenant Parramore, OC A Company, who they say behaved as if he was on the barrack square though he was hit and . . . [*word indecipherable*] a very heavy fire from machine-guns. Even after being hit in the stomach he continued to lead the men till he fell dead. Reliable information is difficult to obtain now the officers and nearly all the NCOs of the leading companies are casualties.'

A subsequent account of the action from men who came in during the night of the 23rd/24th July follows:

'The men all state that the attacking party started off all right in its proper waves. When they approached the German parapet they found *good wire* and were held up by very heavy machine-gun fire. Second Lieutenant (H.) Corbett and most of the leading wave were killed. The second and third waves came up under 2nd Lieutenant (H.I.) Balderson, who was killed. Major (C.E.) Coates, commanding the assaulting troops, then came up with the next waves. Three other officers just behind were wounded and this accounted for all the officers.'

On 21 July the 5th Battalion had faced the slaughter. D Company reached its objective on the enemy front line and went over into a German trench. A machine-gun mounted on a barricade, firing straight down the trench, mowed them down. One of the three officers leading the attack was Second Lieutenant R.E. Knight.

Will Harvey's final contribution to the *Gazette* appears in the September 1916 edition. It is an epitaph to the friend who called him to safety in August 1915 and who had been by his side in danger and 'at rest' throughout the war.

In Memoriam

Second Lieutenant R.E. KNIGHT, DCM
Died of wounds, July 25th

Dear, rash, warm-hearted friend,
So careless of the end,

Lieutenants Harvey (A) and Knight (B), 1916.

So worldly-foolish, so divinely-wise,
Who, caring not one jot
For place, gave all you'd got
To help your lesser fellow-men to rise.

Swift-footed, fleeter yet
Of heart. Swift to forget
The petty spite that life or men could show you;
Your last long race is won
But beyond the sound of gun
You laugh and help men onward – if I know you.

O still you laugh, and walk,
And sing and frankly talk
(To angels) of the matters that amused you
In this bitter-sweet of life,
And we who keep its strife
Take comfort in the thought how God has used you.

Within two weeks of Will writing those heartfelt lines, the newsboys standing at the Cross in Gloucester were calling out a persistent message: 'LOCAL POET MISSING!'

COMRADES
IN CAPTIVITY

Autumn in prison

Here where no tree changes,
   Here in a prison of pine,
I think how Autumn ranges
   The country that is mine.

There – rust upon the chill breeze –
   The woodland leaf now whirls;
There sway the yellowing birches
   Like dainty dancing girls.

Oh, how the leaves are dancing
   With Death at Lassington!
And Death is now enhancing
   Beauty I walked upon.

The roads with leaves are littered,
   Yellow, brown, and red.
The homes where robins twittered
   Lie ruin; but instead

Gaunt arms of stretching giants
   Stand in the azure air,
Cutting the sky in pattern
   So common, yet so fair,

The heart is kindled by it,
   And lifted as with wine,
In Lassington and Highnam –
   The woodlands that were mine.

XII

Capture

On 16 August 1916 Will Harvey's company had moved into a new part of the line in the Fauquissart Sector, south of Laventie. Here, in No Man's Land, there was long grass and a hedge which ran from the British to within a few feet of the German trenches. Seeing this, Will suggested to his colonel that the cover was so good that it would be possible for a scout to be up there the whole night, taking note of the position of enemy trench mortar and machine-gun emplacement positions. Ever restless to prove his courage, he offered to do this himself. 'Umph!' said the colonel with a smile, 'we shall see.'

That first night was given up to trench consolidation, but it was decided that on the second night a patrol should be taken out to explore the land in front. Because of his previous experience, Will was appointed company-commander of the patrolling party. The next morning Will met briefly with Ivor Gurney and lent him his copy of Robert Bridges' *The Spirit of Man*. For the rest we have his own account from *Comrades in Captivity* (See Notes, p. 348):

On August 17 it occurred to me during my 'rest period' that, as I knew nothing of the ground we were to patrol that night, I might as well go out and have a look at it. Long unburned grass between the trenches afforded plenty of cover, and it is common knowledge that the hours between two and five were the quietest period of the day alike for German soldiers and English. During that period everyone except the sentry was asleep, and sometimes – well, there

have been cases in our own Army, and subsequent events go
to prove that probably the Germans were subject to the
same demands of Nature. It had been a practice of mine,
ever since I was made responsible for patrols, personally to
examine the ground before I took my men over it, and this
seemed a good opportunity. The particular object of my
scouting was to become acquainted with the nature of the
ground over which I was to lead a patrol that evening; the
general object to pick up any information likely to be of use
to the battalion in general. Because there was at that time no
experienced patroller in the company (the battalion being
newly out), and because the men were all tired on account
of overnight fatigues, I decided to go alone. My company
officer had gone off somewhere down the line, taking the
other subaltern with him, so I woke up a corporal asleep in
a dug-out, informed him of my intentions, and instructed
him to warn the sentries, and to replace the wire after me in
the sally-port. Then I started.

After leaving the trench, I went crawling along in shadow
of the hedge, which ran through our lines and terminated
just in front of the enemy parapet, at this point about three
hundred yards off. I carried an automatic pistol.

When the hedge ended the grass became short, and before
leaving that cover I lay and listened for about ten minutes. A
bird sang close by, but there was no sound of digging,
talking or firing, nor, incidentally, was there any sign of
German listening posts in the grass.

My primary and particular object was achieved. If I had
had a man with me I should now have gone back, but I was
beginning to be rather pleased with myself, and, there being
no other life than mine at stake, I crawled forward out of
cover.

Shell-hole by shell-hole I worked my way cautiously to a
little ditch or drain which ran through a gap in the German
wire and on to the parapet.

Along this drain, carefully edging my way, I came at last
into the projected shadow of the parapet, where I lay

(holding my breath) to listen. There was not a sound. I twisted my head sideways, and looked up. Nowhere along the parapet, which here jutted out into a point, was there visible either head or periscope.

I wriggled up a little higher and looked quickly over the top into the trench. There was nobody there.

Reason told me at this point that it would be better to go back. What a little thing in human life is reason! Besides, there were at least three reasons against doing so. These were, first, and of course chiefly, that I did not want to go back, having come so far, without some evidence (eg, a cap or a rifle) to corroborate my report, and show to the men who were new to patrol work. This would give them confidence, and show them how easy it was. Secondly and thirdly there were two reasons in favour of the trench being unoccupied: (a) About the same hour the day before I had, in a little fit of rashness, to the consternation of my good sergeant, stepped quickly over our parapet into the borrow ditch at a point just opposite here. Not a shot was fired at me going out, or returning. (b) Though this was mere hearsay, there had been talk in our mess of a certain officer of artillery who, being sent up to find an observation post, had gone too far, and in fact visited the enemy's lines, putting this parapet (so it was averred) to a highly improper and insulting use ere he returned – and without any hostile response.

These things, added to the evidence which I had personally accumulated, were sufficient to persuade me that it was reasonable to do what I wanted to do, go on. The Germans, so I argued, being in need of men for the Somme offensive, which was then in progress, had withdrawn troops, leaving this trench held not at all in the daytime, and only lightly at night. A few machine-guns and some trench mortars were probably all they were relying on. To make sure of *this* was not merely sport, but important work. 'Be damned if I go back!' said I, and slipped straightway over the top into the trench beneath.

It is easier to get into a German trench than to get out. I had barely reached the next bay, which was also empty, when I heard footsteps, and a good many of them, coming along behind me. If I turned back to find my hole in the wire I ran the risk of meeting those feet before I got to it. It seemed better to go on. The trench was a good deal deeper than ours, but I expected to find holes through the parados such as our own trench possessed in large numbers. Through one of these I could creep, finding cover in the long grass behind, and a place where I could watch what was going on around me.

Will now recalled the colonel's tacit approval of his plan to stay in No Man's Land all night. If luck was with him he could now, by force of circumstances, prove his point. But his luck was out.

Nowhere in the parados was there any sign of an exit. The feet were getting nearer. I continued to walk down the trench before them, looking quickly to the right and left for cover. Then, at the end of the bay, I caught sight of a small iron shelter. It was the only place. I approached it swiftly, and was hurrying in when two hefty Germans met me in the doorway. I was seized. My pistol was wrenched away. There was no escape possible. I was cut off from my hole in the wire. The men were shouting something in an excited manner. It was absurd, but – unquestionably I was their prisoner.

It is a strange thing, but to be made prisoner is undoubtedly the most surprising thing that can happen to a soldier. It is an event which one has never considered, never by any chance anticipated.

Yet prisoners are taken pretty frequently. I had myself collared a man the year before on patrol. I had seen German prisoners at work on the river at Rouen. I had heard of our own men being captured, and seen posters in England asking for money to buy food for them.

Yet now I was dumbfounded.

Capture

A few days after Will was reported missing his first collection of poems – *A Gloucestershire Lad* – was published by Sidgwick & Jackson. It was an immediate success.

XIII

Solitary Confinement

Will's first reaction to his capture was, typically, laughter. One of the two German soldiers who took him prisoner looked 'so ridiculously like a certain labourer that I had left working on my father's farm in England that I simply burst out laughing – which possibly saved my life.' Subsequent events were less amusing.

The bewildered captors took Will to their officer who, with his fellow-officers, was equally surprised. They did not believe that he had been patrolling alone in No Man's Land. Where was the rest of the patrol? Where was the attack to be? Clearly this English officer must be interrogated – and quickly.

With very little delay, a motor car, requisitioned by telephone, met Will and his guard on a road to the rear of the German trenches.

It was getting dusk. The car bumped over the cobbles at a rattling pace, overtaking everything we saw which was going in the same direction. Transport was beginning to move. A company of soldiers marched trench-ward, grey in the shadow of the grey poplars which lined the road. It all seemed very queer and exciting. We had wondered so often what it was like on the other side of those German trenches, knowing of course that it must be very similar to our side, yet hardly believing it to be so. Now I was seeing.

After several miles the car stopped at a large house: local headquarters of the German secret service. Will, questioned by a senior officer, gave his name, rank and regiment, after which he lied to any further inquiries.

> It was at this point that the affable gentleman in charge of my cross-examination smiled, and, calling for a map, proceeded to point out places, and to tell me quite accurately all I knew about our regiment, its billets, its periods of rest, its history during the war, its superior officers, and much more that I did not know myself. Then he asked me where our guns were. Not knowing where they actually were, I was afraid to do more than smile, asking him if he really expected me to tell him, for I might have spoken the truth out of sheer ignorance!

Apparently, the Germans knew far more than Will about the Allied dispositions. Further questioning was pointless. The next morning he was taken by train to Douai and imprisoned in the barracks.

> There, alone in a lousy little room for (I believe) ten days, I had leisure to think – to think. All my previous experience of captivity had been so strange and hasty, so kaleidoscopic, that I hardly realized that I was a prisoner.
>
> It was as though I had dropped in to see a lot of rather eccentric strangers, and would presently go back to my friends to laugh over my experiences. I had talked and acted in a queer dream-world, and all the time, interested but slightly incredulous, stood behind myself.
>
> Now I had time to reflect on the reality of it all. 'By God,' I spoke suddenly to the room, 'they've got me!'
>
> Everything – room, lice, solitude, dirty black bread, bowl of brown disgusting soup – corroborated the statement. I was a prisoner. I should be reported missing. My mother would be duly notified, and would grieve, not knowing whether I was alive or dead. My friends in the regiment would go out to look for me. Possibly they would get killed searching. It was horrible – horrible.

F. W. *Harvey* SOLDIER, POET

Will's best friend, not only in the regiment, was certainly grieving his loss. Ivor Gurney, believing Will, like so many other wasted men, to be dead, wrote to Marion Scott;[1]

Willy Harvey, my best friend, went out on patrol a week ago, and never came back. It does not make very much difference; for two years I have had only the most fleeting glimpses of him, but we were firm enough in friendship, and I do not look ever for a closer bond, though I live long and am as lucky in friendship as heretofore.

He was full of unsatisfied longings. A Doctor would have called it neurasthenia, but that term covers many things, and in him it meant partly an idealism that could not be contented with realities. His ordinary look was gloomy, but on being spoken to he gladdened one with the most beautiful of smiles, the most considerate courtesy of manner. Being self-absorbed, he was nevertheless nobly unselfish at most times, and all who knew him and understood him, must not have liked him merely, but have loved him. Had he lived, a great poet might have developed from him, could he only obtain the gift of serenity. As a soldier, or rather as I would say, a man, he was dauntlessly brave, and bravery in others stirred him not only to the most generous recognition, but also unfortunately to an insatiable desire to surpass that. His desire for nobility and sacrifice was insatiable and was at last his doom, but his friends may be excused for desiring a better ending than that probable, of a sniper's bullet in No Man's Land .... If the fates send that I live to a great age and attain fulness of days and honour, nothing can alter my memory of him or the evenings we spent together at Minsterworth. My thoughts of Bach and all firelit frosty evenings will be full of him, and the perfectest evening of Autumn will but recall him the more vividly to my memory. He is my friend, and nothing can alter that, and if I have the good fortune ever to meet with such another, he has a golden memory to contend with. A thing not easy.

Gurney's innermost thoughts on the supposed loss of a dear friend were distilled into deeply-felt lines of melancholy and grief in his poem 'To His Love':

He's gone, and all our plans
  Are useless indeed.
We'll walk no more on Cotswold
  Where the sheep feed
  Quietly and take no heed.

His body that was so quick
  Is not as you
Knew it, on Severn river
  Under the blue
  Driving our small boat through.

You would not know him now . . .
  But still he died
Nobly, so cover him over
  With violets of pride
  Purple from Severn side.

Cover him, cover him soon!
  And with thick-set
Masses of memoried flowers –
  Hide that red wet
  Thing I must somehow forget.

. . . . .

Meanwhile, lying in his cell in Douai, Will Harvey was struggling against self-recrimination.

Again and again I asked myself if I could in any way have avoided being taken. Again and again, wise after the event, I

discovered ways in which I might have done so. Oh, why
did I risk getting into that trench at all? Why, why did I
never guess that there were Germans inside that damned
shelter which had been my hope of cover when I heard
footsteps behind me? and so on and so on – the whole
torturing cycle of vain questions which come tormenting
prisoners at such a time, and even long after, as they prowl
round and round their wire cages, and long after that too,
when they have arrived, by various roads, at the truth of the
whole matter, which is, 'I being I, and the circumstances
being what they were at the time, it was quite unavoidable.'

He bribed his guards to buy him some writing paper, and wrote a
long letter to his mother. Even though he took care to exclude
anything to which his captors might object, this letter was kept
back by them. For several weeks poor Tillie knew only that her son
was 'missing' and had no idea that he was alive and well in
captivity.

In the cell next to Will's was a French girl. In whispers, when the
guards were absent, she told him that she had been imprisoned a
week earlier for distributing cakes to hungry British prisoners who
were being marched through the streets. Will pushed his last
cigarette to her through the keyhole. But already he was acquiring
the suspicion and dislike for talking so unsurprisingly common in
prisoners of war.

> How long was she to be imprisoned? She did not know: she
> must trust in the good God. That was about the extent of
> our conversation, and I never saw her.
> Once I harboured an unworthy suspicion that she might
> be a spy put there to gain information which the Germans
> had not been able to extract; but she never asked any
> questions, and I am ashamed that I doubted her.

Throughout the war Will had carried in his uniform pocket a
copy of Shakespeare's sonnets. This small, trench-soiled volume
was with him now. His other comfort was something which he had

carried since his first successful patrol in 1915. That this also was with him in Douai is surely proof that the Germans failed to search their prisoner.

> When darkness fell and I could no longer read, it became more difficult to forget, but fortunately it had always been my rule since I did much patrol-work to carry in my pocket sufficient morphia to finish myself off in the event of my being left out in No Man's Land, a dying torment to myself and a living danger to such as might be tempted to drag me in.
> This morphia I took in small doses sufficient to induce a nightly forgetfulness of my troubles, physical and mental.
> Shakespeare for the light, morphia for the night, was my motto at Douai for ten days.

> Twice during those ten days, English planes flew over the town and Will cheered them loudly from his window. This infuriated his guards who threatened that he would be shot if it should happen again.
> In spite of the lice which plagued him, dark discomfort, danger, uncertainty about the future and anger with himself, Will knew how to escape – at least from the prison of the mind. Lying in his cell he discovered an old French book and on its flyleaf he wrote lines which are amongst his finest achievement in verse imagery.

Solitary Confinement

No mortal come to visit me to-day,
  Only the gay and early-rising Sun
Who strolled in nonchalantly, just to say,
  'Good morrow, and despair not, foolish one!'
But like the tune which comforted King Saul
Sounds in my brain that sunny madrigal.

Anon the playful Wind arises, swells
   Into vague music, and departing, leaves
A sense of blue bare heights and tinkling bells,
   Audible silences which sound achieves
Through music, mountain streams, and hinted heather,
And drowsy flocks drifting in golden weather.

Lastly, as to my bed I turn for rest,
   Comes Lady Moon herself on silver feet
To sit with one white arm across my breast,
   Talking of elves and haunts where they do meet.
No mortal comes to see me, yet I say
'Oh, I have had fine visitors to-day!'

XIV

Gütersloh

After Will had been held in Douai Barracks for eight days, a captured English patrol was brought in and another officer shared his cell for two nights. On the tenth day all the prisoners, under guard, were put aboard a train to be taken into Germany; officers and soldiers to separate camps.

After the English soldiers and their guards had split away from us – I believe at Cologne – we travelled (for the most part by ourselves) in a clean, comfortable carriage, and when towards the end of our weary travel we were compelled to enter a carriage of German soldiers, not one of them did more than stare at us.

Our guards, too, were quite ready to buy us food where possible, at a slight profit to themselves, and to chat amiably about anything, including the war.

One of them knew a little English. He described and vividly illustrated a bombing raid he had taken part in somewhere near Armentières.

'We throw. They throw. Zip! Zip! Bong! Bong! Oh, malade!'

His Iron Cross had been earned for patrol-work on the Russian front. He was a dapper little man, and looked more like a Frenchman than a German.

The Russian front was, he said, better than the French; but notwithstanding that, he concluded that 'Krieg' was 'nix gut'. His countrymen in general were of a different belief, or concealed their feelings very successfully, to judge by the train-loads of singing soldiers we saw. They had decorated engine, carriages and trucks with green branches, and were obviously possessed of fine physique and *morale*. They cheered and laughed and went by.

I thought of them at the front, killing and being killed, and wondered *when*, though not *how* it would all end. My guard was wondering the same thing apparently. 'Deutschland kaput. France kaput. Russia kaput. England kaput. Alles kaput!' was his desperate verdict.

At about three o'clock on the second morning of his journey Will arrived at Gütersloh, a camp built as a lunatic asylum but now being used as a *Gefangenenlager*. He and the other officer-prisoner from Douai were marched into quarantine, buildings wired and boarded off from the rest of the camp, 'and being dead tired immediately fell asleep upon or under those queer soft bags with which all German beds are covered'. (Strange to hear duvets so described after decades in which even the barriers between British and continental bedding preferences have been broken down.)

Gütersloh camp was surrounded by double, high barbed-wire fencing, illuminated at night by electric lamps. Within this cage much of the ground area was covered by pine-woods, in the shadow of which were the camp buildings. Inside the wire and between the trees, 'generally in couples, prowled the prisoners, a mixed community of English, French, Russians, Belgians, Irish, Scotch, and representatives of the colonies classed indiscriminately by the Germans as "black troops".'

In so cosmopolitan a society language took on an especial fascination in its infinite variety. An amusing mixture of tongues could be heard, especially amongst the orderlies. 'Après la bloody krieg!' was a fragment of a French orderly's earnest argument with a German soldier, overheard almost as soon as Will arrived.

Out of quarantine, after baths, fumigation, medical examination and questioning, Will joined the other inmates and found that his native language was his first passport to acceptance by the foreign prisoners, all of whom were most anxious to learn English.

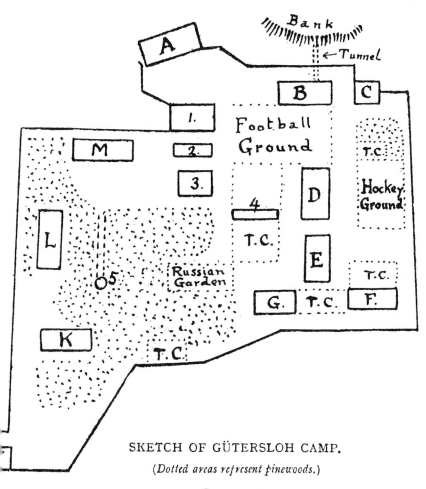

SKETCH OF GÜTERSLOH CAMP.

(Dotted areas represent pinewoods.)

REFERENCES.

A. Camp Offices.
B. English House.
C. Mixed House.
D. Russian House.
E. Russian and Overflow.
F. French House.
G. French House.
H. Quarantine and Prison.
K. English House.
L. Russian House.

M. Civilians.
T.C. Tennis Courts.

1. Canteen, Restaurant, and Kitchen.
2. Dining Hall.
3. Laundry, Theatre, Parcel Office.
4. Private Kitchens.
5. Band-stand.

Gütersloh Camp, from *Comrades in Captivity.*

Amongst the British prisoners there was no instant popularity for a newcomer – one had to prove oneself. It was up to the individual 'to break the ice or thaw it, and it usually took about a month to accomplish'. For Will, however, the process took a little less. He soon proved his worth to the captive community as contributor to the two camp papers, as an actor in little home-made plays, as a singer in concerts, and as a sportsman. He tells us that 'Chesterton's drinking songs set to homely tunes enabled me first to gain admittance into society. After that I wrote poems, essays, and reviews (both of the English and American variety), played hockey, lectured, and attended cheery evenings with consistent regularity.' No longer was Will's nickname 'The Little Man'. Now 'The Poet' was his camp title, 'and though my duties were held to include the writing of topical verses to order, and the carrying to their dreadful conclusions half-recollected songs of George Robey's, I know that never again in this life shall I hold so high and happy a position amid my fellows.'

As always, the public and the private Will Harvey were quite separate people. In his moments of solitude he was working on a new collection of poems born of the bitterness of isolation from all he held dear. For Anne, faithfully waiting at home for who-could-tell how long, he expressed his yearning in 'Loneliness':

> Oh where's the use to write?
> What can I tell you, dear?
> Just that I want you so
> Who are not near.
> Just that I miss the lamp whose blessèd light
> Was God's own moon to shine upon my night,
> And newly mourn each new day's lost delight:
> Just – oh, it will not ease my pain –
> That I am lonely
> Until I see you once again,
> You – you only.

In two 'Ballades', by turns, his anger blazes out at the human price of war and then, in contrast, he celebrates war's inspiriting flame.

'Will you teach me English – yes?' A new arrival and the foreign
officers. Cartoon from *Comrades in Captivity*.

No. 1

Bodies of comrade soldiers gleaming white
  Within the mill-pool where you float and dive
And lounge around part-clothed or naked quite;
  Beautiful shining forms of men alive,
  O living lutes stringed with the senses five
For Love's sweet fingers; seeing Fate afar,
  My very soul with Death for you must strive;
Because of you I loathe the name of War.

But O you piteous corpses yellow-black,
  Rotting unburied in the sunbeam's light,
With teeth laid bare by yellow lips curled back
  Most hideously; whose tortured souls took flight
  Leaving your limbs, all mangled by the fight,
In attitudes of horror fouler far
  Than dreams which haunt a devil's brain at night;
Because of you I loathe the name of War.

Mothers and maids who love you, and the wives
  Bereft of your sweet presences; yea, all
Who knew you beautiful; and those small lives
  Made of that knowledge; O, and you who call
  For life (but vainly now) from that dark hall
Where wait the Unborn, and the loves which are
  In future generations to befall;
Because of you I loathe the name of War.

L'ENVOI

Prince Jesu, hanging stark upon a tree
  Crucified as the malefactors are
That man and man henceforth should brothers be;
  Because of you I loathe the name of War.

No. 2

You dawns, whose loveliness I have not missed,
   Making so delicate background for the larches
Melting the hills to softest amethyst;
    O beauty never absent from our machine;
    Passion of heaven shot golden through the arches
Of woods, or filtered softly from a star,
   Nature's wild love that never cloys or parches;
Because of you I love the name of War.

I have seen dawn and sunset, night and morning,
   I have tramped tired and dusty to a tune
Of singing voices tired as I, but scorning
    To yield up gaiety to sweltering June.
    O comrades marching under blazing noon
Who told me tales in taverns near and far,
   And sang and slept with me beneath the moon;
Because of you I love the name of War.

But you most dear companions Life and Death,
   Whose friendship I had never valued well
Until that Battle blew with fiery breath
    Over the earth his message terrible;
    Crying aloud the things Peace could not tell,
Calling up ancient custom to the bar
   Of God, to plead its cause with Heaven and Hell . . .
Because of you I love the name of War.

L'ENVOI

Prince Jesu, who did speak the amazing word
   Loud, trumpet-clear, flame-flashing like a star
Which falls: 'Not peace I bring you, but the sword!'
   Because of you I love the name of War.

F.W. Harvey SOLDIER, POET

In his account of prison-camp life Will Harvey rarely touches upon the imposed indignities, or what he calls 'disagreeable details concerning the body'. In his view 'those things are not worth remembering. Besides, they have been done – and overdone – already.' When such things are described by him it is in the context of humour, or the German lack of it. The following is typical:

> The Rugby matches always amused the Germans so. They thought (and said) that the English were all mad. The Germans themselves – how much less amusing they would be if they had a sense of humour! Someone thought they had one. What about the great search for hidden articles when they stripped poor old grey-haired Major W., and he dancing about naked and sovereigns falling out of him? 'As good as Maud Allan, and much funnier,' suggests someone. Exactly, but the point was that the Germans never laughed. No, but neither did the Major. He was purple with anger.

The camp day was organised by the prisoners themselves; the Germans seldom interfered. The aim was to keep minds and bodies occupied to fend off the misery of boredom and what Will describes as 'green mould'. The first highlight of the day would be, for the lucky ones, the receipt of a parcel from home. Parcels were both a luxury and a necessity as the Germans food ration was barely sufficient to sustain life.

> It was not possible (usually) to take away one's parcels whole from the parcel office, but all tins were stored away in a locker labelled with the name of the owner or the number of the mess he belonged to. These tins were opened by the Germans before being given out, as a precaution against the smuggling through of forbidden articles, such as wire-cutters and compasses.
>   Cakes also were cut in half, but bread, coming under the Red Cross and therefore on parole, was not. And indeed some of the bread was not at all easy to cut after a delayed journey; in proof of which I might relate how, in attempting so to do,

144

Gütersloh

'Jacko', one of the prisoners – a man over six feet tall and more than proportionately broad, who had played Rugby football for Ireland on several occasions – put his shoulder out and afterwards broke one of his teeth over the same loaf.

This was considered by everyone to be a very good joke, for camp humour tended towards the grim, and poor old Jacko got his leg pulled over it long after his shoulder had been pulled into place.

After breakfast there were the letters.

They were the most delightful, though parcels were the most necessary, things in prison. I find it hard to this day to remember without a tear the first letters I received from home after they had discovered that I was not dead, and one sent on chance before it was known for certain whether I was dead or not. Letters were generally pathetic or funny, and sometimes both. I thought it most kind when one of a circle of pious people, almost hourly expecting the end of the world as a result of prophecy fulfilled during the war, found time to write to me, contrasting the pettiness of all human troubles with the mightiness of the Doomsday which was to end my captivity.

In common with his fellow prisoners, Will felt anger and frustration at the impotence of his position; his inability to help those fighting and dying in the Somme offensive; the lack of any real news from the front; the enforced idleness.

What We Think Of

Walking round our cages like the lions at the Zoo,
We think of things that we have done, and things we mean to do:
Of girls we left behind us, of letters that are due,
Of boating on the river beneath a sky of blue,
Of hills we climbed together – not always for the view.

F.W. Harvey SOLDIER, POET

Walking round our cages like the lions at the Zoo,
We see the phantom faces of you, and you, and you,
Faces of those we loved or loathed – oh everyone we knew!
And deeds we wrought in carelessness for happiness or rue,
And dreams we broke in folly, and seek to build anew, –
Walking round our cages like the lions at the Zoo.

The only thing for an honourable man to do, his positive contribution, his duty in fact, was to escape.

Escape is no simple matter even to men working on farms near the frontier. To officers more closely guarded in strong prisons, hundreds of kilometres away, it is very much more difficult. On arriving at Gütersloh I was told that from this camp only one officer, a Russian, had ever succeeded in getting 'away and over'. The prisoners, and especially the Russians, said the interpreter, frequently tried, but were always caught and punished for their foolishness, in addition to getting restrictions put upon the freedom of the camp generally. The Russians were particularly foolish. The French also occasionally so . . . . 'And the English?' I inquired. 'Ah, they are good – so – like sheep.'
    It would probably have surprised this insolent Hun to learn how at that time certain of the sheep were patiently engaged night after night in driving a tunnel from under their fold, a tunnel which would, when completed, be sufficient to liberate half the camp.

XV

Music

Nothing has the power of music to lift one out of one's surroundings; and to none more poignantly than to prisoners-of-war does Music bring her valiant reminder of things 'outside', the refreshing comfort of a world of realities transcending human chance.

More than anything else which was absent from his life at war, Will Harvey missed good music, and in captivity his longing for it grew intense. To him music and poetry both danced in the same spiritual light; both were needed to tap the rhythm of his creative mind. In his friendship with Ivor Gurney, ideas in music and verse had flowed from one to the other as freely as the sea washing over the shore, bringing and taking inspiration in its ebb and flow. Happily, at Gütersloh, and later at Crefeld, camp orchestras were permitted and the Germans allowed the prisoners to buy instruments and to hire a piano.

I do not need the old programme now before me to remind myself of the burst of sweetness and light which fell upon me at hearing four 'cellos playing together very softly that aria of Bach for strings; and the strange, sudden sense of exultation over circumstances called up by Schubert's 'Unfinished Symphony'.
   . . . The folk-songs of France and of Russia, and that divine prelude and fugue of Bach in E Major (surely the talking of angels overheard), was a joy hard to overrate.

The Bach prelude was one which Gurney held especially dear and referred to often, as in his poem 'Bach and the Sentry':

> Watching the dark my spirit rose in flood
> On that most dearest Prelude of my delight.
> The low-lying mist lifted its hood,
> The October stars showed nobly in clear night.
>
> When I return, and to real music-making,
> And play that Prelude, how will it happen then?
> Shall I feel as I felt, a sentry hardly waking,
> With a dull sense of No Man's Land again?

Every nationality contributed to the musical tapestry 'but the Russians were, taken all round, the acknowledged musicians of the camp'. Will seems to have found a particular affinity with the Russian prisoners, their deep-rooted patriotism, their pride in Russian traditions and culture, echoes of noble souls which had borne past sufferings courageously.

Following one Russian concert, Will wrote a review in which he made no specific reference to the pieces played, but rather gave his vivid imagination wings to fly over the prison wire and to soar with the spirit of beauty to a dream-world of consolation and joy.

THE RUSSIAN CONCERT

An Impression

'Beauty has as many meanings as a man has moods'

Withinside of a rich great garden – in what country I could

not know, since luxury is much the same all the world over
– the morning dew was scarce dry on close-shaven sunny
lawns, and within the shadows of tall trees flowers as yet
unnoticed by the sun stood in rows, begemmed, and swaying
a little to the breeze like impatient, pretty, dancing girls.
Bird-song was in the air, and the plash of playing fountains.
Terribly close to earth, constellations of green stars shone in
the foliage of trees, changing colour as the wind's fingers
adjusted leaves to the light, or in a silver flash turned them
upside down.

Out of the shadow of these bright things stepped presently
the forms of human beings. Men and women they were, and
by their dress foreigners, but of what century I know not,
since elegance remains almost unaltered by the flight of
Time. So, stately as trees and brightly clad as the flowers,
these men and women came with laughter and the sound of
lutes from out the chequered shadow, and on the smooth
lawn ranged themselves in the order of a dance.

> 'Was a lady such a lady,
> Eyes so bright, and lips so red,
> And the breast's superb abundance where
> a man might base his head!'

They danced; and with bird-song and the sound of their
dancing, the walled garden was brimmed with sweetness as
a great cup with wine. Shorn of the blare of brass was their
music, uttered by curious shapely instruments of polished
wood beneath the caresses of the musicians, and so mingled
it was with the movement of the dance that one looked at
the feet of the dancers, expecting a breath of sound to rise
glittering in visible mist of music.

It seemed that the earth was but a sweet unsteady bell, to
be set a-ringing by the beat and rhythm of those twinkling
feet.

And after they had danced, they laughed together and sat

down on banks and sunny patches of the ground . . .

Then arose a dark man of melancholy features – a singer. Tall and handsome he was, but with always-hungering eyes; in the company but not of it; and from his songs I learned how impossible it is that adventure and passionate longing should ever be put to sleep in the unquiet heart of a man; how beneath the glitter of all bright things lurks sadness; that a walled garden, howso lovely, is a prison, and the dancers within it exiles.

And upon that note of sadness (since sorrow is ever soaring) I took flight, and was borne without the walls of the garden. The shimmer of satin and of pearls gave way to that of snow. Brows of men and women shone no more with jewels, but with a nobler crown and tiara – sweat. The century was my own. Out of that song-sweet place of flowers I had come at last to Holy Russia. The gypsies' song floats free on the frosty air, as they wander under heaven, poor yet wanting nothing, homeless but with the horizon for walls and the changing sky for a ceiling. I watch them tramping, tired, to the evening. I see them dancing about their fires.

Meanwhile (for in music this miracle is wrought) sounds on my ear the 'Song of the Workmen'. Its sombre loveliness breaks over the heart in a wave of feeling so tragic that (this is the test of great tragedy) the result is sheer exaltation.

On such a cry a soul is lifted to see (as Moses saw from the mountain) the far-off destiny of man.

The music stops. Again I am in the garden. Darkness has fallen like a garment, and delight of nightingales embroiders it with faint stars. Lovers serenade with sweet melancholy their own desires.

> There is sweet music here that softer falls
> Than petals from blown roses on the grass,
> Or night-dews on still waters between walls
> Of shadowy granite, in a gleaming pass:

Music that gentlier on the spirit lies
Than tir'd eyelids on tir'd eyes,
Music that brings sweet sleep down from
the blissful skies.

Save this there is silence beneath the moon.

Then suddenly, both stars and moon are quenched in the blaze of lanterns carried by gallant gentlemen and fair ladies. Laughter and music break like a flood upon the garden. The dance recommences. Gayer and yet more gay becomes the tune.

Gaiety, a coloured moon-bright bubble, is born, and grows; swims gigantic, opalescent, wonderful, upon the dark waters, . . . grows, . . . grows, . . . yet more wonderful! . . . Ah! will it ever break? . . .

. . . . .

The Russian Concert is ended. My wandering is done. Again at Gütersloh, and in room 65, I sit to write this review of the evening's enjoyment.

After an exhaustive study of Wagner's music, Mark Twain came to the conclusion that it was 'better than it sounded'.

All I can say about Russian music in general, and about this concert in particular, is that it was as good as it sounded – and that is the highest praise.

Music was to Dr Johnson 'the least objectionable of noises'. To me it is not less than a passion. If the gods were moved by such human prayer I should certainly be a musician. Alas! the arts are not chosen. Creation of music is denied me. But not, thank Heaven! appreciation. From a Queen's Hall concert or such evening as this last, I come away literally crammed with *new experiences* – richer by so much *life*.

Why has this Russian music so much power to affect me? I think the answer is:

1. Because it is Music.
2. Because it is Russian.

The chief interest of life is other men and women. The chief interest of our prison life is other nations. But the particular interest of each nation is its nationality, just as individuality is the interest of a man. These are truisms, but like most truisms they are very little realized. Therefore I say: 'Oh, you Russians, Caucasians, French, and you Irish, English, Canadians, and Scots, give us of yourselves'.

It is important to remember that we are all the same. It is equally important to remember that we are all different. That is our most interesting quality.

. . . . .

When the Russian revolution broke out most of the Russian officers were overjoyed. 'Now,' they said, 'the army will no longer be betrayed by the Court-hirelings of Germany. Russia will be Russian, and victory must soon reward her!'

To-day a chill comes over me wondering how many of those true-hearted patriots, whose whole thought was for Russia, lie callously murdered because (disregarding the invitations of their English friends) they bravely and foolishly insisted on returning to their own country in 1918 after the Armistice.

As well as the serious there was, of course, a great deal of light-hearted music in the camp. After the evening roll-call, or *Appell*, the prisoners were locked in their barrack-blocks and, before long, the shout would go up for one or another to sing a song.

Imagine a room tightly packed with people who are sitting on beds, on chairs, and on the floor. A large kettle of punch is brewing on a spirit-lamp. The punch is composed of bad German wine, tinned fruit, and smuggled cognac, raisins, cloves, cinnamon, and a spot or two of Worcester sauce for bite. Each guest had brought his own mug along (for that is the prison custom) or shares his neighbour's if he likes to take a chance.

By general request 'Boats' is singing, for perhaps the
109th time in captivity, an old sea-song concerning

> 'A girl called Mary
> Who lived in Drury Lane,
> Whose master was unkind to her,
> Whose mistress was the same.'

As the evening wore on, and the level in the punch kettle went
down, voices would be raised in the popular songs of all nations
and, in between, tales went around to the accompaniment of great
bursts of laughter. It was here that Will learnt many of the songs
which he so enjoyed singing to inn companions and children alike
in the years after the war. But one particular song was surely
introduced to the camp by Will himself.

> Sooner or later in the evening comes 'The Old Bold Mate',
> the most frequently sung song in *Gefangenenshaft*. The
> words are by John Masefield. The tune, which echoed
> through a dozen prison *Lager* in various parts of Germany,
> is by Ivor Gurney, then a private soldier in the Gloucesters,
> but now a public character in English music.
>   Henry Morgan was the celebrated buccaneer who for his
> services to the Empire was afterwards appointed governor of
> Jamaica. 'The Old Bold Mate' is a fine rollicking song, fit
> company for 'Rio Grande', 'Spanish Ladies', 'A-Roving',
> and the rest of the great sea chanteys, and can be found
> amongst Masefield's shorter poems under the title 'Captain
> Stratton's Fancy.'

Eventually, the sentry would appear, shouting 'Lichts aus!'
Failing to achieve this object, he would go away and

> In five minutes he will reappear with a guard. Then we shall
> disperse to our rooms . . . Silence will creep over the barrack.
> The P.T. (still on night shifts) will recommence work.

XVI

'The Pink Toe'

The British tunnelling party at Gütersloh Camp was led by Captain F. Moysey of the Suffolks, popularly known as 'Mossy'. In typical style, Will described the system used:

It was characteristic of the Russians that they 'took no thought for the morrow', and escaped out of the camp however and whenever possible, without adequate preparations for travel or a clear idea of where the frontier was to be crossed.

It was characteristic of the French to be more deliberate, but yet to follow the nearest road and mar the success of a venture by impetuosity.

It was characteristic of the British to allow themselves to be thought sheep while they worked night after night for months driving their tunnel.

It was very characteristic of the Germans completely to misunderstand this apparent tranquillity, and to taunt them with it.

The main British tunnel (for there were several) started from a disused cellar beneath the English barrack.

The Germans may possibly have suspected that the cellar was being used for illegal purposes, for on two occasions they caused suspension of the work, and the second time by means of heavy concrete.

But they had reckoned without their host, or more accurately without their 'guests'.

A dinner knife and infinite perseverance persuaded one of the heavy granite steps leading to the cellar to slide to and from its place. From beneath these steps work was again begun, and continued with interruptions for over nine months.

Tunnelling was at first carried on only at night, but it was afterwards considered safer as well as more convenient to post sentries and have day shifts.

A certain whistle or a few bars of a song was sufficient warning that the Huns had finished dinner or were in any way dangerous.

Progress was necessarily very slow, because it was not possible to work more than a couple of hours each day, and because the digging implements were improvised out of wood and bits of iron discovered in the camp. The roof of the tunnel was supported with bed-boards and the wood of packing-cases bringing food to the camp. These cases were retained by the Germans, but were constantly stolen back out of the parcel office. The periodic disappearance of bed-boards, and consequent discomfort of that sleeper from whose bed they were abstracted, was indication that a further few feet of tunnelling had been completed.

Abstracted sand was carried away in home-made bags and dribbled about the camp from under cover of Burberrys at dusk when the wearers took their exercise. It was also found that the Church of England chapel, being unused during the weekdays, made a very excellent place of storage. Between the roof and the rafters there must now be several tons of sand waiting the hour when they shall fall upon the heads of a congregation of lunatics to convince them of the day of judgment.

Moreover, the discovery by the Germans of one or two tunnels less cunningly concealed was of advantage in this single sense, that it undoubtedly accounted for some of that sand which must occasionally have struck the notice of the dullest sentry, as being of a different and darker colour than that which covered the ground round about it.

The underground shift consisted of five men, and their order down the tunnel was as follows:

No. 1, the digger.
No. 2, the man behind the digger.
No. 3, the pitman.
No. 4, the sandbagger.
No. 5, the fanman.

Their functions are pretty clearly indicated by their names. No. 1 dug out the sand, stabbing the tunnel with the sharpened leg of an iron bedstead. It was found that this implement had in nine months worn down several inches!

No. 2 knelt behind No. 1, raking back the loosened sand and putting it on 'Westward Ho!' which was the name given to a small sledge fitted with wooden runners, which No. 3 dragged painfully on hands and knees to the shaft where No. 4 packed the sand in bags ready to be disposed of. The fanman worked the fan, keeping the air fresh and cool in the tunnel.

The tunnel was carefully designed to end outside the wire on the opposite side of a high bank standing in the shadow of pine-trees about forty yards away. Between this bank and the wire was the German sentry's beat, and great care had to be taken that he should not guess what was going on beneath his feet. This necessitated a system of telegraphy from the English observation post to the digger at the end of the tunnel, notifying him when he must stop working and when he might go on with it, for the sentry was continually walking backwards and forwards over him.

Especial care had to be taken in roofing also, for if the German sentry should slip through, the tunnel would be discovered and months of labour be made vain. Also it was the malicious custom of Huns on the discovery of a tunnel to fire down it, a proceeding likely to entail unpleasant consequences to the digger, the man behind the digger, the pitman, the sandbagger, old Uncle Tom Cobbleigh and all!

'The Pink Toe'

Great delay and difficulty in working was occasioned by
the heavy rain and snow of Christmas, 1916, which caused
the tunnel to fill with water and to threaten complete
subsidence, which latter was, however, averted by dint of
much hard and ingenious labour on the part of R. and his
followers. About this time the underground workers would
arrive up dripping with water and fairly caked with mud,
which fortunately could generally be brushed off as soon as
dry.

The P.T. (such was the title of the tunnelling party, which
had originated in a small characteristic joke and stood for
'Pink Toe', not 'Party of tunnellers') was frequently troubled
by the unwelcome attentions of strangers, and very
especially by those of a German of such gloomy demeanour
as to entitle him to the name of 'Mouldy Death'. Therefore
it was with particular pleasure that a member of the party,
finding him on an eve in a drunken and sombre sleep amid
the pine-trees, emptied over his face the whole contents of
his sandbag, and vanished.

It was expected that the tunnel would be finished early in
the spring of 1917, when travelling would be more
convenient and cover more plentiful, and by the end of
March it was within a few yards of completion.

The P.T. carried on working until 18 March and then a terrible
rumour began to circulate in the camp that the British prisoners
were going to be moved out. The next day they were ordered to
pack up ready to leave for Crefeld on the following morning.

On 19 March the P.T. desperately added another yard to the end
of the sap in preparation for breaking out. A tube was driven
through to locate the end of the sap; it was now 'over 30 yards
long, and although well beyond the second row of barbed wire it
was immediately below the sentry's beat!'

Depair turned to dispute for the first and last time at a P.T.
meeting. Ought the British tunnel to be used that night in the
possibility that one or two might escape, or ought it to be
considered a contribution to the Allied cause and left for the next

occupiers of the barrack, probably Russians, to complete so that many more might escape? In the end, the painful decision was taken to lay aside all personal and national ambition for the sake of 'the Cause'.

XVII

Crefeld

By the time he arrived at Crefeld Camp in March 1917, Will Harvey had the satisfaction of knowing that *A Gloucestershire Lad* was a huge success, having already gone into a fourth edition. This at least was some consolation in what he found to be a change for the worse.

For all its faults and frustrations, Gütersloh in retrospect now seemed a stimulating place, both 'bracing and strenuous; its work, its games, and its socialism were those of a public school. But to Crefeld hung rather the mouldy atmosphere of a club – a bad one.' Morale was low and many officers, in search of privacy, had moved out of communal rooms and constructed cardboard cubicles in passageways and corners. Soon after the arrival of the British, all the foreign prisoners were moved out to other camps.

At Gütersloh the mix of nationalities had created a constant source of interest in the diversity of languages, ideas, perceptions and backgrounds. Perhaps the Germans had hoped that the nations allied against them in the war would be divided against each other in captivity. If so, the theory had failed, and maybe this was why they now decided to set up single-nation camps.

Many of the British prisoners at Crefeld had been there a long time, and were 'more fed up with it all, and less ready to see misfortunes from a humorous angle.' There was no warm welcome for the new arrivals from Gütersloh, some of whom lost for a while their own once-cheery disposition. However, within a fortnight, under the direction of 'Mossy', the men of the Gütersloh P.T. had started a tunnel and life once more gained purpose. After all, Crefeld was only eighteen kilometres from the border!

Crefeld Camp.

'Getting outside' is generally the least of the escaper's
difficulties – his troubles are then just beginning – but at
Crefeld if you were able to get out the chances were about
two to one on your getting over, instead of about a hundred
to one against. For this reason the German authorities there
were concerned to see that no such chance should be given
to any prisoner. The camp was searched each day for
tunnels; the dust-cart was carefully guarded, and the refuse
stabbed through and through with a long spear before it was
taken away, and the end of the said spear examined for any
trace of gore.

Crefeld was a well-run camp and the prisoners were treated
reasonably: 'one of the best camps in Germany, and one of the
dullest and least sociable'. Letters and parcels arrived regularly and
were quickly distributed; the food was quite good; there was a
theatre, and an orchestra which gave weekly concerts. As at
Gütersloh, lectures and classes were organised.

Our recreations were walks outside the camp on parole; and games – football, hockey, and tennis – inside the camp. The latter were played on the barrack square, which was ridiculously small as well as very dangerous, being composed of stone and gravel rendered septic by the previous presence of many German cavalrymen and their horses. Matches were played every Saturday during the football season between the officers and the orderlies of the camp. Furious matches were also played between Gütersloh and Crefeld elevens, and it was as a result of representing Gütersloh at hockey that I was laid up for eight weeks with a poisoned knee. The ground was, in fact, so septic that any slight fall which caused the skin to be broken was quite sufficient to put you on your back for months.

Unlike the humourless commandant of Gütersloh, Von Groeben, who could be heard shouting angrily at his lieutenants, as was customary for Prussian officers, the commandant at Crefeld 'was a jolly old gentleman whose nose must have cost him a small fortune to colour; but he was jolly, and he was a gentleman, and he treated the officers as gentlemen.' When Will approached him for permission to send home for publication the poems which he had written at Gütersloh, the commandant readily agreed. Not one word of the manuscript was altered. Thanks to this kindness, a companion volume to *A Gloucestershire Lad* appeared later in 1917 under the title *Gloucestershire Friends*, dedicated by Will to 'The Best of all Gloucestershire Friends – My Mother'.

Two months after Will's arrival at Crefeld, the camp was broken up with great urgency but no explanation, only a promise that the next camp would be a good one. Two possibilities were advanced by the prisoners: the first, that the Germans feared a mass break-out assisted by an RFC bombing raid, seems hardly credible, even though the proximity of the camp to the frontier made such a scheme just feasible. The second theory is more likely: 'that the townspeople of Crefeld, who were by this time quite friendly, but desperately hungry as a result of the continuance of the war, were planning to kill two birds with one stone by liberating us and seizing our food.' Whatever the cause, the disappointment to 'Mossy' and the other members of the P.T. was intense; their efforts were for a second time apparently wasted.

The sap which the P.T. was digging had been inherited from Russian prisoners who had been moved out of Crefeld to make way for the British. Its opening was carefully concealed behind a false wall in one of the huts.

It was decided that one of the party should conceal himself when the others left the camp and try to finish the tunnel alone. His place would be faked on *Appell*, and his name answered by friends for as long as this was possible. 'Mossy' was therefore hidden away behind the false wall, together with the tunnelling tools and a store of food; and the rest of the P.T. and the camp in general carried their tempers down into the barrack square, well prepared for any devilry which should suggest itself.

The thought of concealing themselves till everybody had cleared out of the camp had occurred to several more officers, and so it was found on evening *Appell* that the numbers were not correct. We were counted again, and this time enthusiastic but injudicious faking led to the numbers being not less but more than they ought to be. The Germans, who were now thoroughly suspicious, ordered a third *Appell*, and this time each man as he answered his name was required to march through a small opening in the wire fence which divided the barrack square from two tennis-courts. A large number of these officers, however, contrived to crawl back again under the wire, and to answer other people's names; and as a result of this and the mistakes which the Germans themselves were making a ludicrous result was again arrived at. This last roll-call took so long that darkness came on before it was finished.

Meanwhile, many of the officers who had been counted had departed to bring down such furniture and belongings as they could not hope to carry away with them, and were making bonfires. The idea became popular. Fires sprung up all over the barrack square. While the sentries were beating out one, two others were being lighted. The leaping red flames showed men being chased with bayonets and vanishing in darkness. The fires continued to burn, and increased in number. Finally the alarm was sounded, and a battalion marched in to clear the square. We were given five minutes to clear out. After that, anyone seen about would be shot. The Germans were thoroughly apprehensive, their idea of the rag being that an attempt had been made to burn down the camp. Whether the guards knew the reason for our removal or not I cannot say, but certainly they had the wind well up. Sentries and prisoners alike spent a sleepless night, the former carefully watching, the latter packing and arranging what they could carry with them on the journey.

The next morning a motley parade of British officers, straining under the weight of all manner of bags, boxes and parcels, made slow progress to Crefeld railway station, urged on by the shouts and rifle-butts of numerous, impatient armed guards.

Even from Crefeld camp down to the station the road was left littered with breakages and discarded loads, but it was when we had arrived at the other end of the railway journey that the nightmare started. Mile after mile we were urged across country becoming ever wilder and more swampy. The day was exceedingly hot. Weary men hurled aside one by one various loads they had tied to themselves. Finally we arrived into camp furious and utterly exhausted, to find ourselves looking at about four drab, dirty-looking wooden huts roofed with tarred felt. This was Schwarmstedt, the good camp. A barbed-wire fence surrounded, and machine-gun towers dominated, the *Lager* from each end.

A few days later 'Mossy' was discovered by the Germans, hiding behind the false wall. He too was sent on to Schwarmstedt.

XVIII

Schwarmstedt – And a Bid for Freedom

'Achtung!' (Attention) suddenly yelled the Germans. The Camp Commandant has arrived on the scene to have a look at us. We rise somewhat listlessly, and see with amusement a very magnificent figure approaching. He is old, but tall and erect, and wears with very obvious pride the Uhlan Officer's uniform, plastered with enormous decorations gained, I believe, in 1870, when his mind last worked. His manners were theatrical but very courteous. He was what you call 'old-world'. He welcomed us to his camp, which was, he said, not so nice as he would wish for English officers – but there, he had not invited us; we must make the best of it; and he would endeavour to do all that was possible to make our stay comfortable. The rooms held from thirteen to sixteen officers, so that we could be with our friends. He knew all that was to be known about the English, because he had stayed in Scotland. We could dismiss.

Some of us were of the opinion that he was trying to be funny; others that he was not quite all there. Personally I believe that he was quite serious, and merely 'old-world' – yes, 'old-world'.

The rooms he referred to lay in three of the long drab wooden huts. The partition between the rooms was of thin matchboarding. The outside walls were thicker, but the tarred felt had come off in places and the boards had warped, leaving cracks almost an inch wide for the rain and wind. A state of overcrowding could not be avoided, and by whatever mode of arrangement, the beds had often to touch one another.

Sanitary arrangements were very bad, and the latrine so situated that the ends of two living-huts came to within ten paces of it. The drinking-water was brownish, and smelt; but filtered water could be bought in the canteen at ten pfennigs a glass, and boiling water at fifteen pfennigs the kettle. There were two pumps in the camp, and at these and in the wooden troughs near we washed our clothes when they became dirty. To reduce the quantity of things required to be washed, and because the camp was filled with a fine dusty sand, very difficult to remove, most of us went about wearing only gym shoes, a shirt and a pair of shorts. Bodily cleansing was, we discovered, another question and a more difficult one. The camp baths lay outside the wire, and the Germans required parole to be given before we visited them. This parole, some of us considered, we had no right to give, except for reasonable exercise, in accordance with the Army order. The Germans should have supplied baths within the camp, and had no right to demand parole from us for such a purpose as visiting them. We who refused parole were taken across twice a week by an armed guard, who watched us carefully all the time; the other officers were, I believe, allowed four baths for the same period of time.

Owing to the hot weather, and the fleas which infested the camp, a cold swill under one of the pumps seemed highly desirable, but this was forbidden on grounds of modesty, as the two pumps were in the open. The camp lay in the middle of a large moor, and there was not a house for miles round. The only female I ever saw enter the camp was the dentist's assistant, useful as a smuggler of maps and compasses if sufficiently bribed with dripping, but the last person in the world likely to be shocked by such a sight.

What happened in consequence was that there were frequent rushes from the barracks to the pump by naked

officers, a hurried douche, and a rush back. Occasionally
two stolid German guards would appear, to march the
naked men off to prison; and later on they would call round
for their clothes. I recall with some pleasure the time when
an 'Inspector of Camps', or some such personage, was
accosted by a naked officer holding up a flea, which he
desired to bring to notice. 'Dat', shouted the shocked
Inspector 'is der most unverschamter spectacle [with accent
on the second syllable] I have ever seen!'

Conditions at Schwarmstedt were uncomfortable in the extreme.
The grubby, overcrowded huts were infested by bugs. The food
provided by the Germans was exceedingly scanty and bad. Until
extra food arrived in parcels from home the daily ration, for which
a charge of one mark fifty pfennigs was made, comprised the
following:

Breakfast:	black coffee, thought to be made from acorns.
Dinner:	soup, containing cabbage, black peas, mangel-wurzel, occasional pieces of potato, and once or twice a week tiny shreds of meat.
Supper:	thin soup, 'more like pig's wash than anything else'.

When not queuing for letters and parcels or attending to camp
chores, seemingly endless time was taken up in reading, tale-
swapping and song; camp concerts and debates.

Twice a week at Schwarmstedt a party of us met to read
and discuss the lesser-known plays of Shakespeare. The
debate which followed the reading was generally a very
amusing one, for our party comprised men of four or five
nationalities, and included many professionals. There was a
medical student, an Oxford don, a publisher, a professor of
philosophy, a portrait-painter, an architect, and four Regular
soldiers beside myself. There was a dulcitone in the camp
belonging to one of the prisoners, and it sounded very pretty

accompanying the songs at the end of 'Love's Labour's Lost'.

It cannot have been easy to concentrate on writing verse or on serious reading in a room shared with up to fifteen other officers. None the less, Will pursued both in good measure. His reading was very varied and included Saintsbury's *History of English Prosody*, Hardy's *Dynasts*, a work greatly admired by Ivor Gurney who most probably sent it to Will, and Tolstoy's *War and Peace*, which miracle of writing he considered the finest of all novels.

When, in the evening, all the officers were restricted to their rooms, one or another would spin a yarn. Some of these tales were true: personal accounts of derring-do in and out of the war, often exaggerated deliberately to amuse a knowing audience; others were fictitious, sometimes traditional. For some time after Will's arrival, the rooms at Schwarmstedt were unlighted, except for stalking, shadowy beams cast through the windows by the great arc lamps which shone on the wire. In this sinister gloom tales of the supernatural must have summoned up ghostly imaginings indeed. One such tale, told by H.S. (Hugh) Walker, the Scottish hockey international who became headmaster of St Mary's, Melrose, was, in later years, retold by Will in verse-form. The poem tingles along at a 'Tam O'Shanter' pace, but is rather spoilt by a weak ending.

Foul Ford

The Foul Ford glimmers darkly
Where the smooth waters run
Like lidless eyes of a serpent
That basks in the sun:
Like the cold eye of Murder,
Hating everyone.

For years a-many none had dared
Passage at midnight hour,
And men bowed down trembling

Before an evil power.
And faith of God withered
And wilted like a flower.

Twice in the memory of men
In the dark midnight hour
Man had gone forth to prove that curse
Which over the ford did lower;
Twice in living days had men
Witnessed the demon's power.

Twice found they in the morning
A twisted body stark
That had fought in vain the foulness
Of the demons of the dark: –
No wound upon it,
Nor any outward mark.

But unseen hands of horror
Had pawed them suddenly
When their eyes beheld the wickedness
The which no eyes might see,
Yea, the great flame of evil
Had emptied them utterly.

Then boldly cried the young priest
(Though with dread his heart drummed high)
'What talk is this of devils
And wicked mystery –
Nay is God's power our keeper
Or ghosts and wizardry?'

So when the day turned ghostly
He walked into the mist.
They watched his figure dwindle fast
As forth he strode with a smile – the last
That e'er he smiled, I wist.

For soon black rain and thunder
Boomed through the hollow height,
And the sky was wealed with poisonous
Quivering scars and bright,
As the red whips of the lightning
Lashed at the face of night.

Loud, and louder grew the storm,
And ghastlier the skies,
And all the air was foully full
Of hoarse bubbling cries,
And the darkness lit with flickering
As hell blinked fiery eyes.

But when safe dawn had broken
Men laid fear aside,
And, dreading to discover
The way this man had died,
Forth went they and found him
At the Foul Ford side.

His face was furrowed deep:
His fair locks frosty-grey.
The quick horror in his eyes
What mortal tongue shall say?
Joyously ran they to greet him
But in awe shrank away.

What there he had both heard and seen
Of sin too foul to tell
None asked. But all knew certainly
That soul had lain in hell,
Companion unto demons
And dreams detestable.

Yet was the spell of Satan
Snapt: and no more there fluttered

F.W. *Harvey* SOLDIER, POET

Foul things above the water . . .

Wherefore did priest and people,
Giving to Christ the glory,
Ring bells to rock their steeple:
And I have writ this story.

. . . . .

In the enforced togetherness of camp life it was impossible for a
man with Will's intense powers of observation not to scrutinise
those around him, marking every detail of character, both flawed
and impeccable.

Certainly the study of my fellow-prisoners was the chiefest
of my interests while I was at Schwarmstedt. Dull, clever,
good, or thoroughly wicked, these men finally sealed my
philosophy of life. Goodness comes into the world like a
blinding flash; and like lightning it vanishes, or seems to;
but it comes to all. There are no heroes and no heroines – at
least, there are none like those we find in books; but every
man is a hero sometimes, and every woman is a heroine.
Nor is life a piebald thing; nor is it a grey thing; but it is
shot through with shifting colour like the flitting wing of a
hornet, and so quickly it changes. How dare we think
goodness commonplace? How dare we give it permanently
to a few? The glory of God is reflected with a fitful
splendour on a million diverse natures. All reveal it some
time, and in those moments must we not merely love, but
worship them. The worst people I have ever met have
contrived to make me an optimist after the best had almost
succeeded in making me a pessimist. There may or there
may not be blinded and damned souls working willingly for
the devil. I have never met them. I have never seen a man
without some goodness in him.

Schwarmstedt – And a Bid for Freedom

Tunnelling at Schwarmstedt would have been useless. The soil was sandy, with peat a foot down and the water table at a depth of only two feet. No job for the P.T. but, even so, the irrepressible 'Mossy' was determined to make an escape attempt. He and another officer, identified by Will simply as 'M', burrowed a very shallow tunnel from beneath the floor of a hut to the outside of the wire.

The Huns got wind of the attempt and were waiting for them. Poor M. was shot without challenge or chance of life at five yards' range, and 'Mossy' got an arm badly smashed. Nobody whined about it (it would have been the last thing they would have wished; they had taken their risk and paid for it), but I cannot bring myself to imagine any British soldier deliberately killing a defenceless man in such circumstances. He might have shot him running, or said, 'Get back, and think yourself lucky with five months' gaol' – that was the penalty at the time – but since it is the duty of all soldiers to escape if they can, he would hardly have murdered him for making the attempt. Wolf was the name of the Hun who did it – a name which we took in case of any future chance of justice – and a wolf he must have been, with a wolf's heart and a wolf's brain, to shoot a defenceless man without challenge, in cold blood.

The Commandant allowed M. a military funeral, which took place in a small churchyard about six miles away. His particular friends, the members of his room, and a percentage of other prisoners, were allowed to attend, and stood by the graveside when the German soldiers fired a salute of three rounds which echoed back from the overshadowing woods. There, with sunlight, branch-filtered, falling across the brown earth which covered him, we left poor M. when the echoes had fallen to silence and only the sough of the trees could be heard. He was one of the gentlest and bravest souls I ever knew.

Requiescat

(W.M. Shot, June 1917, Schwarmstedt Camp)

Were men but men, and Christians not at all:
Mere pagans, primitive and quick of sense
To feel the sun's great blind beneficence:
The kind hand of the breeze: – nay but to see
Only the brotherly blue that's over all,
And realise that calm immensity
So far-enfolding, softly-bright and still,
Feel only that: – Surely they would not kill!

Beside a new-digged grave beneath the trees
I kneel. The brotherly sky is over all.
It seems to me so strange wars do not cease.

Even so, as well as failures, there were successful escapes by
officers who were able to cut through or climb over the wire in dark
corners of the camp, sometimes aided by elemental distractions
such as thunderstorms and forest fires. Most were recaptured close
to the Dutch frontier, but a few did get across to Holland. Amongst
these were Captains Fox and Caunter, whose success was recounted by Caunter in a book entitled *Thirteen Days*, the time taken for
their perilous journey.

Little by little, and in spite of regular searches by the guards, Will
gathered together the supplies which he would require for an escape
attempt of his own. There was an officer in the camp who
specialised in making improvised compasses, another who forged
keys to camp buildings out of the metal money-tokens with which
prisoners were paid. Sufficient rations had to be secreted away to
enable an escaper to survive for three weeks. Will traced his own
maps, using the grease-proof lining paper from biscuit tins.

All Will lacked now were credible civilian clothes. Then, one day, a
fellow officer offered him just what he needed: a suit sent from England
in a parcel, and which was smuggled past the guard in the parcel room

where all packages were opened and checked. Now he was ready.

Will's first plan involved climbing on to the roof of one of the huts close to the wire at night, waiting until the beam of the roving arc lamp had moved momentarily away, then jumping over the wire to a telegraph pole beyond and sliding down.

Fortunately for Will, on the day before he was to make his bid for freedom, he noticed that new barbed wire had been wound around the lower half of the telegraph pole. Had be been caught on this wire, not only would his legs and hands have been badly torn, but he would undoubtedly have been picked off by one of the machine-gunners who manned each arc lamp.

In an introduction to a selection of poems by Will Harvey, published in 1947, Hugh Walker related how he had seen Will 'carried out of the camp in an ominously creaking wicker basket'. He does not exand on this and no such event occurs in Will's own account of his two years in captivity. However, whilst describing some of the escape attempts from Schwarmstedt, Will tells us, as though of others only, that 'certain officers, bent on emulating St Paul, got into their boxes (as a matter of fact they were large wicker baskets), and arranged that English orderlies should carry them across to the store shed' [which was outside the wire] 'from which they would be able to escape during the night.' Apparently this attempt went badly wrong. Whilst the baskets were being transferred under guard, a German officer called the soldiers away to other work, telling them to leave the baskets for the time being. It was a very hot day and the baskets remained in the sun through the heat of the afternoon. One of the occupants got cramp and 'awful squeakings and scratchings' came from his basket. Prisoners watching all this from inside the wire tried to make a lot of noise to create a distraction, but the sentry became suspicious and looked hard at the basket. 'Fortunately he did not stab it with his bayonet; nor could he open any of them, because they were locked, all the keys being carried by one officer in another basket, who was expected to cut himself out and liberate his companions.' At last the baskets were taken to the shed at five o'clock. Alas, the plan failed, probably because the sentry had mentioned his suspicions. At about eight o'clock a German officer followed by a guard went straight into the shed and captured them all. The punishment was five months' solitary confinement.

News now began to circulate that the prisoners were to be transferred yet again. Will had to bide his time and wait for another suitable opportunity to attempt his escape. That opportunity presented itself on the railway journey from Schwarmstedt to Holzminden Camp.

. . . . .

For several days before our departure the Huns were very busy searching the camp for *verboten* articles in order to prevent escapes on the journey; and to conceal my civilian clothes I resorted to the very simple expedient of wearing them (under a Burberry) when they searched my boxes, and putting them in my boxes when they searched me. Knowing the ways of the Hun, I was almost certain that this bare-faced plan would be successful, and it was. The sentries were, to use the German phrase, 'earnest men', and their very earnestness prevented them from being bright. They concentrated. They didn't *half* search my box, and they didn't *half* search me: they did both thoroughly. And having done so, they felt perfectly satisfied that everything must be all right. I very nearly gave the show away by laughing: it was so ridiculous to watch the funny old things going slowly and carefully through my boxes for the clothes that I was wearing less than a yard away.

The next morning we were marched down to the station to entrain for Holzminden. In a wood where we halted close to the railway-line an officer made a bolt for it through the trees, and rifles went off right and left, although half of the men could not possibly have had anything to aim at. Having fallen into a ditch, the officer was recaptured, and the Germans showed no particular ill-will except one breathless old man, who had dropped a large hunch of bread and lard (his day's rations) during the chase, and was unable to find it again.

We gave him a tin of meat (which cheered him up at once), for it was necessary that the sentries should have something more to do than watch us: and nothing appealed to them like eating.

When we entrained, one sentry was stationed in each carriage, and sat in a corner seat near the door; the other door was locked. Each carriage held, besides the sentry, five or six officers. The train was a corridor, and a lavatory lay between our particular compartment and the next – a fact which I mention because it had considerable bearing on my subsequent escape.

I took off the knapsack in which I had packed food for a three weeks' journey, and placed it in the corridor outside the lavatory door. My map and compass were in the pockets of the civilian suit which I was wearing under a Burberry. The problem was to get myself and my equipment off the train without being seen. There was plenty of time, for it was inadvisable to jump until dusk, both for sake of getting concealment, and because the train was carrying me in the right direction.

For the first hour or two we were watched very carefully and every moment, but as time wore on the guards became more slack. One after another each man in our carriage made a point of visiting the lavatory, and remaining there or outside in the corridor for an increasing space of time, and as they always returned the old sentry became less and less suspicious, and at last quite used to having one short in the carriage.

My first plan was to jump out through the lavatory window, but I found that it was too small. Moreover, it was on the sentry-side of the train, and so my jump would certainly be seen by scores of armed guards in other carriages, one of whom would probably shoot straight.

The window which was in the corridor was on the convenient side of the train, but it, also was too small for me, though it was wide enough for my knapsack.

There only remained the window in my own carriage,

which was both large enough and on the right side of the train. But there was the sentry.

The sentry in our carriage was a kindly old thing, but very weary. He had been up most of the night. He closed his eyes occasionally and blew little spit-bubbles from his lips. But he would not go to sleep. Once or twice we almost believed that he was 'off', but always he would open a watery blue eye at an unexpected moment. It was very trying. We gave him food. He ate it. We gave him wine. He drank it. But he would not go to sleep. He just continued to blow bubbles.

Finally I decided that it was during the bubble-blowing or not at all that I should have to go.

Five seconds was about all I could afford to spend doing the vanishing trick, and I could not rely on that, for at any time his blue eye might open.

The window was down – we had fought hard for that during the first hour – and there was an arm-strap near the window. By putting one foot on the seat, and if the arm-strap was sufficiently strong to bear the weight of a body, it was, I argued, quite possible to be out of the carriage in one moment by diving through the window. The arm-strap would save me from falling head-first on to the line; and by grasping the outside rail with the other hand I could lower myself silently and quickly on to the step by with-drawing my feet from the carriage. I should be less likely to get shot this way, since my feet would be the only part left inside the train after the first spring.

The knapsack I could not take with us, but that could be pushed through the corridor-window by a friend as soon as I had jumped from the step, and so we should reach the ground about the same time. As things turned out, we certainly did, for I got it in the back!

I could not jump while the train was doing more than twenty miles an hour, or I should break my neck; nor must I jump too near a station, or I should be seen; so the proper place was on an uphill gradient in open country. If, on top of this, I could get a wood for cover, conditions would be ideal.

Schwarmstedt – And a Bid for Freedom

It was unlikely that I should have to face a train-load of bullets, because the sentries were all sitting the other side to guard the door which was unlocked, but even supposing some few did get across and fire, it was very unlikely that they would hit me, for not only was I pretty certain to be a moving target, but they would be moving marksmen.

While I was thinking out these chances I heard with horror that we were due to arrive in about half an hour. It was not nearly dusk and dusk was an important link in the chain of my calculations – but then, I seem fated to have to do things in day-light which are generally done at night!

Having been captured in day-light, it seemed (thought I) a sort of poetic justice that I should also escape in day-light – so 'here goes!'

Knowing my plan, and that I purposed carrying it out at once, several of my companions stood up in the carriage on pretext of reaching things from the rack, and so screened me from the sentry, who was not then blowing bubbles. As I pushed off from the seat on which he was sitting I could hear someone directing his attention to the beauty of some stunted hills on the other side of the line. I dived. To withdraw my feet took only a moment, and there I was outside the carriage on the step, watching the ground whiz by underneath. It seemed to be going by very fast; but I had been lucky in the place, for we were doing a bend, and my carriage was then on the outside of the circle, so that no one looking out of the windows in front or in rear of the train could see me.

Then I jumped. The ground seemed suddenly tilted up towards me, and I came down an awful bump with the pack in the middle of my back, and my throat across the opposite rail.

I had jumped forward, but as a marble escapes from the bag which a boy swings, had been thrown outwards from the curving train. For a moment we lay there, pack and man, flat in the trackway, while the train clanked past a few yards behind; then I realized where I was and why. I got up and ran quickly for cover, leaving the pack where it was.

We were on an embankment. I threw myself over the edge
of it and lay down while the train dragged its huge length
past. I saw the German interpreter go by, leaning out of the
window, a cigarette in his mouth. When the last carriage
had passed, I got up and went to get my knapsack. It had
split open in the fall, and many things, which included a
towel, several tins of meat, and some very large hard
Canadian biscuits, lay strewn over the railway-track.

I was hastily picking these things up when I heard
shouting, and saw a stream of people running towards me
from the half-reaped fields below the embankment on that
side – reapers and farm-hands, male and female, headed by
crowds of children and a dog.

I did not wait to collect any more of my belongings, but
shouldered my pack and set off down the opposite slope,
reflecting that if English labourers had seen a man jump off
a train they would not have made all this fuss because it was
verboten, but have thought him rather a sport for 'doing'
the railway company.

'Damn them!' Why must they come chasing after me!
Since I was in civilian clothes, they could not possibly know
that I was anything else than one of their own countrymen.
Why couldn't they mind their own business? Alas! that is
not the German habit.

They had seen me jump from the train. To jump from a
train was *verboten*. There must be something wrong. It was
the duty of all to discover what it was, and have the
offender punished.

I marched on as fast as I could towards a wood which lay
the far side of a village near by the railway. Run, I dare not,
since it would only attract suspicion, and because more
things would fall out of my pack, which I had not had time
to fasten up again at the top. Nobody attempted to stop me,
and by walking fast I hoped to get through the village before
the crowd; but it was round me before I had done so. I kept
straight on, ignoring the shouts and menaces; still nobody
attempted to stop me. I decided that if once I could get

outside the village I would make a dash for it, and get cover in the wood till nightfall.

But I was not allowed to reach the open.

In a place where two roads met before branching right and left out of the village, I was collared by a youth trembling with excitement. I put on my best scowl, and attempted to shake him off, but he held on, shouting. The crowd surged round, and I felt there was nothing for it but to give up.

Had I been a fluent speaker of German I might yet have got off, for I was in civilian attire, and, save that I had been seen jumping off a train, there was nothing against me; but being unable to give any good explanation of myself, I was arrested as a civilian spy, and taken to the police-station. Then I found out that I was suspected of having tried to blow up a tunnel.

This I did not like the sound of at all, for the Germans have a short way with spies; therefore I thought it well to explain quickly that I was a British officer. They could verify my statement, said I, by telephoning to Holzminden. This was done, and as by that time the officers had been counted and I had been missed the message soon came through that my statement was correct, and that I was to be brought immediately in to the prison.

While waiting at the station with my guard to catch the next train on to Holzminden, I was amused to see several of the large hard biscuits which I had left on the line lying on a table in the station-masters's room. They had been brought there by those who found them under the impression that they were slabs of dynamite, and hence the rumour that I had come to blow up the tunnel!

I was able to destroy my maps on the journey down, and to get rid of my compass, which things (being *verboten*) would mean imprisonment additional to the fortnight's confinement given for simple escape; but contrary to my expectations I was not searched when I arrived at the *Lager*.

I passed my old guard as I went in and winked at him, but he did not respond in any way to my salutation. The door slammed behind me, the key turned in the lock, and I lay down to endure a second spell of solitary confinement, and to write an acrostic on the word DAMN!

XIX

Gloucestershire Friends

At the time of his train-jumping exploit Harvey had been in captivity for just one year. It was now August 1917. Late in the previous October his comrades in the 2/5th Battalion Glosters, including brother Eric and Ivor Gurney, had moved down from Laventie to occupy trenches in front of Grandecourt on the Somme, close by the men of the 1/5th Battalion.

> The contrast between the sectors in front of Laventie and the Somme crater fields was striking. Here were primitive conditions – men clinging to shell holes, mud deep enough to completely submerge a gun team and limber, masses of unburied dead strewn over the battle fields; no sign of organised trenches, but merely shell holes joined up to one another – and, last, but by no means least in importance, no landmarks anywhere. The whole scene was one bleak wilderness of death.

An officer of the battalion, Captain Sinclair, gave a graphic account of reconnoitring in this part of the line.

> From Mouquet Farm guides took each of us to our appointed sectors. I shall never forget this day as long as I live. My guide took me on to the tramway which ran from Tullock's Corner to Rifle Dump in Zollern Trench. There was a white November fog and a pretty thick one at that. When we got to Rifle Dump we left the tramway and

N° 16   DECEMBER 1916

5th GLOUCESTER GAZETTE

A Chronicle, serious and humorous, of the Battalion while serving with the
BRITISH EXPEDITIONARY FORCE

Tanks again

" Why not make use of our mobile veterinary section ? "

ploughed across the open. We had started from Albert at
about midday and it was now 3 p.m. We got hopelessly lost.
I have dim recollections of shell fire, of fog, of dead bodies,
of Hessian Trench and of eventually striking that cheerful
spot appropriately named Death Valley. The guide had
completely lost his bearings. He left me on a duckboard
track somewhere near Hessian Trench, promising to return
after finding out where he was. He was away about an hour
and a half and when he did return, it was getting dark.
Somehow or other we struggled on through the mud,
stumbled over dead bodies and floundered into water-logged
shell holes, till we luckily struck the Ravine. It was now
about 7 p.m. Three hours later we set out on the long trail
back to Albert, which, thanks to a 'lorry jump' from
Pozieres, we eventually reached more dead than alive in the
early hours of the morning. The average rate of progression
over that crater field could not, at the most, have been more
than a mile in two hours. Then came the job of leading the
various companies to their sectors. We started off at 2 p.m.
on the 21st and met our guides at Tullock's Corner. We were
shelled the whole way up to our positions and the relief was
not completed till 2 p.m. on the 22nd, the code word for
'relief complete' being 'another little drink won't do us any
harm' – another invention of the Practical Jokes Department.

In the front line the mud made movement of any sort
practically impossible until the frost hardened the ground;
shaving was not to be thought of; ration parties were held
up in the mire and so we were down to one cup of cold tea
per man per day, hence the aptness of the above code word.
The shelling was so incessant that we were compelled to live
more like rats than men. After three or four days of this
existence, we were relieved on November 26th and marched
back to Wellington Huts.[1]

Gurney was a signaller, his duty being to keep the lines of
communication intact under all circumstances, and in so doing was
often called upon to face the gravest risks:

The scene is Headquarters Signal Office in Zollern trench. The operator receives a report from A Company, who are holding the front line, of heavy enemy shelling; he communicates the message to the CO who asks to be put through to the Company; the operator plugs in, but gets no reply. The line has been broken. A corporal and a linesman prepare to go along to A Company's line; they dash up the steps of the dugout and dive into the trench to wallow knee deep in slush. After plunging along for fifty yards, the linesman taps in and calling Battalion, is answered immediately: the break is further afield – they must go on. Presently the line disappears over the top and they follow it out into the open ground where their only shelter from continuous gun fire is water-logged shell holes. They scramble on, holding the telephone line for guidance until ahead of them they can dimly see the white outline of Regina trench. There is the screaming sound of a shell and they drop into the nearest shell hole just as, with a blinding flash, the earth ten yards ahead is churned up; they rush into the trench, tap in again and again are answered by Battalion, but still there is no reply from A Company. On they must go again, out into the open and into Death Valley over which a barrage is raging – evidently this is where the line is broken. Ultimately after much stumbling, searching and a few comments on shells and Germans in general, one broken end is found and then the other, some forty or fifty yards away. The two men now crouch in a pot hole and join the end; a phone, which the linesman always carries with him, is connected and at last A Company is spoken to. It looks as though their task is now done, but alas! it is now found that no reply is forthcoming from Battalion – another breakage – two more loose ends to be found and repaired – more comments on shells and Germans. All the above experiences have to be gone through again and again till finally complete communication is restored and the signallers return to the shelter of their dugout, worn out but proud in the knowledge that their duty has been well and bravely done.[2]

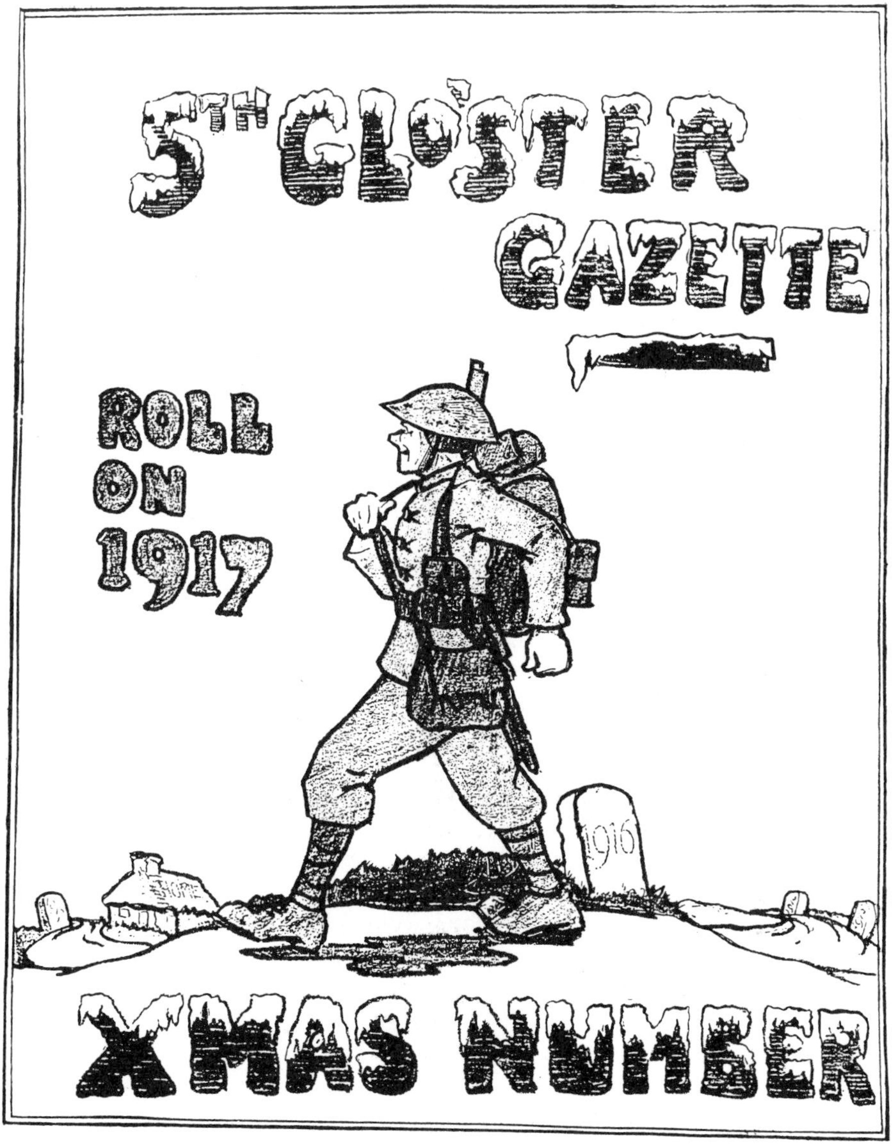
5TH GLO'STER GAZETTE
ROLL ON 1917
HOME
1916
XMAS NUMBER

In spite of all, Ivor Gurney composed four of his finest songs whilst in the trenches: 'By a Bierside', a setting of Masefield's poem which contemplates the nature of death; 'Only the Wanderer' to words of his own; 'Even Such is Time', a setting of Sir Walter Raleigh's farewell to life; and 'In Flanders', Will Harvey's master-piece of yearning for Gloucestershire. The manuscript of this last is marked: 'Crucifix Corner, Thiepval, 11th January 1917'. Harvey's words and Gurney's music are so much the perfect complement to each other that no other setting of 'In Flanders' can be imagined.

In the middle of March the Germans began a tactical withdrawal from the Somme, eastwards to the St Quentin front and the Hindenburg Line. The Allies set off in pursuit.

The Germans had done things very thoroughly: villages were devasted, all fruit trees cut down, all cross-roads mined, all wells rendered useless. Knowing that the allies would follow them in their withdrawal, the enemy had made the pursuit as difficult as possible. It reminded one of the man who, because his loving spouse had expressed her intention of dancing on his grave, left instructions with his executors to bury him at sea.[3]

On 1 April Ivor Gurney wrote to Marion Scott:

The day has been springlike on the whole, and last night's sky was gloriously tragic; I sang 'In Flanders' to myself, facing the West, alone in a lately ruined house, spoiled by that unutterable thoroughness of the German destruction; and was somewhat comforted thereby. That has all been said for me in 'In Flanders'. What you said about the sense of being out under the stars, in 'By a Bierside' pleased me very much. The scene of 'In Flanders' is obviously Coopers Hill. O times! O saisons, O chateaux![4]

On the following days the men of the 2/5th Battalion took part in an attack on the village of Bihecourt which fell to them for the loss of 15 dead and 34 wounded. Gurney was shot in the arm and sent to hospital in Rouen for six weeks. From there he wrote again to Marion Scott:

> Will Harvey is getting his parcels, and has a new book of verse almost ready. This is good news: and it will be very interesting to see the difference between the two; for of course there will be a difference.
>
> Though this Spring is cold and inclement, I cannot keep out of mind what April has meant to me in past years – Minsterworth, Framilode, and his companionship. And my sick mind holds desperately on to such memories for Beauty's sake; and the hope of Joy.[5]

By now the battalion was so depleted in numbers that it was necessary to scrap one of the four companies and to reduce each of the remaining three to only three platoons each. Even so, they pressed on towards St Quentin and went into trenches in the Fayet Sector. Here the British were overlooked by the belfry of St Quentin's cathedral; every movement in their lines was observed by the Germans, even at night when a continuous stream of star shells filled the sky with brilliant light. 'At first there were no communication trenches, movement had to be made across the open, and a good deal of ingenuity was needed in order to keep on the reverse slopes and so avoid the malignant eye of the Cathedral belfry which appeared never to cease its vigil.' Then, in mid-May, the Glosters marched north-west to the Arras front.

At last, in July, reinforcements arrived and the battalion was brought back up to strength ready for the journey north to the third Battle of Ypres, remembered now in one dreadful word – Passchendaele.

> The ruined town of Ypres was the centre of what is known as the Salient, which was lightly held by British troops. Eastward, beyond the British line, lay a vast low-lying and slightly undulating plain running down to the sluggish and dirty River Steenbeeke. Beyond this stream the plain rose slowly till it culminated in the famous Passchendaele Ridge.

Behind this ridge, which was the objective of the attack, sat the German gunners with perfect observation over the plain right up to and beyond Ypres. The Germans with characteristic thoroughness had fortified this plain with great concrete structures, all arranged on a mutually co-operating plan. Some of the concretes were veritable fortresses. There is a certain irony in the rumour that a large amount of the concrete used had come from British firms through neutral countries. The plain itself was a desolate pock-marked area, ripped to pieces by gun fire almost since the commencement of the War. All drainage was destroyed and the advent of rain at once turned the whole place into one vast bog of pestilential slime and filth. It was across this plain that the advance on Passchendaele had to be made. Duckboard tracks were laid and along these the men moved in single file. To slip off these tracks, as sometimes happened at night, often meant drowing in slime; to remain on them was almost as perilous since the German guns had every track taped.[6]

Field Marshal Haig's plan, pushed through in spite of opposition from fellow generals and the disquiet of Lloyd George and the British Cabinet, was to mount an offensive at the Ypres salient which would break through and roll up the German line from the north. An advance of only thirty miles and the Allies would be in Ostend. He took no account of the fact that, to the north, the Belgians had broken the dykes and let in the sea. The ground at Ypres was heavy clay from which the water never drained away; bombardment churned it into deep mud. Foch warned that it would be impossible to fight both Germans and mud, but Haig, ignoring the lessons of the Somme, was determined.

The offensive was a disaster. British casualties exceeded 300,000; the Germans almost 200,000. When on 8 November Haig's Chief of Staff, Kiggell, got close to the battle zone for the very first time he burst into tears. 'Good God, did we really send men to fight in that?' And the young subaltern who was accompanying him said, 'It's worse further on up.'

Shell-shocked and suffering badly from trench fever, Eric Harvey was invalided home and remained there until April 1918 when he returned to the front.

In September Ivor Gurney, transferred from signals to machine-guns, was at St Juliaan, overlooking the Passchendaele Ridge, when a spume of gas filled his lungs. He too was invalided home, but for him there was to be no going back.

. . . . .

Early in October Gurney wrote to Marion Scott from his ward in the Edinburgh War Hospital:

A certain Sister borrowed *Gloucestershire Friends* and has not yet returned it. My first impression is disappointment. He is farther away – FWH – from the reader than in *A Gloucestershire Lad*. 'My father bred great horses', if it were a little better would be first-rate. 'The Ballad of Army Pay' is good. 'Seth bemoans the oldest inhabitant'. And a poem which includes a line 'with one high morning note a drowsing man'. The poem written at Douai (O questions!) has very good stuff in it. That, also (though I do not like 'big' glory) which has a refrain, 'and in the little valleys thatch and dreams'. The best thing I believe is – 'We have taken a trench'.

My poor friend was tired: do not judge him by this. It is the ineffectual beating of wings, a sick mind's desire. So fine a footballer, cricketer, man, cannot wait many years after the war for his fulfilment. *This* is not it, anyway. It will do as a source of quotation for Bishop Frodsham, who will also obtain a pleasurable glow of satisfaction at his great work of uplifting the People by Literature. Obelise him!

Will Harvey is an untidy careless dreamer, who has known much sorrow, chiefly because his mind was not occupied as fully as it needed to be. He is chivalry itself, and the detection of Fear within his heart is merely the spur of action. He sings well, and is indeed born a lover of all Beauty. He is capable of great Wisdom, of glorious foolishness. Loves Life which loves not him.

Some men have to form themselves, to control their every tiniest movement of spirit, and indeed to create their own world. And such is he; who has now learnt all bitter things, and has only to gather the sweet with experienced hand. A mind of sweetness allied to strength which has never known itself and cannot live as most men by habit. But don't look at *Gloucestershire Friends* to find all this.[7]

This is a remarkable letter. Gurney expresses his views with absolute honesty, holding nothing back for friendship's sake. And for friendship's sake we can be sure that he expressed the same thoughts on the poems to Will Harvey himself. It is remarkable too in the totally accurate pen-picture which he gives us of Harvey the man. The two friends shared a love of beauty, a sense of fun, a depth of literary knowledge and, above all, an overwhelming awareness of their belonging to Gloucestershire. Where they differed was in their perceptions of heroism and of faith. Gurney, brave enough for the fight, was essentially anti-heroic, sometimes humorously so. His war was seen from the viewpoint of the private soldier, not afraid to question authority or the purposes of God (if purposes there were), as can be seen in 'Billet':

O, but the racked clear tired strained frames we had!
Tumbling in the new billet on to straw bed,
Dead asleep in eye shutting. Waking as sudden
To a golden and azure roof, a golden ratcheted
Lovely web of blue seen and blue shut, and cobwebs and tiles,
And grey wood dusty with time. June's girlish
kindest smiles.
Rest at last and no danger for another week, a seven-day week.
But one Private took on himself a Company's heart to speak,
'I wish to bloody hell I was just going to Brewery – surely

To work all day (in Stroud) and be free at tea-time – allowed
Resting when one wanted, and a joke in season,
To change clothes and take a girl to Horsepool's turning,
Or drink a pint at "Travellers Rest", and find no cloud.
Then God and man and war and Gloucestershire would have
a reason,
But I get no good in France, getting killed, cleaning off mud.'
He spoke the heart of all of us – the hidden thought burning,
   unturning.

Will Harvey's attitude on the other hand was, for the most part, staunchly heroic; seeing God's hand in deeds of valour. Of course, their poetic languages were quite different, but even so, nothing could be further from the voice of Gurney's reluctant soldier than this poem from *Gloucestershire Friends*:

Sonnet

(To One Killed in Action)

My undevout yet ardent sacrifice
   Did God refuse, knowing how carelessly
   And with what curious sensuality
The coloured flames did flicker and arise.
Half boy, half decadent, always my eyes
   Sparkle to danger: Oh it was joy to me
   To sit with Death gambling desperately
The borrowed Coin of Life. But you, more wise,
Went forth for nothing but to do God's will:
   Went gravely out – well knowing what you did
   And hating it – with feet that did not falter
   To place your gift upon the highest altar.
Therefore to you this last and finest thrill
   Is given – even Death itself, to me forbid.

No wonder Gurney did not like it. Nor would he have enjoyed much those sections of *Gloucestershire Friends* which are given over to slight verses for children, delightful as they are, and to parochial pastorales of Minsterworth folk. Even so, there is perhaps a bitter-sweet irony in one of these pieces which gives voice to a wizened and toothless old woman about to die, hearing noises in her head and fearing fire and flood in purgatory. Could Will possibly have been conscious of the contrast between her passing in village tranquillity and that of men 'dying in ditches' out of their time, hearing the guns' roar, seeing hell-fire and drowning in mud?

The Oldest Inhabitant hears far off The Drums of Death

Sometimes 'tis far off, and sometimes 'tis nigh,
Such drummerdery noises too they be!
'Tis odd – oh, I do hope I baint to die
Just as the summer months be coming on,
And buffly chicken out, and bumble-bee:
Though, to be sure, I cannot hear 'em plain
For this drat row as goes a-drumming on,
Just like a little soldier in my brain.
And oh, I've heard we got to go through flame
And water-floods – but maybe 'tisn't true!
I allus were a-frightened o' the sea.
And burning fires – oh, it would be a shame
And all the garden ripe, and sky so blue.
Such drummerdery noises, too, they be.

There are, undoubtedly, some trivial pieces in *Gloucestershire Friends*; equally others fall just short of perfection. One of these is 'The Horses' (p. 28) which in mood recalls A. E. Housman's 'A Shropshire Lad'. But whereas Housman wrote exquisitely of a

Gloucestershire Friends

Shropshire he hardly knew, Harvey's Gloucestershire landscapes are filled with real people and places he loved. In 'Solitary Confinement' (p. 135) the vision of

> Comes Lady Moon herself on silver feet
> To sit with one white arm across my breast,

is hauntingly lovely. 'What We Think of' (p. 145) deserves a better title.

In his introduction to *Gloucestershire Friends*, the Canon Residentiary of Gloucester, Bishop Frodsham (Poor Bishop Frodsham! How Gurney takes him down) gives a kindly-meant eulogy in which his only regret is that 'the poems are all short – too short'. This is hardly the case; the length of each poem is appropriate to its content. Two of the best comprise one very long and one very short. The first of these owes no small debt to Kipling. This is army life seen from the bottom up:

Ballad of Army Pay

In general, if you want a man to do a dangerous job: –
Say, swim the Channel, climb St Paul's, or break into and rob
The Bank of England, why, you find his wages must be higher
Than if you merely wanted him to light the kitchen fire.
But in the British Army, it's just the other way,
And the maximum of danger means the minimum of pay.

You put some men inside a trench, and call them infantrie,
And make them face ten kinds of hell, and face it cheerfully;
And live in holes like rats, with other rats, and lice, and toads,
And in their leisure time, assist the R.E.'s with their loads.
Then, when they've done it all, you give 'em each a bob a day!
For the maximum of danger means the minimum of pay.

We won't run down the A.S.C., nor yet the R.T.O.
They ration and direct us on the way we've got to go.
They're very useful people, and it's pretty plain to see
We couldn't do without 'em, nor yet the A.P.C.
But comparing risks and wages, – I think they all will say
That the maximum of danger means the minimum of pay.

There are men who make munitions – and seventy bob a week;
They never see a lousy trench nor hear a big shell shriek;
And others *sing* about the war at high-class music-halls
Getting heaps and heaps of money and encores from the stalls.
They 'keep the home fires burning' and bright by night and
    day,
While the maximum of danger means the minimum of pay.

I wonder if it's harder to make big shells at a bench,
Than to face the screaming beggars when they're crumping up
    a trench;
I wonder if it's harder to sing in mellow tones
Of danger, than to face it – say, in a wood like Trones;
Is discipline skilled labour, or something children play?
Should the maximum of danger mean the minimum of pay?

The second, thought by Gurney to be the best piece in the book,
sees the war from the top down. It is a gem of compaction which
stabs at cant with a stiletto:

At Afternoon Tea

(*Triolet*)

We have taken a trench
    Near Combles, I see,
Along with the French.

We have taken a trench.
(*Oh, the bodies, the stench!*)
Won't you have some more tea?
 We have taken a trench
Near Combles, I see.

 Gurney's dislike of '"Big" glory' in 'A Rondel of Gloucestershire' is understandable: the word sits awkwardly on the page. However, when read aloud it does work and the whole poem has great lyrical beauty. The composer Alan Paynes has included 'A Rondel of Gloucestershire' in a delightful set of choral pieces, 'Songs of Gloucestershire', and at the first performance in 1987 Harvey's words found their ideal expression – in song.

A Rondel of Gloucestershire

Big glory mellowing on the mellowing hills,
And in the little valleys, thatch and dreams,
Wrought by the manifold and vagrant wills
Of sun and ripening rain and wind; so gleams
My country, that great magic cup which spills
Into my mind a thousand thousand streams
Of glory mellowing on the mellowing hills
And in the little valleys, thatch and dreams.

O you dear heights of blue no ploughman tills,
O valleys where the curling mist upsteams
White over fields of trembling daffodils,
And you old dusty little water-mills,
Through all my life, for joy of you, sweet thrills
Shook me, and in my death at last there beams
Big glory mellowing on the mellowing hills
And in the little valleys, thatch and dreams.

F. W. *Harvey* SOLDIER, POET

At least two poems establish beyond doubt Harvey's eligibility to the title 'War Poet':

The Sleepers

A battered roof where stars went tripping
    With silver feet,
A broken roof whence rain came dripping,
    Yet rest was sweet.

A dug-out where the rats ran squeaking
    Under the ground,
And out in front the poor dead reeking!
    Yet sleep was sound.

No longer house or dug-out keeping,
    Within a cell
Of brown and bloody earth they're sleeping;
    Oh they sleep well.

Thrice blessed sleep, the balm of sorrow!
    Thrice blessed eyes
Sealed up till on some doomsday morrow
    The sun arise!

And one of the best poems to have been written on its subject:

Prisoners

Comrades of risk and rigour long ago
Who have done battle under honour's name,
Hoped (living or shot down) some meed of fame,

And wooed bright Danger for a thrilling kiss, –
Laugh, oh laugh well, that we have come to this!

Laugh, oh laugh loud, all ye who long ago
Adventure found in gallant company!
Safe in Stagnation, laugh, laugh bitterly,
While on this filthiest backwater of Time's flow
Drift we and rot, till something set us free!

Laugh like old men with senses atrophied,
Heeding no Present, to the Future dead,
Nodding quite foolish by the warm fireside
And seeing no flame, but only in the red
And flickering embers, pictures of the past:
Life like a cinder fading black at last.

But perhaps, taken as a whole, the finest poem in the book, which is also the best known, is 'The Bugler'. Here we have Will Harvey's affirmation of unbroken faith and dedication to his art.

The Bugler

God dreamed a man;
Then, having firmly shut
Life like a precious metal in his fist,
Withdrew, His labour done. Thus did begin
Our various divinity and sin.
For some to ploughshares did the metal twist,
And others – dreaming empires – straightway cut
Crowns for their aching foreheads. Others beat
Long nails and heavy hammers for the feet
Of their forgotten Lord. (Who dare to boast
That he is guiltless?) Others coined it: most
Did with it – simply nothing. (Here, again,

Who cries his innocence?) Yet doth remain
Metal unmarred, to each man more or less,
Whereof to fashion perfect loveliness.

For me, I do but bear within my hand
(For sake of Him our Lord, now long forsaken)
A simple bugle such as may awaken
With one high morning note a drowsing man:
That wheresoe'er within my motherland
The sound may come, 'twill echo far and wide
Like pipes of battle calling up a clan,
Trumpeting men through beauty to God's side.

Gloucestershire Friends was published by Sidgwick & Jackson in
September 1917. But in that same month Will Harvey was far
away from the satisfaction of a literary launch: locked in solitary
confinement at Holzminden Camp.

XX

Holzminden

After ten days in solitary confinement at Holzminden, when his only companion was a little mouse which peeped out occasionally from behind the unlighted coke-stove in his cell, Will was joined by another prisoner: an Irish officer who, poor man, was suffering from diarrhoea. They were allowed out of their cell only at certain hours, and when Will opened the window the guards threatened to shoot him.

For three weeks the two men endured this fetid misery and, at last, the 'green mould' of prisondom began to get the better of Will. Throughout the previous year in captivity, no matter how adverse the conditions, he had retained his sense of humour and kept alight his creative spirit. He was a man given to self-doubt and soul-searching who needed physical activity to counterbalance a tendency to depression. At Schwarmstedt, a foul camp, he had at least been able to walk, albeit under guard, in the wild but beautiful country surrounding the *lager*. 'There were woods in which to lie talking while tea was boiled on a stick fire; gorse and heather to smell; and streams to bathe in as long as we remained unseen. It was possible to wander for miles amid the red heather and the golden gorse without seeing a house, or a human being within shade of the dappled pine-woods which dotted darkly green the countryside.' Not so at Holzminden, where walks outside the wire were forbidden.

Will tried to write poetry, but his melancholy refused to be defeated as it had been at Douai. The words just would not come. No doubt some of the anguish which he felt was a reaction to the

Holzminden Camp.

failure of his enormously brave escape-attempt. To have risked so much only to return to seemingly endless captivity must have been unbearably frustrating. The outward proof of his mental state was a neglect of his personal appearance. He grew a beard 'and looked like Judas Iscariot'.

> I had been a prisoner not much more than a year, and my temperament is not naturally a mouldy one; but captivity is an insidious evil which saps one's vitality and eats away one's spirit. I have come to the conclusion that to give a man 'five years' may be necessary, but it is damnable cruelty. Whether a man highly strung feels it more than a duller and more animal type, or less, I cannot tell, but with a little more than two years' experience of it, I can say with certainty that it is by far the worst thing that ever happened to me, and a thing from which I shall possibly never recover. It is not the physical hardship, it is the purposelessness of it, and the awful monotony, that sickens the heart. And I only did two years, and I had books, and I had the finest friends

Will Harvey (centre) with comrades in captivity, Holzminden.

man could wish to share it. I mention all this now because
this was the first time that I had begun to feel mouldy, and
because up to that time I had always despised those who
gave way to the disease. But some had done three years
when I had ony done one, and how was I to know that
mouldiness accumulated at compound interest!

Out of his cell after a month, Will discovered that even the small
pleasures possible at his previous camps were now to be denied.
Holzminden could and should have been a good camp. Its solid
brick buildings contained comfortable, airy, uncrowded rooms;
there was a large bathroom with hot water on tap; the countryside
around the camp was beautiful. But all this counted for nothing
because one man determined that life at Holzminden would be as
unpleasant as possible for prisoners of war. This man was Hauptmann Niemeyer, the camp commandant. He was 'a cad, a boaster,
and a bully of the worst type. He had lived in America, and was
commonly known as "Milwaukee Bill". He talked broken American under the impression that it was English. "I guess you know",
his commonest expression, became a catch-phrase with all who
knew him.'
Niemeyer ensured that every aspect of camp life was made
unduly difficult: queuing for letters, parcels, food, firewood, bread-
cards, wine-cards, inoculations, sick parades and baths. He decided
that the bathroom was a good place to kennel the police dogs and
signed the following notice: 'When a more suitable place in the
camp can be found for the dogs, officers may have baths on
Tuesdays and Fridays.' Thus men, given a lower priority than dogs,
were obliged to bathe in the open under a cold pump, subject to the
ridicule of passers-by.

Under anyone but Niemeyer we might have had walks, and
a playing field; games, and baths after games; and so kept
ourselves fit and hard, but he made such things quite
impossible. Also he disallowed our little entertainments,
concerts, and so forth, which we gave in the dining-rooms,
where planks on trestles did for a stage and the dulcitone

"MILWAUKEE BILL."

Hauptmann Niemeyer, the commandant at Holzminden Camp.
Cartoon from *Comrades in Captivity*.

replaced a piano – and this merely because he felt annoyed
that somebody had got away. On such occasions he would
order all the officers into their barracks, and forbid them to
open the windows or to look out of them. People who
showed themselves were shot at, and I shall not forget the
splintering and smashing of glass which went on the day
when Bobbie rigged up a dummy figure at one of the
windows, and worked it up and down with a string; the rest
of us, crawling about on our hands and knees, were
laughing until we could hardly move, but Bobbie was just
absorbed and proud, like a child with a new toy.

Whenever there was an escape or an escape attempt, and they
were many, Niemeyer reacted and over-reacted in the barking,
puerile, spiteful manner which earned for him the loathing of
prisoners and Germans alike, such that the camp quickly became
known as Hellminden. However, each outburst only strengthened
the resolve of the captives to escape.
  Will was pleased to find himself put into a small room at the top
of a block along with seven particular friends, amongst them 'R' the
P.T. engineer, and 'Mossy'.

  . . . there is no need to say that it was soon as full of moving
  panels, planks which lifted, and sills which slid, as any
  medieval castle. It was simply honeycombed with hiding-
  places, and half the escaping kit in the barrack was stored
  there, if only the Huns had known.

The Huns most certainly did not know that a major tunnel was
even then being dug from a cellar, under concrete flooring, to the
farther side of a stone wall surrounding the camp, intended to
emerge in a field of corn on the other side of the roadway. Because
Will had been in the cells he missed his chance to apply for a place
on the escaping party which was to use the tunnel, but in any case
there was a hopelessly long waiting-list. On 23 July the tunnel at
Holzminden was ready for use:

Two days before Niemeyer, boasting of camp arrangements, had said: 'Well, gentlemen, I guess you know if you want to escape you must give me a couple of days' notice!' Notice was not given, but two days later, almost to the hour, twenty-nine officers crawled out through the sap, and though nineteen of them were retaken in various parts of Germany, ten got right away into England, a record for any camp in Germany during the war. The fugitives included two Lieutenant-Colonels, and the German authorities offered £250 for each prisoner brought back. As soon as the members of the party were out, they very wisely separated, travelling in little groups, or alone, for the rest of the journey. Several of them, to avoid suspicion, started off in a direction directly opposite to the frontier; and curiously enough it was some of these who were first to 'get over'. A fortnight was about the average time taken to reach the border, and during that period the men tramped 180 miles or thereabouts. Naturally most of them travelled only at night, but a few, I believe, risked daylight marching; and one or two, who spoke German fluently, and had supplied themselves with forged passports, saved their legs and took the train.

It took Niemeyer and his staff about two hours to find the tunnel on the following day, and he then ordered it to be opened up. This work would take his soldiers several hours to carry out, said he, so it would be impossible to censor any parcels. The officers were therefore deprived of their food during that time, and had to live on German rations. This resulted in an additional queue. At mealtimes the officers would stand in a long line with dishes and plates in their hands, and as they passed by one German would fling a few potatoes into the dish, while another thrust his dirty hand into a great cauldron to deposit a piece of fish upon the plate. Niemeyer, thoroughly pleased, stood by to taunt his victims, saying, 'Ach, it is not so goot as Piccadilly, zo?'

I hear that on the morning following the escape, when his *Feldwebel* reported 'Twenty-nine missing, Herr Captain',

The tunnel at Holzminden after it had been opened up.

Niemeyer was so full of evil rage that he almost lost his reason. He simply raved. Calling out the guards, he commanded them to fire on any British officer who dared as much as to look out of the windows. After that, he ordered a parade on the barrack square; and several senior officers who appeared in shoes instead of boots were sent immediately to cells. As a reprisal, on the following morning everybody came on parade without either hat or tunic. Niemeyer, furious with rage, ordered the sentries to charge, but as they hated him more than they did the British, the thing was a ridiculous farce. One officer had lost a leg, and so could not disappear into barracks so swiftly as the others. Him the sentries collared. He was put into cells and kept there for three weeks.

The success of the tunnel was a tremendous blow to Niemeyer's pride, and completely killed his prestige in the army corps. He was never quite the same blustering bully afterwards, and finally, hated alike by Germans and British, became a mere laughing-stock. After the Armistice he was (I am told) relegated to cells by the Workers' and Soldiers' Council, which, if true, is surely one of the best bits of work it ever did.

The walls of the room which Will shared had been covered with chalk drawings by 'Mossy', perhaps as much for camouflage as decoration. There were prehistoric animals of frightening look and great spiders hanging from exaggerated webs. Over Will's bed 'Mossy' had drawn a pool of water and 'amid the rushes floated some fine white ducks', a happy reminder of the little pond at The Redlands perhaps.

One night (it was soon after I had come out of solitary confinement) everybody was drifting off to sleep when there came sudden peals of laughter from my bed. Sponges were thrown, and boots, and voices demanded what the devil was the matter; to which I replied, 'I was just thinking what an extraordinarily funny thing a duck is!'

And the next morning, to make clear my meaning, and to explain the secret beauty and humour of that bird no less than its relationship and significance to the heavens above and to hell underneath, I wrote the following poem:

Ducks

*(TO F.M., who drew them in
Holzminden Prison)*

I

From troubles of the world
I turn to ducks,
Beautiful comical things
Sleeping or curled
Their heads beneath white wings
By water cool,
Or finding curious things
To eat in various mucks
Beneath the pool,
Tails uppermost, or waddling
Sailor-like on the shores
Of ponds, or paddling
Left! right! – with fanlike feet
Which are for steady oars
When they (white galleys) float
Each bird a boat
Rippling at will the sweet
Wide waterway . . .
When night is fallen *you* creep
Upstairs, but drakes and dillies
Nest with pale water-stars,
Moonbeams and shadow bars,

Holzminden

And water-lilies:
Fearful too much to sleep
Since they've no locks
To click against the teeth
Of weasel and fox.
And warm beneath
Are eggs of cloudy green
Whence hungry rats and lean
Would stealthily suck
New life, but for the mien,
The bold ferocious mien
Of the mother-duck.

II

Yes, ducks are valiant things
On nests of twigs and straws,
And ducks are soothy things
And lovely on the lake
When that the sunlight draws
Thereon their pictures dim
In colours cool.
And when beneath the pool
They dabble, and when they swim
And make their rippling rings,
O ducks are beautiful things!

But ducks are comical things: —
As comical as you.
Quack!
They waddle round, they do.
They eat all sorts of things,
And then they quack.
By barn and stable and stack
They wander at their will,
But if you go too near
They look at you through black

209

Small topaz-tinted eyes
And wish you ill.
Triangular and clear
They leave their curious track
In mud at the water's edge,
And there amid the sedge
And slime they gobble and peer
Saying 'Quack! quack!'

III

When God had finished the stars and whirl of
   coloured suns
He turned His mind from big things to fashion little
   ones;
Beautiful tiny things (like daisies) He made, and then
He made the comical ones in case the minds of men
Should stiffen and become
Dull, humourless and glum,
And so forgetful of their Maker be
As to take even themselves – *quite seriously.*
Caterpillars and cats are lively and excellent puns:
All God's jokes are good – even the practical ones!
And as for the duck, I think God must have smiled a
   bit
Seeing those bright eyes blink on the day He
   fashioned it.
And He's probably laughing still at the sound that
   came out of its bill!

'Ducks', conceived in Will Harvey's deepest gloom, proved at birth to be his best-loved expression of humour and joy. The poem became the title-work of his third book of verse, published in 1919 and dedicated to Anne. It travelled the world, found its way into many anthologies and was highly praised by G.K. Chesterton.

When, years later, Will was told that during the Second World

War one of the English exercises in German schools had been to translate 'Ducks' into German, his reaction was: 'Serves the Germans damn well right!'

XXI

Bad-Colberg

At the end of February 1918 Will and a number of other officers, most of whom had been sentenced for escaping, were transferred from Holzminden to Bad-Colberg. The new camp was a great improvement on the old, with comfortable rooms, good baths and, best of all, permission to walk in the surrounding countryside. However, whereas Niemeyer at Holzminden had been an insufferable bully, the commandant at Bad-Colberg, Kröner, was a weak old fool; quite 'under the thumb and the intellect' of his malignant adjutant, Captain Beetz.

Soon after his arrival at Bad-Colberg, Will's sense of humour returned. The Irish officers had hoodwinked Kröner into believing that St Patrick's Day 'was a great Irish feast and anniversary of the bloody Battle of the Boyne, when proud England was beaten to her craven knees by the sword of Erin.' So convinced was the commandant that he allowed oysters, hock, burgundy and champagne to be brought into camp to ensure that the feast was befitting the celebration of a victory over England!

On the day after the feast of St Patrick, we got up early and walked about nine miles to Mass. It was a trying business and needed a stern effort of will, but the country was very lovely in the morning light, and the shade of the pine-woods like a cool hand laid upon brows which certainly needed it. Afterwards, out of remembrance of my own country, so different from this, and from Ireland, but so equally beautiful in approaching Spring, I wrote a poem under the title:

Bad-Colberg

Gloucestershire from Abroad

On Dinny Hill the daffodil
  Has crowned the year's returning,
The water cool in Placket Pool
  Is ruffled up and burning
In little wings of fluttering fire:
  And all the heart of my desire
  Is now to be in Gloucestershire.

The river flows, the blossom blows
  In orchards by the river.
O now to stand in that, my land,
  And watch the withies shiver!
The yearning eyes of my desire
  Are blinded by a twinkling fire
  Of turning leaves in Gloucestershire.

The shadows fleet o'er springing wheat
  Which like green water washes
The red old earth of Minsterworth,
  And ripples in such flashes
As by their little harmless fire
  Light the great stack of my desire
  This day to be in Gloucestershire.

The camp was situated in a valley set among low hills clad with pine-woods in which many rare butterflies were to be found. Several prisoners were enthusiastic entomologists, amongst them one of Will's friends, 'Mac'. Whenever Mac set out to catch butterflies he was accompanied by an aged German guard who carried the killing bottle

. . . and was positively angry when the butterflies which Mac was chasing refused to come and be transformed into

---

'specimens' for the glory of their country. It was a gross breach of discipline on the part of a German insect, and he resented it in a delightful and characteristic expression of feeling, which the following tale relates.

Imagine Mac (that nice fat little man) panting in pursuit of a beautiful swallow-tail. Behind him, carrying the bottle, galumphs the perspiring Hun. Mac makes a slash with his net, but misses his footing and falls headlong into a prickly bush. The guard rushes up; the butterfly hovers exasperatingly near, fluttering yet above the bush. Mac, picking thorns out of himself, looks up to see his old sentry standing impotent, but furious with rage, shaking a fat fist at the lovely swallow-tail now fluttering away upon its innocent airy course, and shouting 'Schweinhund!'

Mac recounted this delicious little nonsense to Will who was so amused by it that he felt the need for an immediate celebration – he shaved off his beard!

But of course no prison camp could be all comfort and humour, and at Bad-Colberg there was Beetz who hated the British in general and those who had tried to escape in particular. Following the discovery that an attempt had been made by somebody from Will's building to cut the wire, the atmosphere became ugly. The rooms were searched and several escape kits discovered.

The Commandant was furious, and ordered all the officers in the three suspected rooms to report themselves at the interpreter's office every hour of the day until further notice. This was clearly a flagrant case of collective punishment which the German and British Governments had agreed should not be inflicted. The result of it would be that the officers who had to report themselves would thereby be deprived of walks; not to mention the obvious disadvantage of having to stop doing whatever they might be doing, and run off to the interpreter's office every hour of the day. We therefore decided that we would not go.

Finding that his order had been ignored, the

But M. and W. did not live to serve their sentences. Before they could be taken away they made a desperate and courageous escape and were free for several days before recapture. On Whit Sunday 1918 Beetz sent eight carefully-chosen soldiers to collect the prisoners from a railway station about eight miles from the camp. That afternoon both men were brought into the prison on stretchers – dead.

Piecing together the evidence of friendly sentries it became clear that the guards picked by Beetz had been the most brutal and anti-British in the camp; that Beetz had said of M. and W.'s many escapes: 'Yes, they are two very brave men, but they will be shot'; and that he had told them that they would never escape again.

> Now at the time at which they were shot it was broad daylight; they were presumably without their packs, unless purposely allowed to keep them as a temptation to escape; they had four armed guards each; they were seventy yards apart, so that there could have been no collaboration; it was a lonely spot; they were both shot dead, and neither merely wounded.

No inspection of the bodies by British officers was permitted and nothing could be proved. But all were convinced that there had been foul play and that it had been orchestrated by Beetz.

After this, Will's days at Bad-Colberg were occupied mainly with being 'prisoner's friend' –

> – an employment kept entirely unofficial and secret, though the Germans certainly had their suspicions of what I was doing, as shown by a remark made at one of the courts-martial when Beetz snarled suddenly, 'And these lies have been carefully made up for you by Lt. Harvey, I suppose?' – a suggestion which was, of course, indignantly denied by the prisoner.
>
> What, in fact, happened was this: the best line of defence to whatever questions had to be answered was thought out,

A COURT MARTIAL

From *Within Four Walls* by M.C.C. Harrison and H.A. Cartwright
(Edward Arnold & Co., 1930). Drawn by H.A. Cartwright.

written down, and learnt by heart. It was then translated
into German. At trial the translated defence was handed to
the judges. The prisoner did not require a German counsel.
He had written out his defence. He had got it translated for
the convenience of the court. He had no more to say. The
court was naturally pleased at this saving of time, and to
the chagrin of the camp authorities showed its first
appreciation of such a frank and concise explanation by
inflicting only three weeks' imprisonment upon an officer
whom Beetz and Kröner had accused of burglary, being in
possession of stolen goods, destruction of German property,
and attempted escape.

The Germans asked some very curious questions at their
courts-martial, and solemnly took down some very curious
answers – e.g. 'Where were you born?'

Answer. 'Dixie.'
Q. 'What was your mother's maiden name?'
A. 'Pinkum.'
Q. 'Christian name?'
A. 'Lydia.'
Except in their often very unpleasant consequences these German courts-martial of British officers were a comic farce; and as for justice –!

Under international conventions it was possible for prisoners of war to be repatriated to neutral territory. A number of British officers were sent over to Holland by the Germans according to the length of time which they had spent in the camps. 'Details of all bad cases of injustice or ill-treatment were memorised by officers being sent to Holland on repatriation, and so taken through one by one to the British authorities, causing dignified protest on one side and insolent denial on the other.'
In June 1918, Will's name appeared on the list of those to go to Holland. He had been in captivity for almost two years.

On the day of departure we were subject to a very rigorous personal search, and required to give up all camp money in our possession whether notes or otherwise; the reason for this being a trick played on Germany by repatriated Frenchmen in another camp. Our Allies, having taken away with them some of the paper which passed for money in that camp, proceeded to forge thousands of notes, which they sent concealed in parcels of food to their friends who remained in the camp they had left, where such paper had, of course, the purchasing value of money. There resulted an unheard-of boom in the canteen (money is no object when one has only to go up to a friend and say, 'Give me a thousand marks'), and the Germans, who made a profit on everything sold, must have thought that they were making a fine fortune, till they discovered at the end of several months that more money had been spent than was ever issued, and that a vast percentage of notes for which value had been

given was absolutely worthless. Our search over, and
nothing of importance found, we drove light-heartedly away
to the station in a rickety one-horse char-à-banc. The
guards who accompanied us were stolid amiable men, and
the driver a village 'character'. On our way to the station we
passed through Parson's Wood (Pfaffenholtz), near
Heldburg, and had pointed out to us by the driver the exact
places where poor M. and W. had been shot. The two spots
pointed out were certainly seventy yards apart.

Saddened with the memory of that tragedy, and
gladdened at the thought of quitting the place of it for ever,
we boarded the train and were soon being carried swiftly
away on our road to freedom.

XXII

Morgenfrüh

Will Harvey's expectations of early repatriation were quickly dashed. He and his companions arrived at Aachen (Aix la Chapelle) on about 24 June and entered yet another camp. Day after day they asked the Germans when they would be moving on. Day after day they were told, 'Morgenfrüh' ('tomorrow morning') and this soon became the worst kind of torture. As the days passed into weeks of angry frustration, Will began once more to plan his escape.

On 16 August Will and a friend made their attempt to get away, only to be caught by a guard whose silence they were fortunately able to buy. That same afternoon they were put aboard a train on their way to another camp on the island of Stralsund in the Baltic.

At Stralsund Will came close to nervous collapse. Giving in to the 'green mould' he once again grew a beard, his symbol of depression, spent most of his days lying on a bug-infested bed, and, in spite of a good camp library, was unable to read anything other than a dictionary. The threads by which he held his mind together were spun from words, drawn from the dictionary for their beauty or curiosity, and written down in numerous lists. Then, as before, the threads were woven into verse.

The Treasury

I have such joy in my heart's coffer,
Little I care what Life may offer;

Little it matters if I lie
In dungeons, who possess the sky.

The sparkling morn, the starry night,
Are locked away for my delight.

But in my heart there hangs a key
To open them, called Memory.

How should I ever lack a friend
Who so have lovers without end?

How can I ever lose my home
Who bear it with me where I come?

My home is in my heart, and there
In dreadful days I do repair;

And I have broken off the seal
Of that Dream-box, whose dreams are real.

So rich am I, I do possess
Their overpowering loveliness;

And have such joy in my heart's coffer,
Little I care what Life may offer.

It is a strange thing, this power of poetry, to substitute life,
or recreate it, when life has failed us. It is responsible for all
the fine poetry which has come, surprising us for no reason,
direct from the trenches.

Whilst in Stralsund Camp Will did not write a single letter home
and later acknowledged that this had been unkind. He could hardly
have known just how unkind. At the beginning of September his
brother Eric was awarded a bar to the MC for his inspiring

leadership during the advance on Sailly, west of the River Lys. Eric never wore his decoration. On 30 September he was killed by a machine-gun bullet while walking back to his company headquarters from the front line in daylight. The chronicler of the 2/5th Battalion wrote of him:

> Capt. Eric Harvey's death was a loss the Battalion could ill afford. The best of company commanders and the cheeriest of comrades, he displayed the utmost gallantry on every occasion. His disregard of danger inspired his men, who would go anywhere under his command.
>
> Early in the morning Capt. Harvey was buried in the Estaires cemetery with full military honours. 'Last Post' was blown and volleys were fired. The service was attended by most of the officers and the whole of A Company who, owing to the early hour, came on parade just as they had left the line, unshaven and with the mud of the trenches still on them. The service was none the less impressive on that account.[1]

Eric's widow, Gwen, was left to bring up her baby son alone, and Tillie's grief can only have been deepened by Will's silence. Five days after Eric's death Germany and Austro-Hungary asked President Wilson for armistice talks.

At last, in late October, Will Harvey was on his way to Scheveningen in Holland, via Aachen.

> After another wearisome journey we arrived at Aachen for the second time, a thoroughly mouldy party, not really believing that we should ever be allowed over the border. But we crossed it a few days later, and, where the sleepers changed from iron to wood (the escaper's invariable assurance that he is 'over'), saw incredulously a crowd of Dutch children cheering us and blowing kisses. It was a very choky feeling that we had then, a lump in the throat which almost prevented our returning their pretty welcome; but soon we were all shouting back lustily to greetings which

met us as the train rocked quietly through that low-lying land of bell-towers and canals. If we found later on that Holland and Heaven chiefly resembled one another in the fact that both were extraordinarily difficult to reach, we seemed certainly to be getting into Heaven the day we crossed over from Germany.

At Scheveningen station we were met by hundreds of friends, both officers and orderlies, pressing round and cheering us as we came off the train. I believe there was a reception somewhere, but am not sure, for I was immediately whirled off to The Hague by dear old R. There suddenly and with violence our swiftly running tram was boarded by two highly excited officers, O. and D.S., who had seen us from the roadway. Then altogether we stood up and sang 'The Old Bold Mate'.

Even then, Will Harvey was denied the reward of repatriation. He and five other officers and a number of soldiers were sent to a central camp at Leeuwarden to distribute food and clothes to returning English prisoners. This work completed he went with another officer to feed Italians and Portuguese at Harderwijk by the Zuider Zee.

During his last days in Holland Will fell victim to the Spanish 'flu epidemic which began in April 1918 and for a year swept the world, leaving 25 million dead. And so, at last, in February 1919, weak and ill, his skin yellowed, he came back to England: first to a camp at Seaton Delaval in Northumberland for demobilisation and then, at Eastertime, to Minsterworth.

HOME AGAIN

After Long Wandering

I will go back to Gloucestershire,
  To the spot where I was born,
To the talk at eve with men and women
  And song on the roads at morn.
And I'll sing as I tramp by dusty hedges
  Or drink my ale in the shade
How Gloucestershire is the finest home
  That the Lord God ever made.

First I will go to the ancient house
  Where Doomsday book was planned,
And cool my body and soul in shade
  Of pillars huge which stand
Where the organ echoes thunder-like
  Its paean of triumph and praise
In a temple lovely as ever the love
  Of Beauty's God did raise.

Gargoyles will thrust out heads to hearken,
  A frozen forest of stone
Echo behind me as I pass
  Out of the shadow alone
To buzz and bustle of Barton Fair
  And its drifting droves of sheep,
To find three miles away the village
  Where I will sleep.

Minsterworth, queen of riverside places
  (Save Framilode, who can vie?),
To her I'll go when day has dwindled
  And the light low in the sky;
And my troubles shall fall from me, a bundle,
  And youth come back again,
Seeing the smoke of her houses and hearing
  The talk of Minsterworth men.

I'll drink my perry and sing my song
  Of home and home again,
Pierced with the old miraculous pleasure
  Keen as sharpest pain;
And if I rise to sing on the morrow
  Or if I die in my bed,
'Tis all the same: I'll be home again,
  And happy alive or dead.

XXIII

Home Again

It is wonderful to get home – home: in the grave beauty of night to lie wakeful, disturbed only by the delicious unrest and distress of the trees – kept awake, as by a lover, all night. It is happiness. There is the moonlight cold and quiet, and bars of darkness, within the room; and outside in the whiteness of moonshine my dear hills, so blue, phantom-fast, and shadowy – the hills that I shall see again (and so changed) at dawn.

But as I was sitting reading to my mother in her bedroom (for she was ill at the time), talking occasionally or listening to the little lapping voices of the fire, I said to myself, thinking of all I had seen and experienced, 'This is the most wonderful thing that has ever happened to me!'

For several weeks after his return to The Redlands, Will Harvey was far from well, but as he slowly regained health and strength a new creative fever compelled him to write.

In February 1918, whilst Will smouldered in Holzminden camp, Ivor Gurney, concealing his own suffering, had written to him:

My Dear Old Willy: It's a dull day. I will comfort and renew myself by writing to you, friend of orchard and river; drawing life from memories of blue and silver seen together and great sights of sunset from the little hill . . . .

Dear chap, there's so much to talk about. I'll put my hand on your shoulder, and we'll wander about the fields and

roads to talk of the Georgian Book, No. 3 – which has
several new names. (Willy, I hope you'll be in No. 4.)
Turner, Sassoon, Munro, J.C. Squire, Stephens, Graves.
And old names. Drinkwater (a good selection), Gibson (a
poor one), Walter De La Mare, Davies (poor), Hodgson.
These young writers are very interesting, very much in
earnest, and very gifted; out of them a great poet should
come. Make haste Willy and start it!

O we'll do such things together yet!

You must be stale with imprisonment; but still, unless
weak with hunger or sickness – force yourself: write . . .

Do you remember how, in Spring evenings, the gold of
late sunlight used to be heavy on the floor of the orchard,
that lies to the right of the road, nearing your house on a
journey from Gloucester. And great sunsets? And Autumn
afterglows, most tender, most 'thronged' (you know what I
mean). You'll make words to catch that charm, and I'll make
music, combine the result. Cheerio, Willy, things will come
right in the end. Look at me – the sick creature of 4 years
ago, and what I am now. If *I* can do it, what can you do?[1]

Back home in Gloucestershire Will certainly forced himself to
write, but not in the over-simplified lyric vein of some of the models
listed in Gurney's kindly-meant letter: those poets whose work
Cyril Connolly wittily called an 'explosion of Georgian Marsh-gas'.
Harvey's message was to be deeply personal, sometimes angry and
often astringent.

On 28 June 1919, the Treaty of Versailles was signed. In the
evening Will Harvey paused amongst the elm trees which he had
kissed goodbye five years before, trees which had anchored his
memories to the lost world of yesterday.

Victory Night, 1919

Trees posture to a dog holding a bone:
Change magically to a silhouette

Of giant lovers whispering alone:
Then, as I pass them in the dark and wet,
To one queer ebony blob upon the sky;
Then suddenly back to elms – elms that I
Have known so long that they are part of life,
The soldierly elms that line the road to home.
Home . . . Father and two dead brothers come
Suddenly round the bend, and all the strife
Of years is blended into whispering
Of trees familiar, lisping leaves, and dropping
Of rain upon this curled dark strip of road.
All I would not forget in this wild mood
Of victory is whispered here in trees,
The heavy elms which hold my memories.

This is one of the jewels of a collection dedicated to Anne, made up of new work as well as prison poems, which was published by Sidgwick & Jackson in November 1919 under the title *Ducks and Other Verses*. If the book sold on the deserved popularity of 'Ducks', its readers found in it much of beauty, depth and perception besides; and even in 'Ducks' there is a touch of the profound.

A whole section of the book was devoted to 'A New England' which is prefaced by Harvey's apologia for all that follows; his prayer that the immense sacrifices of the war would at least fuel a new understanding amongst his fellow-countrymen:

'Who is here so vile that will not love his country?'
All save one of the poems, under the title of 'A New
England', were written in German prisons in an attempt to
treat my captivity as a 'retreat' (sternly enforced) wherein I
might attain perspective of life which would enable me to
return to England a more useful and considerate child.
    Reconstruction is their theme; love of England their
inspiration.
    Though openly propagandist, they are not political, save
only in the sense that all poetry is so. I am in no way

concerned to discover which 'party' will outwardly achieve a reform which must be born first in the heart: – an immaculate conception.

Practically I am against any man being too poor for the reason that he is my brother, and because it is bad for the State, just as I am against any man being too rich for the same reason and because it is bad form.

What England needs is a spiritual ideal. But how hard it is to be spiritual with toothache!

So poverty which cripples the beautiful body of a State, not less than luxury its inevitable companion, must be dealt with ere England can be free to live healthily. And since health (however robust) in an idiot or a moral degenerate is of little value, England must realise these two dependent and supreme mysteries, namely: 'the Fatherhood of God' and 'the Brotherhood of Men'. Otherwise the war will have been lost, the sacrifice in vain.

In pocket we, like every other European nation, are poorer than before.

We have gained only in national experience, and now is the time to invest it.

A comradeship of ghastly experience knits up all classes.

Now is the time to reconstruct; to understand; to get unity of aim; to fashion A New England.

No one can deny the fact that Peace has never seized the national imagination as War has done.

Peace was not spoken of as 'The Great Adventure'. For Peace we never poured out blood and gold like water. Art, housing, education, science, employment, have never received endowment of x^t millions. To organise efficiently for War took us nearly two years, but for Peace we have taken two thousand: – and failed.

Let us admit it: our hearts were not in the work. When our hearts are in the work we shall succeed, for in truth:

> 'Whatever thing we love as the supreme
> Import of life, that surely we achieve.

Home Again

Man cannot fail to do if he believe,
And follows still the angel of his dream.
For gold is not of all this world the core,
But God from whom our strength is evermore.'

'Requiescat' (p. 172) appears in this section of the book and provides a keynote for the other poems. Particularly fine is 'Ecce Homo'.

Ecce Homo

Quiet he lies
All day beneath a hood of horrible flies,
For Death has put the dark into his eyes;
    And in the night
    A rat now finds delight
Therein – *this* is the heir
Of Time: for this did bear
A woman pangs of childbirth: Lo, this thing
    Is Man, and king
Of all the strangely beautiful years that were!

Travail and tears
Of all men's mothers, and God's mother-years
Lie here bemocked of dark and witless rage: –
    The bloody heritage
Of men who cast out Love and clung to Fears.

In a radio interview shortly before he died, the late Lord Stockton (Harold Macmillan), remembering the horrors of the Great War, said of the men who survived it: 'The experience was like that of men who have been prisoners of war; it put something *on* them.' Will Harvey both survived the horror and had been a prisoner of war. Highly-strung before 1914, in 1919 he came home

231

a changed man; he had 'something *on* him' which his family could not dispel.

Always fond of a glass of cider or beer, Will found that these friends had the power to still his jangling nerves and to set afloat his thoughts in verse. The men whose inn-company he sought had shared his bitter cup of war and understood his pain. But inevitably there were those who, not having ached in Flanders fields, censured his behaviour and company. To these Will reacted in verse worthy of John Clare in its denunciation of cant.

Apologia for a Merry Rogue

Rogue and drinker men call me: I am!
For abstinent virtues I care not a d—:
But from stinginess and hypocrisy,
From envy, meanness and cruelty
May God of His grace deliver me.

I live to affirm my zest of things
    In life, be they seemly or otherwise,
    And reckon the Creator wise
That men from creeping tramps to kings
    Are not a crowd of holy, bloated
    Shiny-hatted, grave, frock-coated,
Damnably obedient, good,
Fat people, doing all they should.

I do not choose to justify
    My ways by any holy name
    Because our Gods are not the same:
For me, I count it blasphemy
To fail in any zest of living,
Or sniff at what our Host is giving
In this fine house of Life, wherein
Ingratitude's the basest sin.

Home Again

So let me be 'a d—d bad lot'
But glad to live: for he who is not
Is worse than I, and fit to be shot;
The which I will maintain till when
I lie at last in earth. Amen.

To Certain Persons

('*I would rather see England free than sober.*')

Did you think (fools!) I hated men?
   If so you thought, go think again.
And thought you that when I wrote 'If
   We Return' that we'd return to sniff
Over the drinkers of ale, the smokers
   Of 'baccy, the human vulgar jokers,
Best of what God and good green earth
   Have made; that I meant *lemonade*,
And not a valiant great birth
   Of Freedom, of men unafraid
Claiming a man's just right to eat,
   Drink, live and love, and breathe the sweet
Air of old England? Now as then
   I stand for men – just men, the men
Who saved from violence that skin
   Of yours: – God pardon them the sin!

Do I loathe drunkenness? I do, –
   Just half as much as cant, and you!

A gentler Will, singing softly of his love, returns in a prison-winter poem dedicated to Anne.

233

To S.A.K.

Snow covers the ground
  Save where in a little ring
Cold crocuses are showing
  With green grass round,
As if their fire glowing
  Had melted the snow, and Spring
    (When all was bare and bound)
  Kept there her dwelling.

Even so in the snowy cold
  Of Life shine you, my dear,
A sunny place, a flaming
  Small ring of crocus-gold,
    And taming –
Yet with no fiercer thing
  Than innocence, the sheer
Savageness of Winter to crocus-crowned Spring.

By the summer of 1919 Will had completed his only prose work, *Comrades in Captivity*, an account of his experiences in the German camps and dedicated to:

ALL OLD GEFANGENER FRIENDS
but particularly to the
P.T. AND TO MY FRIEND IVOR GURNEY

The dust-jacket, originally intended for *Gloucestershire Friends*, was a pen-and-ink sketch by a fellow-prisoner at Crefeld called Jackson. However, this had been disallowed by the commandant 'on the ground that the decorative barbs had been drawn too big'! Happily, the design was much more appropriate for *Comrades in Captivity*.

The book is like no other prisoner-of-war story, and from the First World War such stories are in any case few. This is no catalogue of barbarous atrocities, or even of heroism, although

COMRADES in CAPTIVITY
A Record of Life in Seven German
Prison Camps.   By F. W. Harvey.

The dust jacket of *Comrades in Captivity*.

both are present in carefully limited measure. Rather it is an amalgam of absorbing documentary, personal philosophy, political ideals and appreciations of music and literature. It also contains the full texts of three of the lectures which Harvey delivered whilst a prisoner. These deal with such widely differing subjects as: 'Men and Books', 'War – Its Causes and Remedy' and 'The Case against Bernard Shaw'. This last was given in response to an appreciative lecture on G.B.S. which had been delivered by Hugh Walker, who remained one of Will's staunchest friends to the end of his life.

Comrades in Captivity holds another distinction – in the world of popular music. It is understood to have been the first publication in which the full words and melody of the Australian song 'Waltzing Matilda', a great favourite in the camps, appeared in the United Kingdom.

Through *Comrades in Captivity* Harvey balances the spirit-sapping demoralisation of his confinement with testimony that the spirit can rise above adversity. Boredom and monotony had been his chief enemies and he says of his book:

Readers who desire to know more than it tells them about how it feels to be a prisoner need only read it over again, and after that over and over again till they are sick. Then, when they have thrown it on the floor in disgust, let them remind themselves that this was precisely what prisoners were not able to do, though many tried hard and some paid their lives for the attempt. And not only must they read everything I have written in this book a thousand times (if anything so horrible as that can be contemplated) but a thousand times also they must read blank pages. It is the blank page which kills you in the end; even nonsense is better than that.

Will's first weapon against adversity had always been humour, and in *Comrades in Captivity* he returns to the expression of his belief, first set out in 1906, that humour is the companion of fortitude:

Home Again

I have heard it contended with some skill, and demonstrated with convincing evidence such as Bernard Shaw, that the Irish have no sense of humour, but only a very great store of wit; and certainly there is a great deal of difference between those two things, for wit is mainly intellectual, but humour of the immortal spirit. Of course, a man may have both (I believe Sydney Smith had, and very certainly Shakespeare had), but that does not alter the fundamental difference, nor the fact that, of the two, humour is the much more desirable gift of God.

There are people who would measure the amount of a man's humour by the amount of laughing he does. They should keep a hyena. Others treat it as if it were a set of false teeth, to be kept in the mouth all day and laid aside when there are no more chestnuts to chew; but humour is mainly silent, and can never be laid aside. One sees it in people's eyes, but chiefly in their conduct towards life. I believe that its dominating note is courage (and who are more courageous than the Irish?). It is a Christian thing (and Ireland is almost the last Christian country left), founded upon faith, hope and charity, those three cardinal virtues of Christianity. Its courage derives out of a sense of the final invincibility of the soul, and comes out of a deep, though often unconscious, belief, as well as from a certain abstraction from worldly affairs which is not far off contempt for them. This misfortune, these insults, are unpleasant, annoying to the mind and to the body (and what a funny old thing the body is!); but how grotesquely laughable they must be to the soul! – such is the unconscious reasoning of humour in human life. Humour is wonderfully sane; it is a cooling medicine for all the fevers of life. Humour is a passionate, laughing impulse of the soul which saves men from committing suicide by preventing them from ever despairing. A man might commit suicide very wittily, it might well be the wittiest thing he ever did; but he could not do it humorously. Wit is a diversion; humour an employment. Wit is an after-dinner element;

237

humour a world element. Wit flashes out occasionally, but best in prosperity. Humour shines always, but most clearly in adversity. Wit is the laughter of a full man, but humour is the laughter of a man who is probably starving. Oh yes, there is a great deal of difference between the two!

· · · · ·

Soon after his return from Holland Will was visited by Ivor Gurney and the old friendship was renewed. In the previous eighteen months Gurney had suffered terribly. Invalided home in September 1917, he was admitted to the Edinburgh War Hospital in Bangour, Scotland. There he fell in love with one of his nurses, Annie Nelson Drummond, and for a while believed his love returned. He wrote to Herbert Howells: 'O Erbert, O Erbert . . . I forgot my body when walking with her: a thing that has not happened since . . . when? I really don't know.'[2] Ultimate rejection brought despair.

In November 1917 Gurney was discharged from hospital and returned to Army duty at Seaton Delaval, but in February 1918 he was back in hospital, this time in Newcastle, 'through stomach trouble caused by gas'. Returning to duty once more, he was sent to Brancepeth Castle, Durham, but now the true seat of his ills began to be revealed. At the end of March he wrote to Marion Scott:

Yesterday I felt and talked to (I am serious) the spirit of Beethoven.

No, there is no exclamation mark behind that, because such a statement is past ordinary ways of expressing surprise. But you know how sceptical I was of any such thing before.

It means that I have reached higher than ever before – in spite of the dirt and coarseness and selfishness of so much of me. Something happened the day before which considerably lessened and lightened my gloom. What it was I shall not tell you, but it was the strangest and most terrible spiritual adventure. The next day while I was playing the slow movement of the D major [sonata] I felt the presence of a wise and friendly spirit; it was old Ludwig van all right. When I had finished he said 'Yes, but there's a better thing than that' and turned me to the 1st movement of the latest E flat Sonata – a beauty (I did not know it before). There was a lot more; Bach was there but does not care for me. Schumann also, but my love for him is not so great. Beethoven said among other things that he was fond of me and that in nature I was like himself as a young man. That I should probably not write anything really big and good; for I had started much too late and had much to do with myself spiritually and much to learn. Still he said that he himself was not much more developed at my age, and at the end – when I had shown my willingness to be resigned to God's will and try first of all to do my best, he allowed me (somehow) to hope more, much more. It depends on the degree of spiritual height I can attain – so I was led somehow to gather.

There! What would the doctors say to *that*? A Ticket certainly, for insanity. No, it is the beginning of a new life, a new vision.

I could not get much about Howells off L van B: (the memory is faint) he was reluctant to speak; whether Howells is to die or not to develop I could not gather. How I would like to see your face! No, you'll take it seriously, and decide I am not unbalanced or overstrung. This letter is quite sane, n'est ce pas?[3]

But, of course, it was not quite sane.

By May, Gurney was sufficiently disturbed to be admitted to Lord Derby's War Hospital in Warrington, a hospital which specialised in nervous disorders. In spite of his pre-war history of 'neurasthenia', itself a coverall diagnosis, Gurney's illness was vaguely described as 'Nervous Breakdown from Deferred Shock'. On 19 June he wrote again to Marion Scott:

My Dear Friend: This is a good-bye letter, and written because I am afraid of slipping down and becoming a mere wreck – and I know you would rather know me dead than mad, and my only regret is that my Father will lose my allotment.

Thank you most gratefully for all your kindness, dear Miss Scott. Your book is in my kit bag which will be sent home, and thank you so much for it – at Brancepeth I read it a lot.

Goodbye with best wishes from one who owes you a lot. May God reward you and forgive me.[4]

Gurney got as far as the canal, but courage to take his life deserted him. He was escorted back to hospital where he asked the doctors to send him to an asylum. Marion Scott and John Haines visited him and on 1 July Haines wrote to Miss Scott:

I heard from Ivor this morning – a postcard, and have written to him again. I enclose two letters received by me today from Abercrombie: they speak for themselves. I hope Canon Stevens will look him up soon. Warrington is the most detestable place I have ever spent six hours in, without exception, and the place would drive me mad, despite my lack of genius, in a very few weeks. How Gurney must dislike it I can well imagine. On the other hand I don't recommend the idea of any mental place very near Gloucester (they abound), nor do I think he should be allowed to go to his people until he is better than he is now: the father is too delicate and the mother too nervy.[5]

In fact, Gurney's father was suffering from terminal cancer. On 4 July Ivor was transferred to the Napsbury War Hospital, St Albans. At the beginning of October 1918 he was discharged from the hospital and the Army, and sent home to Gloucester, a dying father and a preoccupied mother. Within days John Haines was writing again to Marion Scott:

Home Again

I saw Ivor for most of yesterday. Perhaps you had best not tell him I have written to you. He spent an hour at the office and I was horrified – at all events at first. Quite evidently his trouble was on him especially badly and, at first, I thought him in a pretty serious way. After a while I began to see that his ideas about the voices and so forth, though extravagant, were in themselves ordered and sensible – granting the fact that they existed, and I became more comfortable. It was a beastly day but I cut the office and took him for a walk (rain or no rain) over the Cotswolds; Crickley, Birdlip and so forth, for the whole of the afternoon; tired myself out and I hope him. He was much more normal and left me happy enough with plenty of books and less annoyance from his voices – I think. I think something must be done with him soon. Is it any use for him to think of music or work connected therewith – yet? He talks of the sea. His shrunken appearance is not satisfactory, nor his quietness and humility. He left at 7 and I was so exhausted and drained that I slept the clock round![6]

In the following weeks Gurney alarmed his family and friends with erratic behaviour, irregular eating habits and frequent disappearances. John Haines took him off on a walking tour of the Black Mountains, Herbert Howells came to see him from London, and then came good news: the Armistice, notification from Sidgwick & Jackson that his second volume of poems, *War's Embers*, had been accepted for publication, and Will Harvey came home.

In March 1919 John Haines was able to report to Marion Scott:

He himself is wonderfully normal and well. I have had two or three evenings with him and he appears to be composing both verse and music with the same extraordinary rapidity still. F.W. Harvey gave a poetry recital at Stroud on Saturday and it was illustrated by several songs set by Gurney and accompanied by him: 'In Flanders', 'Horses', 'The Red Farm', 'Piper's Wood', and 'Minsterworth Perry'. Next to 'In Flanders', I like 'The Red Farm' best. 'Horses' is fine but requires exceptional singing and Harvey was not in the best of voice . . .[7]

Given the condition of both men it is remarkable that the recital took place at all.

In the spring of 1919 Gurney went to stay at The Redlands to share with Will the old inspiriting, healing pleasures of countryside and river. Will, after a great deal of effort, was able to obtain a small war pension for his friend (12 shillings a week) and for both him and Ivor Gurney 1919 and 1920 were to be the most fruitful of their creative years.

On 10 May David Gurney died at the age of 57, severing Ivor's strongest bond with his home. The Royal College of Music invited him to take up his scholarship once more and so, in the autumn of 1919, Ivor Gurney returned to London.

XXIV

'Farewell'

By 1919, in addition to the volumes published by Sidgwick & Jackson, examples of Harvey's work had appeared in various newspapers and magazines. One of these was *New Witness*, the successor to *Eye Witness*, a weekly journal which sought to uphold straight dealing in public affairs and whose regular contributors included Hilaire Belloc, Bernard Shaw, Ernest Newman, Alice Meynell and G.K. Chesterton; the editor, until his death in the First World War, had been Chesterton's brother, Cecil. Although from writing he had received little financial reward, Harvey's name had been noticed in the world of letters.

In November 1919, following Will Harvey's initiative in an effort to do something more for Ivor Gurney's support and recognition, both men were invited to visit John Masefield at his home near Oxford. It seems that, in addition to talk of poetry, Will sang some of Ivor's settings of Masefield's poems to the composer's own accompaniment. Both men wrote about the visit to John Haines, but only Gurney's letter survives:

> On Saturday as you will hear from F.W.H. we visited Masefield in his proper haunt at Boar's Hill, where are Graves, Nichols and Bridges also. He was extremely nice, a boyish, quiet person with a manner friendly enough and easy to get on with . . . .
>
> Neither F.W.H. nor myself thought Masefield cared for 'By a Bierside', but the 'Old Bold Mate' and 'The Halt of the Legion' and 'Upon the Downs' pleased him . . . .[1]

A family album photograph shows Will and Gladys Harvey with
Mr and Mrs Frank Sidgwick.

After the visit Will sent his newly-published *Comrades in Captivity* to Masefield for an opinion. In a letter dated 15 December 1919, Masefield replied:

> So many thanks for sending me your *Comrades in Captivity*.
> It has been a great delight to me. I have enjoyed it more
> than any book about the war that has come into my hands.
> It is a most strong and exciting tale most admirably told.
>   I am so glad that you have done this. I am quite sure that
> it will have a great success and add to your already
> flourishing laurels . . . .[2]

Harvey's literary star was in the ascendant, but, even so, he was far from satisfied with his efforts. In 1920 he wrote in his notebook:

> I say too much. Poetry should say nothing and show
> everything. The best literature is that which 'approaches a
> state of music'. Poetry is the best literature.[3]

He was under the spell of Edward Thomas and W. B. Yeats, writing down quotations from both in his notebook. These enthusiasms were shared by Gurney who set poems by both men to music and even contemplated the composition of a series of operas based on the shorter plays of Yeats. Another love shared with Gurney was of Elizabethan poetry and, again in his notebook, Harvey quoted from Alice Meynell:

> 17th Century Anthology (Red Letter Library): 'the
> Elizabethan poetry is the apple blossom fine and fragrant.
> The 17th century the apple fragrant and rich. The change
> from the 16th Century to the 17th is a process while that
> from the 17th to the 18th is a catastrophe.'[4]

In his own work he was striving to achieve success on two levels: popular poetry, easily accessible to ordinary folk, and the lyrical expression of deep personal emotion. His notes include two pieces of self-instruction, the first with reference to his 'Ballads':

F.W. Harvey, 1920.   Ivor Gurney, 1919.

Herbert Howells, 1920.

Do not compare with the high music of Spenser's
Epithalamion, Milton's Lycidas, Keats' Nightingale but
genuine poetry written for the people (that is the point),[5]

and the other of poetry generally:

Adjectives = colour. Use sparingly like rhyme, alliteration
etc.
Music pours on mortals a beautiful disdain.
All art strives constantly to the condition of Music.
Music is poetry without adjectives.
Intellect is human; change all: progression.
Prose is concerned with intellect.
It reasons.
Poetry does not. Poetry is emotional.
The child here is as wise as the man.
Hazlitt said that he had spent his whole life
writing down things he knew before he was 17.[6]

Everywhere in his notes lie references to his belief that, for him,
no art is possible in the absence of a rhythm sympathetic to nature's
realm. He expressed this in a quotation from Traherne:

You never enjoy the world aright till the sea itself floweth in
your veins, till you are clothed with the heavens and
crowned with the stars.[7]

. . . . .

In 1920 Harvey reached a crossroads in his life. He was thirty-two
years old, not yet established as a solicitor, coming to the real-
isation that he might never earn sufficient money from his writings
to sustain a family, and deeply in love with Anne. No doubt Tillie
lectured him on the necessity of establishing himself in his adopted
profession. She did not wholly approve of her eldest son's wish to
marry his Irish nurse,[8] but probably realised that a love which had

endured seven long years of waiting could not be resisted. Even so, if the match was to have any chance of success, financial stability would be essential.

Under these pressures it seems that Will seriously considered setting aside literary ambition and turning reluctantly to the single path of the law. In the preface to his fourth book of poems, published in 1921, he wrote:

> In spite of all the soulful utterances of people comfortably off, economic independence remains the first condition of happiness.
>
> This is not to say that people aren't great fools for preferring law to literature. It is rather to imply that a poet who can do both is a fool if *he* does not.
>
> I am not a fool.
>
> Farewell!
>
> F.W.H.

The book is entitled *Farewell* also; Harvey poured his heart into it. Set amidst nature poems, prose poems and poems of reflection is a group of sixteen love poems for Anne. His publisher, Frank Sidgwick, considered these to be the high point of Harvey's work. Here then was the paradox of a poet reaching towards his full maturity, but bidding goodbye to his art.

The Golden Snake

Her body's glory is a golden snake
  Around Life's tree
Coiled: the tree shall break
  In the blast of Eternity
  And the coil be crushed.

Too late! immortal poison has rushed
  Through more-than-veins.

Beauty remains
Though bodies rot. The fang
(Though flesh the pang
    To flesh deliver)
Strikes down more deep
Than flesh, to trouble
Even the ultimate sleep,
    The eternal dream.

Though all she seem
To be, like a golden bubble
Shall break at the prick of Death,
    This shall not break:
Her beauty's sting: sharp as the sting of a snake:
The sting of Beauty failing not with breath.

The Lanthorn

(*'I never saw a soul save in the body.'*)

Haply within the woods of Paradise
We see unblinded of our earthly eyes,
Kiss with unthwarted lips, and taste our one
Desired and complete communion.
There scabbards that do sheath the gleaming blade,
There globes which muffle in the naked light
Aside being cast, naked and unafraid,
Lovers may stand in one another's sight.

Now since through fleshly glass Thy flame, O Love,
Shines clear, and nowhere else doth visibly move;
That lanthorn bright I will bow down before,
Kneeling the crystal body to adore.

Safety

You are like a pool reflecting shadowy trees
Of green and glint of sunbeams mixed together
(And I had forgotten both) in water clear.

Full of the foulness of blood and lust and fear
Is the past now. I break its holding tether,
And stand once more with guiding Innocences.

You are like silence in which I can be myself.
You are the truth of music: something lost
Ages and ages ago, and forgotten, and found.

Ere death my feet are set upon holy ground,
I, wanderer amid a wandering host,
Come home, led by the magic of one sweet elf.

'That I may be Taught the Gesture of Heaven' (p. 33), 'After Long Wandering' (p. 226), 'Gloucestershire from the Train' (p. 32) and 'Elvers' (extract p. 11) appeared for the first time in *Farewell*. There are examples also of Harvey's charming dialect poems:

John Helps

John Helps a wer an honest mon;
    The perry that a made
Wer crunched vrom purs as honest
    As ever tree displayed.

John Helps a wer an honest mon;
    The dumplings that a chewed
Wer made vrom honest apples
    As Autumn ever growed.

John Helps a wer an honest mon,
   And I be sorry a's dead.
Perry and honest men be scarce
   These days, 'tiz zed.

There is Harvey in angry mood, recalling W.E. Henley's 'Invictus' in:

The Rabble Fates – To Hell With Them!

They fling at me stones and mud,
   My clothes are tattered and foul,
My face is covered in blood;
   But they haven't hurt my soul.

They have beaten me sore – in truth
   No part of me stands whole!
They have stolen away my youth:
   But they could not steal my soul.

Robbed, baffled, and broken,
   Something lives in me whole;
And I hold by that for a token
   That they cannot conquer my soul.

Let them thrash me with knotted sorrow,
   Stone me with sharp regret;
I shall be their king on a morrow,
   My soul is a monarch yet.

And the quietly reflective Harvey:

The Philosopher visits the Night Club

Fair and worthless things that die
Praising their goddess Vanity
Here gather. Like a violin
Many a sweet-scented Sin
Whispers. Many a bright-wreathed Folly,
Finding its roses turned to holly,
Seeks with Pleasure's aid to fend
That Boredom which is Folly's end.
Wherefore the violins make moan.
For these 'the visible world' alone
Exists; and 'ah that it should pass!'
They cry, and fill a trembling glass.
'Here's to Beauty!' (surnamed Lust)
They cry; and e'er it falls to dust,
'Love it,' they cry, 'and hug it well.'

'To whatsoever heaven or hell
Fate builds for fools, these surely go,'
Thought the moralist watching this tinsel show.
'Yet is it not difficult to know
Who best deserve the name of Fool,
These or those more respectable
Most moral folks I know so well? . . .
These make of living a foolish sham,
These play a silly blind man's game,
Chasing bubbles like a fool.
But the others like a sullen mule
Play at nothing at all, and so
Think they're good because they're dull –
Where, in the name of sense, will *they* go?'

Upon which curious reflection
The sad and wondering sage arose,

Paid for his drink and blew his nose,
Brushed the confetti from his clothes,
And shuffled forth in deep dejection.

Almost as though he never expected to write again, Harvey
included in *Farewell* one poem in which he commits his soul
to God ('Last Word') and another which is most certainly his own
requiem:

Out of the City

Here in the ring of the hills,
  Under a cloudy sky,
  Content at last I lie
Where Peace o'erspills
  Like a cool rain which giveth
This brave daisy scent
And wine of sacrament
  Whereby he liveth.

The big hooters may howl,
  Men quarrel, whistles screech,
  I will hear only the speech
Of my forgotten soul,
  Which is the speech of trees,
Soft yet of clarity
And brimmed with verity
  And all gay peace.

. . . . .

In the summer of 1920, Will and Roy Harvey took their mother,
undoubtedly at her request, on a motoring tour of Flanders and the

Will, *c.* 1920.

Will Harvey and his mother in Douai, 1920.

Outside the barracks, Douai.

By the Menin road, 1920.

Somme, with Douai as their ultimate destination. Roy drove the
car and took photographs of his passengers amongst the ruins of
Ypres, by the Menin road and in Douai, scene of Will's first
solitary confinement. They also visited Eric Harvey's grave, marked
as it then was by a temporary wooden cross. What thoughts must
have passed through all of their minds on this journey: Tillie seeing
for the first time the ruined scenes which had swallowed her son
and a generation of youth; and the brothers walking quietly in
smart clothes where once they had crawled in rat-infested mud-
holes?

On returning to Gloucestershire, Will resumed his place in the
Gloucester City cricket team. In August of that year Herbert
Howells married his Dorothy, a girl whose home in Churchdown
hugged the side of Chosen Hill where he and Will had loved to walk
with Ivor Gurney. And, whenever he could escape from London,
Gurney came to visit his own beloved county.

By this time Gurney's behaviour had become ever more erratic.

Eric Harvey.

He had found a cottage at Dryhill Farm on Crickley Hill, over-looking the Severn Vale.

> An old Cotswold stone house with one pretty good upper room, but draughty. There are holes in the floor – to be dodged. There are two square places in the roof which will need stopping. The garden was long ago a ruin, the stream dried up, and weeds grew in it; no one came save the curious; and now under the shadow of the great rise of Crickley – here am I.[9]

Gurney spent long days working in the fields to earn a few

shillings, and walking in the Cotswolds, often staying out all night. At The Redlands the dining-room window would be left propped open for him before the family retired to bed. Then Ivor would climb in, muddy from his travels, help himself from the pantry and play the piano for hours before snoozing in a chair. Unfortunately, Tillie's sister Kate Waters' bedroom was directly above the piano and she was less than appreciative of Ivor's renditions of Mozart sonatas, complaining bitterly to Will about the music disturbing her sleep.

At last Will was obliged to tell Ivor that Auntie Kate objected to his over-loud nocturnes. 'Oh, the world is *full* of Auntie Kates!' said Gurney.[10]

. . . . .

On Christmas Day 1920, Will drafted a letter, almost certainly to Anne, in his notebook:

Just off Birdlip you may find anything but whatever you find it will be just what you most want as this afternoon. A little old church in a dark valley of woods threaded with streams shining in the late light

'In valleys of springs of rivers etc:
The quietest under the sun'.

But here on another day in Minsterworth farmer Mogg's house seen with its black timbers and old red masonry through farmer Mogg's January orchard will meet you with an equal surprised delight.

Gloucestershire is like the poems of Edward Thomas wherein you are always finding something new and stirring no matter how often you pick up the book.

A memorable evening at home in the music-room after 10 miles walking with Gurney – O joy of that companionship!

Golden curves of Beethoven matching the fire of pear wood burning in the grate with no calm glow of blinking embers but in a golden torrent of fantastic flame. Peace was in that room. Faith-blinding loveliness. Store of courage against life and all it brings. Hinted glory – glimpses of Heaven.

On some future day this pencil note shall recall it to me and I shall rise up in strength of remembered beauty to meet all that I thought I could not meet – all that is terrifying to the forgetting mind of a man compassed about with darkness shall become a sighing wind in the night around that stout tower of remembered Beauty.[11]

XXV

Happy Singing

Men have made songs,
   And I among them,
Because some hell
   Of grief had wrung them.
The tolling bell
   Will often bring
Torture to force
   A man to sing.

But I this day
   A song will make
Only for joy
   And my sweet love's sake:
And will employ
   No sorrowful thing
For making it –
   That song, I'll sing.

But lovely laughter
   Of singing thrushes
When dawn has broken
   And heaven flushes,
Shall be the token
   Of one whom days
Nor death can rob
   Of joyous praise.

Happy Singing

On 30 April 1921, Will Harvey married Sarah Anne Kane at the Holy Rood Church in Swindon. Will's best man was Arthur Frith, a sculptor friend from Gloucester. Anne's sister, Agnes Attracta, came over from Ireland. Will cut out the announcement of his marriage from the local newspaper, pasted it into his scrapbook and wrote by it Anne's first words to him as they stepped out of the church together into the Groundwell Road:

'Love is a private thing my dear',

and after this he added:

'Ours is.'[1]

Earlier in the year he had been seeking a post. Still bound by his Articles of Indenture to work at least thirty miles from Gloucester, the best position he could find was in Swindon, industrial centre of Wiltshire and home of the Great Western Railway wagon works. He rented lodgings at 152 Goddard Avenue and, once settled with his new employer, sent for his bride. Starting afresh as a solicitor was not easy after so long a gap.

Law is a tricky business and my office hours are crammed with excitement now that I have been out of it for six years and forgotten the little I once did know. The bluff required is abnormal, and one is constantly 'having the wind up' one by the sudden discovery that something most essential to procedure has been overlooked and that there may or may not be *just* time to conform to precedent which has no care for ex-warriors.[2]

Swindon then was a depressing place; the Harveys' lodgings even more depressing, with a surly landlady who hedged their lives about with restrictions. To her, even their use of the bath was an inconvenience for which she charged an extra shilling.[3] For Will and Anne the only joy was in each other, but, as in the past, discomfort could be dissolved in a cup of verse.

In Lodgings

Nothing sounds in the house
   Except the owner's snore.
A little silent mouse
   Flits over the floor
Spring-cleaned so proudly
   By the woman whom
We hear doing nothing so loudly
   In the next room.

He is doing a lot . . .
   With a frisk
He scales her marmalade pot;
   Taking his risk
Of falling headlong into
   That sticky heaven of his.
She sleeps. It would be a sin to
   Disturb his ecstasies!

And so I pause in scribbling,
   Lest, turning a sheet over,
I should stop his sweet nibbling
   At the pot's cover.
Dishonest, no doubt,
   For it isn't my jam,
And should not have been left out
   Nor the ham!

But here are we three –
   I, and the mouse,
And the snoring landlady
   Of the house,
Each assisting each
   (Though I alone know it)
Laughing patience to teach
   An impatient poet.

Happy Singing

Whose little pen would scrape
  Like a mouse's nail
The cloths which drape
  Joys that not fail,
In a house where Death
  (That landlady so grim)
Snores yet, but tarrieth
  Not long to trap *him*.

On 23 January 1922 the Harvey's first child, Eileen Anne, was born in the Swindon lodgings. The following December, the conditions of his Articles completed, Will took the decision to leave Swindon. Happily, John Haines gave him a post in Gloucester. As soon as Anne and the baby could be moved, he took them back to the light and air of Minsterworth and, until a home of their own could be found, the family moved into a room on the first floor of The Redlands. Here a proud father celebrated his baby daughter.

Eileen Anne

Frond-like your tiny fingers curl,
  Dear baby-girl, around my own.
Fern-like your little life doth twine
  With mine.

Thus Fate may set a green spray dancing,
  Sunnily glancing on a stone,
And wake miraculously some riven wall
  To spring-tide festival.

Further cause for celebration came in May 1922 with the publication by Sidgwick & Jackson of *Poems of Today* (Second

Series) in which two of Harvey's poems appeared: 'Ducks' and 'The Bugler'. *Poems of Today* was sponsored by the English Association and the first edition had appeared in 1915. In a prefatory note the editor observed that 'the interval that has passed has brought to all experience which the imagination of a few has transmuted into poetry. This second volume is an attempt to bring together such poems as represent, not indeed all the shifting tendencies of the period, but those moods which have proved most permanent, persisting through all the changes of events and of public feeling, linking the poetry of today with that of yesterday, and looking forward to the poetry of tomorrow.' Harvey now took his place alongside Yeats, Belloc, De La Mare, Hardy, Thomas, and many more. Will presented a copy of *Poems of Today* to his sister Gladys and inscribed the flyleaf with a poem (unpublished) which gives proof that he had been prevailed upon to continue writing verse. *Farewell* would not be Harvey's last collection.

> Life's wheel will turn, and turning bring
> Round many a gay and sorry thing.
> Vain are all wishes. He's a king
>   Who faces gaily
> Those various bolts of Fortune's sling
>   She scatters daily.
>
> Yet (since some wish I needs must write)
> May you when wishing, wish aright!
> Then finding, you will find delight;
>   But should it fly you,
> *Still will that wish be yours.* No might
>   May *that* deny you.

In addition to Gladys, it may be assumed that Sidgwick, Gurney and Haines had all encouraged Harvey to continue with his art. In 1921 a collection of the poems of John Haines had been published by Selwyn & Blount. As in so many of his books, Will heavily marked his copy to highlight the several passages of which he clearly approved, or to edit those poems which he thought too long. It is interesting to compare Haines' work with that of Harvey and to see the friendly rivalry arising as in Haines' 'The High-Road', and Harvey's 'The Little Road' published in *Gloucestershire Friends*. Here are the first verses of both.

The High-Road

The little roads are quaint roads
   That wander where they will,
They wind their arms round all the farms
   And flirt with every hill.
But the high-road is my road
   And goes where I would go,
Its way it wends as man intends,
   For it was fashioned so.

The Little Road

I will not take the great road that goes so proud and high,
Like the march of Roman legions that made it long ago;
But I will choose another way, a little road I know.
There no poor tramp goes limping, nor rich poor men drive by,
Nor ever crowding cattle, or sheep in dusty throng
Before their beating drovers drift cruelly along:
But only birds and free things, and ever in my ear
Sound of the leaves and little tongues of water talking near.

. . . . .

Ivor Gurney still visited The Redlands and still played the piano late into the night, waking the baby and upsetting Auntie Kate. By the summer of 1922 his mental health was causing serious concern to his family and friends. For a short time he had secured a job in the Gloucester Income Tax office, working under Will's friend, Pat Kerr, but this undertaking had been a failure.[4] He would neither eat nor sleep for long stretches and then gorge himself on cakes, ice-cream or a loaf of bread and a pound of butter at a time. He had moved in with his less than sympathetic brother Ronald and his wife, and frequently disturbed them by coming into the house from the fields, covered with mud, and sitting in their best chair, burying his head in a cushion to guard against the electric waves which he believed were coming from the wireless. At last, in September 1922, they could take no more.

Ivor was certified insane and committed to Barnwood House, a mental hospital near Gloucester. However, he escaped from there, cutting his hands badly on broken glass in the process. It was decided that he should be sent to an asylum a long way from Gloucester and from which he could not escape. On 21 December 1922 he was committed to the City of London Mental Hospital at Dartford in Kent.[5] No worse fate could have been determined for a young man who so loved Gloucestershire, freedom and beauty.

The effect on Will of Gurney's confinement may be imagined. His own experience of two years in captivity, allied to his understanding of the sensitive mind and needs of his friend, must surely have heightened his distress, bringing a chill end to 1922.

. . . . .

Arthur Frith, his wife and three young sons, Colin, Brian and Geoffrey, came to visit Will and Anne at The Redlands and found them living not too comfortably in the now crowded house. The Friths were able to suggest the ideal solution, at least for a while.

Although the Friths' home was in Barton Street, Gloucester, they had invested in a cottage at Cranham, a village set amidst the thick woodlands which cloak the shoulder of the Cotswold escarpment where, south-east of Gloucester, it descends steeply to the Severn Vale. Cranham Cottage was empty and available for rental; Will readily accepted the offer.

Gladys travelled over from Minsterworth ahead of her eldest brother and his family, cleaned the little house, hung pretty curtains at the windows and placed flowers in the homely rooms. Young Colin Frith had painted a sign for the gate: 'El Trocadero' it brightly announced! Will greatly enjoyed this joke and insisted on calling the cottage 'El Trocadero' thereafter.[6]

> O, Cranham ways are steep and green
> And Cranham woods are high,
> And if I was that black rook,
> It's there that I would fly.

Early each morning Will cycled down into Gloucester and at the end of each day he rode or pushed his old bicycle back up the hill to the dusky woodland. His first stop would be the Royal William Hotel for a tankard of his favourite brew and then, guided by a narrow river of stars, he would pedal his unlighted bicycle home down invisible lanes, singing happily to the enveloping, moon-silvered trees.[7]

> And in the evening when I walked apart
> For joy of that I carry in my heart,
> The song I made brave thrushes did complete,
> Shouting, 'O, pretty joy!' and 'Sweet! Sweet! Sweet!'
>
> This is my glory, this the crown of me:
> That I hold joy of my love, and she of me;
> And though my song be but a breath of air,
> Yet is it greater than death and all despair.
>
> For howso poor and of what base estate
> I be, this love shall make me proud and great.
> And howso deep in care I lie, there are words
> Shall build my heart a nest of singing birds.

XXVI

Broadoak

Spring 1924

Spring came by water to Broadoak this year.
I saw her clear.
Though on the earth a sprinkling
Of snowdrops shone, the unwrinkling
Bright curve of Severn River
Was of her gospel first giver.
Like a colt new put to pasture it galloped on;
And a million
Small things on its back for token
Of her coming it bore. A broken
Hawthorn floated green,
Gem-bright upon the sheen
Of the moving water. There past
Hay-wisps which showed the fast
Of winter was over for cattle,
Who needed no longer battle
For food in some far meadow.
Soft as shadow
There glided past a skiff,
Heavy with mended nets for salmon. If
Spring dreamed
Lazily in Earth's half-frozen blood,
On Severn's flood
Her presence bravely gleamed.

Broadoak

Yea, all who sought her
Might see, wondering, how Spring walked the water.

On a cool but bright day in the summer of 1987, my wife and I set
out by car from Gloucester with Will Harvey's daughter Eileen and
her artist husband, Tom Griffiths, to seek more of the Forest of
Dean scenes which the poet knew so well. Our first stopping-place
was Broadoak, a tiny Severnside village by that wild contortion of
the river known as the Newnham bend. Leaving the car on the main
road, we walked down the lane called 'The Strood' in the hope of
finding at least some landmark which would evoke for Eileen
memories of childhood and of the unusual house which Will had
rented here in 1924 on moving from Cranham: a pair of converted
railway carriages.

Eileen had not been back to Broadoak for sixty-two years and,
apart from the bold river and a sense of village shape, there was
nothing upon which her recognition could fasten. We were about to
return to the car, when my wife suggested that we should try to
reach the riverbank by walking through the overgrown garden of a
seemingly deserted cottage which stood gable-end on to the lane. In
spite of my reluctance to invade private property, she was off
through the gate, the rest of the party following timidly behind. As
we passed between the cottage and a tree, I was suddenly aware
that we were walking beside a small railway carriage of the
branch-line type. Quite by chance we had found Eileen's first
remembered home, little changed apart from the addition of some
timber-cladding and a pitched roof.

Will could not have selected a site closer to his beloved river,
which flowed only a few paces from the back door. No conven-
tional house, requiring foundations, could have been built in such a
place and the friendly owner, for indeed it was *not* deserted, told us
how he had often been washed out of bed at high tide!

For Eileen, the gap of long years was closed. Amongst happy
Broadoak recollections there were two childhood frights. Here was
the spot where as a toddler she had fallen into the river and clung
frantically to bulrushes until her mother, hearing her cries, had

Broadoak.

lifted her to safety. There, through the window, was the little waiting-room fireplace which one winter's day had blazed so high that the carriage panelling had overheated and burst into flames, to be quenched just in time by her father.

This unconventional dwelling in Broadoak had become the family's home when Will had taken up a post in the nearby Newnham office of his friend John Haines. But devoted as ever to his mother, he regularly cycled the five miles to Minsterworth to see her.

The following year, 1925, was a Three Choirs Festival year in Gloucester. Leonard Clark later described how, as a young teacher, he had played truant from his Forest of Dean school and walked to the city to hear Handel's *Messiah* in the cathedral. The performance was due to begin at 11.30 a.m. and Clark had set out in the 'frail sunlight' of very early morning. By 10 a.m. he had reached Minsterworth and decided to call at The Redlands to see if his friend Will Harvey was at home.

> He was not only at home but he welcomed me as if I had been the Prodigal. 'Come in, boy. Come in. And where might you be going at this time of day on a new September morning?' When I told him, he broke into peals of laughter, and called out to his mother who was somewhere about the house, 'Mother. Where are you? Come and see a prize exhibit. Here's a chap who is walking to music all the way from the Forest.' Mrs Harvey wanted me to have another breakfast but I told her I hadn't time. But Will broke in with 'O, but my sister and I are going into Gloucester by car. We'll give you a lift. Plenty of time. I suppose you've got a ticket.'
>
> So there I was sitting down in the Harveys' front parlour, at half past ten on a Friday morning, with dusty shoes and a hole in my right sock, eating a bacon sandwich. And I was only an hour away from Dr Herbert Brewer, Flora Woodman, Astra Desmond, John Coates, Robert Radford, and the London Symphony Orchestra. It did cross my mind that Standard 5 would now be doing arithmetic. Then Will asked me if I would like to spend the night with them. They were going to have some friends in, there would be music,

songs by Ivor Gurney, and probably Herbert Howells
playing Bach on the sitting-room piano. Mrs Harvey
promised to get a message to my mother, so I decided to
stay the night.

The car dropped us in Westgate Street a few minutes
before all the clocks in Gloucester began to warn the city
that it was 11 o'clock. There were flags and bunting flying
everywhere and great excitement in the festival air. I was
tingling with expectancy. College Green, neat and inviting,
with its old trees and older houses still drugged by the sleep
of centuries, was all top hats and morning dress, as if a
royal wedding was about to take place there and then. Cars
and carriages came and went, depositing their silken loads.
Everyone was happy on that wonderful morning as if kings
had come to the brightness of His rising. The little knots
and bunches of people were already breaking up and moving
steadily into the Cathedral through the south porch and the
other doors. I was impatient to get to my place. The
Harveys were about to leave me for their seats beneath the
great west window when Will suddenly clutched my arm.
'Look, boy. Over there by the deanery door. That's Elgar
and Bernard Shaw.' Spellbound, I watched them as they
disappeared into the Cathedral, the tall, saturnine, hatless,
knickerbockered, playwright, and the immaculate, stately,
trilby-hatted, grey-moustached composer. Just to see them
had been worth my long walk, and losing a day's pay –
about 6 shillings. Yet, my conscience began to prick me
when I thought again of my deserted Standard 5. I
wondered what was being said in the staff room about the
truant teacher.

I made for my seat in the north aisle. It was now nearly
11.30. I could just see, between the mighty Norman pillars,
the massed choir and the London Symphony Orchestra,
with the principal first violin, W.H. Reed, waiting patiently
for the conductor to appear. The Cathedral was packed,
with a subdued rustle of conversation still going on. I looked
round in gratitude. I smelt that peculiar must of the ages

which old cathedrals have. Shafts of broken sunlight streamed through the windows like prayers flashing from heaven. One patch of red mingled with purple falling on a memorial tablet nearby fascinated me for the whole of the service. The history of my county was written around me on wall and marble tomb. The dead city fathers slept on in their carved urns in sure and certain hope that in their flesh they would see God. The stone cherubs stared at me, eyeless, as if I were no part of their eternity. The man who was sitting next to me seemed to be a white-haired angel.

At last the four soloists came in, and then Dr Brewer. I could just see a crimson left arm and side, for he was wearing his doctor's robes. The congregation fell to quiet and my heart to a deep thankfulness, as if some blessing were about to fall on me. I was twenty, and the bloom was still on me.

The choir sang an unaccompanied motet. *Hosanna to the Son of David* by Orlando Gibbons. And then, after a short pause, the orchestra struck that noble tonic chord of E minor and, at last, I was listening to *Messiah* in my Cathedral.

I sat enraptured until the end of the morning's performance, for the oratorio was to be sung in two parts. I have no clear recollection of what I did at lunchtime but I know that I was sitting in my place again in the north aisle when the performance began at a quarter to three. My head was full of Handel and history. I remember Astra Desmond telling good tidings to Zion, Robert Radford reminding us of the light that shone on the people that walked in darkness, Flora Woodman lifting us to the vaulted roof as she preached the gospel of peace, and John Coates dashing them in pieces like a potter's vessel. And there were the tremendous waterfalls of harmony from the choir. Hallelujah. Hallelujah. The Kingdom of this world is become the Kingdom of our Lord. When the trumpet sounded, and let loose a flight of echoes, I was raised with the dead, and for that small moment in time, I was changed.

With the final Amens still rolling round the nave, and all through me, we went out into the afternoon sunlight of College Green. I met Will Harvey again who, face transported, was mopping his brow with a red-and-white spotted handkerchief. He stood bareheaded there beneath the soaring tower. He pointed out some of the notables who were talking to their friends – Vaughan Williams, Walford Davies, Granville Bantock, who were all having works performed at that year's Festival. Then some of Harvey's friends joined him. I was introduced to Herbert Howells who had had two new works performed that week and later to Dr Brewer himself, as the chap who had walked from the Forest that morning to hear *Messiah*. 'But,' chuckled Harvey, 'he hasn't thought of how he is going to get back.'

Get back. How to get back – to Standard 5, my Head Master, the Managers, to a day's pay lost. But all that could wait. It was here and now that mattered. I had heard *Messiah* in Gloucester Cathedral in the company of Will Harvey, Bernard Shaw, Sir Edward Elgar, and all the other great ones. And the glory of the Lord was around me.[1]

On the same evening as the performance of *Messiah*, and before what must have been a very late-night party at The Redlands, there was another concert, this time at Gloucester Shire Hall. The date was 11 September 1925 and the concert was of particular importance to Will as it included the first performance of a work of his own. Harvey had been asked by Herbert Brewer to collaborate in the writing of a song cycle and the result, described by Dr Lee-Williams as 'a tasty feast of double-Gloucester', was *A Sprig of Shamrock*. Will had written four poems to be sung to traditional Irish airs, adapted and arranged by Dr Brewer for contralto or baritone voice with string quartet or piano accompaniment. Flora Woodman was the soloist, accompanied by a quartet of players from the London Symphony Orchestra. The four songs are: 'When the World of the Eyes', 'A Queer Story', 'When I Went Out A-Walking', and an Irish hop-jig, 'Don't Say No'.[2] In these poems Harvey captured by turns the romance, fairy folklore, humour, and rustic fun of the Irish people whose country he never visited, but whose spiritual ideals and character he so admired. But his own Irish love, Anne, was not in the Shire Hall to hear her husband's tribute to her birthplace. She was at home in Broadoak caring for Eileen and for her baby son, born in the spring of that year and baptised Patrick.

To Music

('Music pours on life its beautiful disdain.')

In scarlet shall thy sorrows pace
  Like queens the pathway thou dost dread:
Death shall fall down and hide her face
  And bow the head,
While music upon life's despair
Triumphs, an angel in the air.

Joy is mere pleasure if music lend not
  Magic to hold that heart of fire;
In red and fleeting sunsets end not
  The heart's desire
When music over life's dark dream
Runs singing like a silver stream.

No bars of speech, or blood, or creed,
  Trammel her magic. Wheresoe'er
The heart of man can break and bleed,
  Her healing rare
Falls like the speechless dew whose word
The listening desert-flower has heard.

Pour thou thy beautiful disdain
  On insufficient dreams and days:
Touch with thy wand the iron chain

Which to earth's ways
Binds down the still-aspiring soul:
And make us free: and make us whole!

The last collection of Harvey's poems to be published by Sidgwick & Jackson appeared in 1925 under the title *September and Other Poems*. The year and the book together marked the high point in the poet's creative life. In poems of great beauty, sometimes nostalgic, sometimes disturbing, always sincere, we feel the heart's deep unease of one 'compassed about with darkness'. Harvey does not pipe soft airs of the shallow melancholy which permeates so much of the work of the 'Georgian' poets: he gives totally of himself. The title poem is not simply a lyrical epilogue to a passing season, but a lament for the never-to-be recaptured summer of his life. It points the way to the disillusion and world-weariness which, masked by conviviality and fought against with humour, beset his later years.

September

She walketh like a ghost,
  Lovely and gray
And faint, faint, faint . . .
  Ere Autumn's host
Of colours gay
  Breaks on the year, September
Comes sighing her soft plaint,
  'Remember!'

Remember what? All fair
  Warm loves now wan:
All fleet, fleet, fleet
  Flowers in the hair
Of Summers gone!

Though fruit break rosy, of these
Are her most sweet
    Sad memories.

Most faint and tender
    Music awaketh,
Sighing, sighing, sighing,
    A voice to lend her.
Surely it breaketh
    Even Death's heart, as he goes
To gather in Summer's long-dying
    Last rose.

So drifting like a ghost,
    Lovely with dream
And faint, faint, faint,
    Sighing 'remember', almost
September did seem
    My gray soul's image, as she
Whispered over that plaint
    So musically!

In 'Unstable' (p. 29) Harvey admits to the inconstant spirit which
rules his thoughts and severs him from his desire. In 'Forsaken' the
sense of abandonment cuts much deeper than mere self-pity; it is
absolute, and throws the poet to his knees in 'Prayer'.

Forsaken

Silent it comes
With no dark pageantry
Or drums.
Naught's to see.
    Only the horrible shadow bends
Over me.

Where wait ye, friends?
   Not even Satan with me!
So all ends.
And will ye
   Also forsake this head,
My dreams? They flee.
Discomforted
   My very self has flown.
I am dead,
Less than alone,
   Less than a worm, a tree,
A stone.

Prayer

More than man's strength I need
   For a man's fight.
Fetter of dream and deed
   This nature wears: its might
   Turns feeble at the flight
   Of Thee its Light

So save me, Lord from all
   Sin's treacheries,
Let the magnifical
   Mystery of Mysteries
   Weave my Heart's tapestries
   With Holy Presences.

And when I would put by
   The good, being blind:
Throw down the light of Thy
   Bright lamp into my mind,
   That I may find
   Self's shadow gone behind;

Broadoak

And view again my lost
  And sweet delight,
Even the Holy Ghost,
  Thy beauty sprite:
The sword and the gay might
  Of all who fight.

Many of the poems in *September* pre-date 1924, such as 'In Lodgings' (p. 262) and 'Eileen Anne' (p. 263), written in Swindon. 'On Painswick Beacon' clearly marks Will's joyous return to Gloucestershire, and in 'November', probably inspired by Cranham woods, Harvey the artist paints a perfect word-picture using colour and lines sparingly to achieve a stark and stunning effect. 'November' gained inclusion in the *Oxford Book of Twentieth Century Verse*.

On Painswick Beacon

Here lie counties five in a waggon wheel.
There quick Severn like a silver eel
Wriggles through pastures green and pale stubble.
There, sending up its quiet coloured bubble
Of earth, May Hill floats on a flaming sky.
And, marvelling at all, forgetting trouble,
Here – home again – stand I!

November

He has hanged himself – the Sun.
  He dangles
A scarecrow in thin air.

He is dead for love – the Sun;
    He who in forest tangles
Wooed all things fair.

That great lover – the Sun,
    Now spangles
The wood with blood-stains.

He has hanged himself – the Sun,
    How thin he dangles
In these gray rains!

The influence of Edward Thomas is in evidence in some of the poems in the *September* collection. Harvey follows Thomas into that borderland where nature enfolds artefact and makes it part of its own. Ending a *Daily Chronicle* review in August 1908 Thomas wrote:

> But because we are imperfectly versed in history, we are not therefore blind to the past. The eye that sees the things of today, and the ear that hears, the mind that contemplates or dreams, is itself an instrument of antiquity equal to whatever it is called upon to apprehend. We are not merely twentieth-century Londoners or Kentish men or Welshmen. We belong to the days of Wordsworth, of Elizabeth, of Richard Plantagenet, of Harold, of the earliest bards. We, too, like Taliesin, have borne a banner before Alexander, have been with our Lord in the manger of the ass, have been in India, and with the 'remnant of Troia', and with Noah in the ark, and our original country is 'the region of the summer stars'. And of these many folds in our nature the face of the earth reminds us, and perhaps even where there are no more marks visible upon the land than there were in Eden, we are aware of the passing of time in ways too difficult and strange for the explanation of historian and zoologist and philosopher. It is the manifold nature that responds with

such indescribable depth and variety to the appeals of many landscapes.[3]

Harvey shares with Thomas that 'sense of oneness with man in his natural surroundings'. Compare, for instance, Thomas's poem 'Tall Nettles' with the second stanza of Harvey's 'These Fields'.

Tall Nettles

by Edward Thomas

Tall nettles cover up, as they have done
These many springs, the rusty harrow, the plough
Long worn out, and the roller made of stone:
Only the elm butt tops the nettles now.

This corner of the farmyard I like most:
As well as any bloom upon a flower
I like the dust on the nettles, never lost
Except to prove the sweetness of a shower.

These Fields

Dream not the English meadows dead.
I heard some fields in Gloucestershire
Whispering ere the sun had kist
Their level faces clean of mist.
And very sweet it was to hear
The secret words they said
Clear-spoken by green little lips
Of grass with dew upon the tips.

And mingling in the gossip spoke
With softly-rustling leaves the oak;
Elms too, and the gray willows that look
Into the little twisting brook,
And a garrulous old scythe that lay
Under a bramble hidden away,
Together with a drinking-horn
Fashioned long ere I was born. . .
They spoke the language they had heard
Since they had listened to any word.
They were more English than our tongue:
Old already when words were young.

They said that life ran much the same
Or ever Caesar's army came.
Norman and Saxon were but words.
The men went, the men came;
They took them, but forgot the name.
They took them, these mild fields, these birds,
These streams, these oaks, this grass, and wrought
Within their minds an English thought.
And moulding thus, they made amends
For bloodshed and much labour: gave
Content of thought and food to friends:
Shade to labourers and to lovers:
Water to wash to the world's ends
The care a living man discovers,
And all anxiety and fear
Which life and love may bring too near.

Thus to an immemorial plan
They fashioned and kept the Englishman
A coin of England ringing true:
A bloom of England under blue
Or dark skies: thus for many a day
Past. *And so still purpose they.*

Broadoak

It is perhaps no coincidence that both Thomas and Harvey wrote poems with the title 'Rain'. In a prose account of his response to rain Thomas wrote:

> I lay awake listening to the rain, and at first it was as pleasant to my ear and my mind as it had long been desired; but before I fell asleep it had become a majestic and finally a terrible thing, instead of a sweet sound and symbol. It was accusing and trying me and passing judgment. Long I lay still under the sentence, listening to the rain, and then at last listening to words which seemed to be spoken by a ghostly double beside me. He was muttering: The all-night rain puts out summer like a torch. In the heavy, black rain falling straight from invisible, dark sky to invisible, dark earth, the heat of summer is annihilated, the spendour is dead, the summer is gone.

The sound of the rain brings that sense of oneness with nature to both poets but, whereas for Thomas, writing in 1916, it increases his feeling of isolation and weariness, for Harvey it is a welcome voice in the sleepless, peacetime night.

Rain

by Edward Thomas

Rain, midnight rain, nothing but the wild rain
On this bleak hut, and solitude, and me
Remembering again that I shall die
And neither hear the rain nor give it thanks
For washing me cleaner than I have been
Since I was born into this solitude.
Blessed are the dead that the rain rains upon:
But here I pray that none whom once I loved
Is dying tonight or lying still awake

Solitary, listening to the rain,
Either in pain or thus in sympathy
Helpless among the living and the dead,
Like a cold water among broken reeds,
Myriads of broken reeds all still and stiff,
Like me who have no love which this wild rain
Has not dissolved except the love of death,
If love it be towards what is perfect and
Cannot, the tempest tells me, disappoint.

Rain

From every side there comes
Sounds of the rain tapping its little drums:
    Through darkness calling
        Quietly: but how
Insistently, as it comes falling
        Against my window.

All the night fills
With the excitement of those soft syllables
    Incessantly falling
        Outside: insistently
Giving great news: calling
        Haply to me.

What secret would you tell,
Tale-bearing rain, could I but listen as well,
    And patiently, by chance,
        As the brown earth
Whose nodding nettles in the dark now dance
        Moved to strange mirth?

September and Other Poems, dedicated to John Haines, was an
unsuccessful but worthy candidate for the Hawthornden Prize,

awarded annually for work of imaginative literature by a British subject under the age of 41 and published during the previous year. However, that disappointment was more than offset by high praise from a friend and correspondent of Haines: the Poet Laureate, Robert Bridges. Bridges considered one poem in the collection, 'Ghosts', worthy to stand comparison with the best of all supernatural ballads, 'The Wife of Usher's Well'. Indeed for one reader at least, 'Ghosts' is more effectively chilling than the great medieval model.[4]

Ghosts

A very old woman sat over the fire.
  One came to the door
Whose tap loud-echoed. She did not hear.
  He crossed the threshold o'er.

'Come with me, ancient mother,' he beckoned.
  'Nay, I be too old to move;
Where do 'e want ver I to journey?'
  Croaked she. Death bent above.

'You had ('twas many a year now past)
  A son dread waters drowned.'
At that the aged body started
  To twist herself around.

'He sailed with me, I loved him better
  Than any.' 'Then ye lie!'
Flashed back her answer. 'For nobody
  Loved him so well as I.'

'To you I bear a message
  And a message that is his . . .'
'Tell it, tell it, sweet Death!' 'Nay, mother;
  First – a kiss.'

F.W. Harvey SOLDIER, POET

Then the old trembling woman uprose
   From her low seat, and
Gave her lips to the stranger,
   Her lips; her hand.

'You are too old to journey, mother,
   I'll stay with you here instead.'
'Who speaks?' 'Your son, your dear son, mother,
   – Dead to the dead.'

. . . . .

One year after the publication of *September*, Harvey's poems were selected for inclusion in the prestigious *Augustan Books of Poetry* series; acknowledgement of his acceptance as a major British poet.

FOREST
OFFERING

To Old Comrades,
A Forest Offering

Knowing that war was foul, yet all a-hunger
For that most dear companionship it gave,
I wished myself once more on lousy straw;
And in a trice was there, and ten years younger,
With singing soldiers scornful of the grave:
The tough mates, the rough mates that lay on lousy straw,
And since have laid them down in earth . . .
                              I saw
Again their faces flicker in the light
Of candles fixed most dangerously in rings
Of bayonets stabbed in wooden beams, or stuck
   Down into the floor's muck . . .

   The woods are bright
With smouldering beech. Only a robin sings.
Alone to-day amid the misty woods,
Alone I walk gathering fallen leaves,
For it is autumn and the day of the dead.
I come to where in solemn silence broods
A monument to them whose fame still rings
(Clear as a bugle down) to him that grieves,
And lay my leaves for crown upon each head.
Here, my old Forest friends, are your own flowers!
Beautiful in their death as you in yours;
Symbol of all you loved, and were, and are.
Beautiful now as when you lived among us!
And in their heart I place this spotted fungus,
Symbol of war that slayeth all things fair.

XXVII

'Faery-Crazed or Worse'

F.W.H.

(A Portrait)

A thick-set, dark-haired, dreamy little man,
   Uncouth to see,
Revolving ever this preposterous plan –
Within a web of words spread cunningly
To tangle Life – no less,
(Could he expect success!)

Of Life, he craves not much, except to watch.
   Being forced to act,
He walks behind himself, as if to catch
The motive: – an accessory to the fact,
Faintly amused, it seems,
Behind his dreams.

Yet hath he loved the vision of this world,
   And found it good:
The Faith, the fight 'neath Freedom's flag unfurled,
The friends, the fun, the army-brotherhood.
But faery-crazed or worse
He twists it all to verse!

In 1926 the Harveys left their riverside home at Broadoak to move deeper into the Forest of Dean. From Lydney the road into the Forest rises steeply for three miles by woodland and stream, leading to the villages of Whitecroft, Pillowell and Yorkley. Whilst looking for a permanent home the family rented houses, first in Yorkley and then in Pillowell. From here, Will could walk down to his office in Lydney, gaining inspiration for verse on the way. He joined the Whitecroft Male Voice Choir, not only singing with them but also acting as compère and reading his own poems at concerts. He continued his strong links with 5th Battalion friends through membership of the Royal British Legion Club in Lydney. All appeared set for a contented life, and yet something was amiss.

The men who fought, suffered and saw their comrades die in the Great War believed that they would return to a 'new order' at home; that the pre-war, class-divided society would have given way to fairness and opportunity; that the rising cost of living which had led to widespread labour-unrest, rioting and even, on occasions, bloodshed between 1910 and 1912, would be swept away. Harvey's poem, 'If We Return' (p. v), underlines their sense of obligation. And yet by 1926 little had changed. The politicians had failed. The poor were still desperately poor. Having 'seen the price of Liberty', Will now saw the country plunged into a general strike. He saw, too, the soup-kitchen set up on Pillowell Common and the daily queues of out-of-work Foresters. He became angry and disillusioned.

Beggars

> You without heed or pity
>   Of men who slink
> From city to city
>   Lacking food, lacking drink:
>   Fluttering
>   Foul tatter;
>   Muttering
>   Poverty's whining patter:

For alms
  Stretching blue palms . . .

When you have died:
  When tramp and king
Lie gowned alike in emerald, and crowned
  Golden with buttercup:
  Be beggars still! Rise up
And beg the Crucified
  That He forgive the world your suffering!

As well as disaffection with the political leadership of his country, Will continued to struggle against the 'black hues of melancholy' which beset him. After his prison-camp experience he could hardly bear to be shut indoors. More and more he left the routine work of his office to his clerk, Harold Brown, whilst he, the dreamer ever, wandered into the woodlands to find spiritual strength and release from stress.

Havoc

Out of the reach of man's black fratricide
Let us flee to the clefts of the hills, with beasts to abide!
There if the frost bite deep it shall gnaw without hate.
Let us climb to the rocks of the hills with foxes to hide:
Timid and beautiful things, not man-like they wait
To filch of their kind. They war but with hunger and with fate.
They steal not for gain, nor amass they gold for their pride.
If the adder strike, she shall surely strike not her mate.

There though we die, we die 'neath the eye of a star,
Not the dull gaze of envy and hate. Unbar
The doors of this dark prison wherein we move!
Let us flee to the rocks of the hills that softer are

Than hearts which are shrivelled husks – empty of love!
Not frozen snow nor ice of winter shall prove
Cruel as they; nor with keen frost-like scar,
The savage teeth so dent when wolves do rove.

. . . . .

Let us flee to the clefts of the hills, with beasts to abide!

This poem is one of a collection entitled *In Pillowell Woods and other Poems*, suggested, printed and published in 1926 by Mr Frank Harris of Lydney. In a preface, Harvey explains that:

> Without any clear-cut division the book arranges itself under three heads, viz. –
> *Nature Poems*: these centring largely upon the Forest.
> *Poems written for public occasions*: Gloucester Musical Festival, Regimental Reunions, Remembrance Day, Hospital Day, etc., and
> *Religious Poems*: Occasionally, as is but natural, these three overlap.
> There is also (consisting of only two poems) a
> *Bucolic Section*. Local opinion being not undivided with regard to the subject-matter, which is the desirability of drinking beer, these two poems are printed on one page, which can easily be excised with a scissors or safety-razor blade without detriment to the remaining portion of the book. Thus a sort of local option may be exercised.
> F.W.H.

As early as 1921, in response to an enquirer from the USA seeking 'facts and figures' about his life for an American Roman Catholic journal, Harvey had replied:

> You ask for facts and figures concerning F.W. Harvey. Here are the facts (so far as I know he never had any figures).

He writes about his childhood, his war-time experience and his poetry, and then continues:

> So much for his work! – For the man himself, his portrait
> has already appeared in two of his own books, once by
> himself and once by a friend (?). See 'F.W.H.'
> (*Gloucestershire Lad*) and page 64 *Comrades in Captivity*.
> [Reproduced on p. 101] If (which God forbid) we were to
> conduct an enquiry into his character after the manner of
> ancient birthday-gift books, it would run somewhat as
> follows: *Virtues* – God only knows! *Vices* – ask his wife!
> *Favourite drink* – beer! *Favourite occupation* – drinking it
> and listening to Gloucestershire stories (he maintains that all
> good poems are born in pubs!) And here we touch on one of
> Harvey's peculiarities, namely that so long as he is writing
> of things usually termed 'serious' he is content to be taken
> flippantly, but so soon as he turns to things like beer, or
> birds like ducks, he turns deadly earnest and demands
> seriousness in his readers. In fact he has built up a
> philosophy upon and around these two things! The war (he
> says) has affected nothing so important as a moral
> readjustment. The soldier (he says) sees drunkenness a vice
> (though a good man's vice!) just as much *now* as he did
> before the war. He sees sobriety a virtue (though often a bad
> man's virtue) just as much now as ever he did. But the war
> (he declares) has widened men's vision to *positive* virtues,
> and shut it to the *negative* virtues. Knowing the men (and
> the lives of those men) who made the supreme sacrifice he
> (and he believes all soldiers) are ready to say that it is not
> refraining from *bad* things that makes saints so much as
> doing *good* things. The perfect type of saint is St Peter who
> although he denied his Lord yet died for him crucified head
> down. And his disciple is every soldier who in the hell of
> Flanders died and died ungrudgingly for his God and his
> country.
>   Let us keep our sense of proportion in morals. Moreover
> he absolutely denies that it is necessary for a man to get

drunk because he drinks beer, as is shown by his reply to a lady who had remarked loudly to his billeting officers: 'I hope this man never returns home the worse for drink.' 'No Madam' (broke in H.) 'always the better.'

As to 'Ducks' – Harvey says that God made them – and therefore God must be a very funny fellow! When I look shocked, he says that unless God had made *me*, I shouldn't be as funny as I am. Comicallity (he says) is as much an aspect of God as holiness. The fact that there are comical men and comical ducks proves that there is a comical God. *One does not love one's Father any less because one suspects Him of a sense of humour.*

Perhaps Harvey is right!

Yours sincerely: – his best friend.[1]

If, by his own criterion, we are to take Harvey seriously in this letter, and I believe that we are, it is clear that the drinking of beer had, in 1921, attained a position of major importance for him, far above that of a social lubricant, and for which he felt the necessity to make an apologia. By 1926 Will Harvey was unable to exercise for himself the type of 'local option' with regard to beer which he had offered to his readers in the preface to *In Pillowell Woods*. Even so, at that time his enjoyment of beer in pubs and clubs probably seemed no more than the recreation of a merry soul, and he still *could* rely on his sense of humour. 'The Foresters', wrote Leonard Clark, 'loved every inch of him. They knew he was a good lawyer, admired his cricket, but most of all enjoyed his company. A miner once said, "Mr. 'arvey, he's like a lovely, wicked old gnome. I only has to look at him to bust out laughing."'

'Bust out laughing' he might well at the bucolic humour of one of Harvey's hilarious poems, written in a railway station waiting-room and dedicated to a certain lord of the manor.

After an exhausting walk with some friends, Harvey arrived at the village to find there was no train for several hours and that the said lord did not allow a licensed house on his estate. Will Harvey, deprived of his beer, knew no mercy!

A Curse

God burn this place called Soddington
  And tread it out to ashes,
And welt the slaves therein right sore
  With whips of many lashes.

But for the lord of Soddington,
  Who grudges men their beer,
Let Satan hound him swift to hell
  With hot and pointed spear;

And ladle down his parching throat
  A quart of molten lead,
And heap the coals of Hades-fire
  Blue-hot upon his head,

And twist his thumbs, and pluck his beard,
  And rend him clean asunder,
And shrivel up his shrieking soul
  In brimstone and in thunder.

. . . . .

XXVIII

Trials

Harvey described his having been articled to a solicitor as 'the beginning of his downfall. He began writing his poems instead of living them. Fat, flatulent poems they were, and the only thing that can be said for them is that they were not about himself, but about the wonderful things he was just beginning to see and love – Gloucestershire, and Gloucestershire men and women. During his 5 years' articles he read and wrote a prodigious deal, but did very little honest reading at law. There is not time for everything in this life, and he was otherwise engaged. Hazlitt says that most of his life was taken up with expressing things he knew before he was 18. Most of Harvey's life has been spent in finding verbal clothes for the ideas he acquired between the ages of 19 and 21.'[1]

If Harvey blamed his profession for robbing his verses of vitality, it was the experience of war and the comradeship of good men which restored them to vigorous life. It was the war, too, which gave purpose to his legal training. Continuing in his characteristic, third-person style, Will wrote of 1914: 'For the first time in his life law became really useful since he was able as prisoner's friend to appear in two courts martial of men accused of sleeping on guard and (by dint of a ruthless cross-examination of his superior officers) obtain their acquittal. This one may imagine gave great pleasure to the little man.'[2]

As a private soldier, Will Harvey had gained experience as an underdog successfully defending other, less eloquent underdogs. During his captivity, although an officer, he was again underdog to his captors, but still well able to conduct an effective defence of his fellow-prisoners. After the war his humanity and legal ability found expression in advocacy, frequently in defence of similar underdogs. During the years of the Depression, and long afterwards, poverty-stricken labouring men, Forest miners and their families when in trouble found in him a friend who would appear for them in court for very little fee, or for a few eggs, a chicken, a pint of beer, or for nothing at all. It was written of him that 'In his best years he was an extremely able lawyer and advocate with outstanding ability which sometimes reached brilliance in court. His eloquence moved magistrates almost to tears; he was a student of the humanities and many of his most potent defences were successful because he based them on the humaneness of the law and presented to the presiding judges in compelling and convincing phrases the best he could find in the man he was defending.'[3] Or again: 'Everybody in trouble went to him. He would defend widows threatened with eviction from their cottages, girls who, in his racy language, had "slipped a bit", and all those people who, otherwise blameless in their lives, suddenly found themselves on the wrong side of the law. I doubt if the courts of West Gloucestershire ever heard better oratory. I have seen a bench of the most matter-of-fact justices listening entranced as that swarthy, kind little man pleaded passionately that the case against some poor unfortunate should be dismissed.'[4]

Sometimes his advocacy was not only brilliant but also very amusing as, for instance, in the case of the Bream man who, having fallen asleep in his car at night whilst waiting for the railway crossing gates to open, was charged with being drunk in charge of a vehicle. In his defence Harvey pointed out that those particular gates were well known for remaining closed for long stretches of time, and asked the magistrates: 'Who would *not* fall asleep during such wearisome waiting?'[5]

On another occasion, when some Gloucester hockey players were prosecuted at Pershore for drinking before the official opening time, Harvey was called upon to defend them. He pointed out that since the Pershore players, who had finished their drinks, were allowed to go free, it was hardly fair that the Gloucester men, who were slower 'on the bend', should have to suffer.[6]

Unsurprisingly, neither defence, in spite of Will's ingenuity, was successful.

The Gloucestershire writer Brian Waters, in his delightful book *The Forest of Dean*, recalled walking with his friend Harvey along the rim of the forest one day. 'The poet lamented the felling of several fine sycamores that had shaded the road, and then confessed that as a solicitor he had brought about their downfall. He had represented a skidding motorist and had shown to the court that this had been due to the propellor-like seeds shed by the trees, which when squashed became a jelly.'

Between 1925 and 1934, Harvey appeared regularly in the courtrooms of Lydney and Coleford, travelling the six miles by train, a railway journey no longer possible. For him the slow forest ride was a time for dreams and escape.

Lydney to Coleford (By Rail)

All creeping things the Lord God made.
  And thus 'tis demonstrated
A railway-line may be divine;
  This engine God-created:
This thing which wakes and sleeps again,
Which crawls and stops and creeps again,
Up slopes and into deeps again,
  Through forest shine and shade.

Is yon the driver? *Driver*! Nay!
  'Tis one who leads, I wist,
Upon his crazy way and mazy
  Some dark Somnambulist,
Within whose dim and sleep drugged brain
Thoughts move. *Call not this dream a train*!
This sleeping-beauty, sweetly fain
  To loiter through a day.

Trials

Who would *not* loiter? Here the bracken
  Gleams green and densely spread,
Here call the birds their pretty words
  In leafage overhead.
A butterfly has kept with me
  His innocent wavering company
For miles: at moments *slept with me*
  When as our pace did slacken.

Abandon hope all ye who here
  Enter to keep appointment!
A gift more fair, a gift more rare,
  A kind and healing ointment,
This train provides. Then cast away
Dull care, and for a Summer's day
Ignore as dross Time's 'Yea' and 'Nay',
  Discard Life's fret and fear.

Too oft doth hurry rule us. Let
  For once the tumult fade:
Fade into humming of bees coming
  Sweet-laden down a glade:
Fade into glint of fern and flower,
Where quarries gleam and foxgloves tower,
And for one lovely lazy hour
  Forget – forget – forget.

You *will* arrive – impatient ass –
  Too soon! and then alighting
Meet kith and kin and wag a chin
  O'er wrongs past human righting.
Discuss old strife; new scandal: such
Soft social soot as serves to smutch
A life once tuned to Nature touch
  Now seldom felt – alas!

Of the same journey he told a priceless pub story:

The following tale is told (with what truth I know not) by a popular Lydney innkeeper:

'One day I was in the bar-room when a man entered in an exhausted condition, sank into a seat, and called for whisky and soda.

' "You look tired, "I said.

' "I've had an awful journey," he answered. *"Thank God the worst of it is over."*

' "Come a long way?"

' "From Coleford."

' "And where might you be going?"

' *"To China,"* he said.'

No fortunes are to be made defending the poor, and Harvey lacked the blade of determination edged with ruthlessness which is essential equipment for the successful businessman. His interest was in people not profit and, when not in court or wandering the woodlands, he would usually be found in the bar of a village pub, sitting amidst the Foresters, enjoying a joke or reading to them from some well-thumbed book of verse. Inevitably, his practice declined.

In 1927 the landlord of a local pub had told Will about a stone-built, four-square house with a walled garden which had come up for sale at Yorkley and from which there were views of 'forest and vale and high blue hill'.[7] With the help of Anne's hard-earned savings the couple bought the property and, for the first time, set up home permanently. Ten years later, Will closed the Lydney office and withdrew to his Forest retreat, where he put up a brass plate which read: 'F.W. Harvey, Solicitor and Commissioner for Oaths.'

For the rest of his life Harvey's income was barely sufficient to live on. His royalties declined to a mere trickle. His increasing need to find in Forest inns the antidote to stress and disillusion cost more than he could afford in either money or health.

As when, under the 'green mould' of prison-camp conditions, he had neglected his personal appearance, so in his years of decline he became increasingly careless about his dress and, in Leonard

The Courtroom, Littledean.

Clark's words, 'He had certainly, except on special occasions, a fine disregard for clothes and, when among his own familiars, of razors also. I remember him best of all ambling along the country roads, wearing a rather stained navy-blue suit, a battered trilby hat planted firmly on his head, gold-rimmed spectacles on nose, and cigarette between tobacco-stained fingers.'[8]

After the Second World War Harvey was a familiar if unconventional figure in the courts of Gloucestershire. He and Anne sometimes took the bus to Littledean where the eighteenth-century Forest gaol was situated. The courtroom at Littledean was a part of the gaol building and so Will could interview his prisoner-client and then, with Anne acting as his clerk, represent him before the magistrates on the same day.[9] Again, this was work with little reward and quite often Will received scanty payment for his time and effort. He would never have sued a client for debt.

In spite of his reduced circumstances, the Foresters never ceased to respect Will Harvey as a learned, professional man amongst them. To them he was always 'Mr Harvey'. In court the police prosecutor, Arthur James, gave him unreserved friendship. Although Will may have been criticised by some barristers in the county for his unconventionality in a changing world, recognition eventually came from a senior and unexpected quarter.

One day Will Harvey was obliged to attend the Quarter Sessions in Gloucester to deal with a case, at the end of which Mr Raglan Somerset K.C., the recorder presiding over the court, said, 'I'm glad to see somebody in court today who has done so much to enrich the English language.' Modestly unaware for a while that every eye was upon him, Will suddenly realised that the unaccustomed words of praise were meant for *him*. With great dignity he turned to the judge, smiled and quietly bowed his head.[10]

XXIX

Gallant Friends

Here's a health to every brother in arms,
  Safe returned from war's alarms;
Maimed and merry, hale and bold,
  To pledge our fellowship of old.

And now (in silence) another toast –
  To gallant friends – a mighty host
Asleep, with foreign earth for bed,
  Till Doomsday reveille – the Glorious Dead!

Throughout his life Harvey maintained contact with old wartime comrades. He was present at the reunion of the 2/5th Battalion of the Gloucestershire Regiment at the Shire Hall, Gloucester, on 6 September 1919. Three weeks later he attended the first reunion of the 1/5th Battalion at the Old Drill Hall, Brunswick Road, Gloucester. Prison-camp friends, such as Hugh Walker, living far from Gloucestershire, kept in touch by letter. And when, on Saturday 28 March 1925, at a service of dedication, Field-Marshal Lord Plumer unveiled a memorial to perpetuate the memory of the men of the 1/5th and 2/5th Battalions, Harvey was there; his words formed part of the ceremony.

Remember –

Forget not us, O land, for which we fell,
May it go well with England, still go well!

Armistice Day, Yorkley, *c.* 1930. Lord and Lady Bledisloe stand next to F.W. Harvey.

Keep her bright banners without spot or stain,
Lest we should dream that we have died in vain.

They died, whatever lie be spun,
Less for Old England than, each one,
For the New England which shall shed
Her sorrows.

. . . . .

Harvey never missed an opportunity to share his love of literature
and music with whosoever would listen. His neighbours became
accustomed to his reading verse to them over the garden wall;

children stopped him in the street with 'Give us a poetry, Mr
'arvey.' He would stop and recite to them, 'never from his
published work, but something improvised from the workshop of
his mind'.[1] He brought Shakespeare and Chaucer into Forest pubs
and, when he had captured the imagination of hard-working men
and women, he would, in the evening glimmer, take his seat at the
piano to play and sing, invariably beginning with the folk-song,
'Golden Slumbers'.[2] His personal crusade was to bring good
literature and music to ordinary folk and to persuade them of their
relevance and benefit to real life.

On the evening of Monday 13 December 1926, Harvey was
invited to address the Gloucester Old Comrades Association. Once
more he took up his theme. The following report appeared the next
day in *The Citizen* newspaper:

'POETRY CURE'

Mr F.W. Harvey with
Gloucester Old Comrades

An interesting recital

Under the auspices of the Gloucester Old Comrades'
Association (1/5th Bn. Gloucestershire Regiment) a social
evening was held at the Services Club, Westgate Street, on
Monday, when Mr Walter Bailey (President) occupied the
chair.

Mr F.W. Harvey gave an address on 'Poetry Cure', in the
course of which he said that they should throw away the
popular superstition that poets were either effeminate gods
or disreputable half-men. That view was historically
incorrect. They must throw away the popular heresy that
poetry was something pretty but ineffably remote from
everyday life, because the exact opposite was the truth. The
poet was the man of all men most keenly alive to the world
about him, and to the world within him, most sensitive to

the bruises of the one and to the joys of the other and to the meaning of both. As for poetry being remote from life, on the contrary it was man's most enduring oath and testament that life was in all its manifestations most wonderful and miraculous. Poetry was praise of life. To quote Ruskin, it was 'Man's delight in God's work'. There was no essential difference between Wordsworth's 'Lines written in Early Spring' and Wilfred Owen's terrible war poem 'Mental Cases', for different as the two poems were in manner and in matter, yet the principle behind was identical, for the one directly by its idealism and the other indirectly by realism were praise of life. In dealing with poetry they were not dealing with a drawing-room accomplishment, for poetry was the oldest of the arts and was man's perception of the rhythm which evidenced life, whether revealed by the pulse in his wrist or by the rolling seasons, or the rising and setting of worlds.

There were many worthy people who did not read poetry, and all one could say of them was that they missed a great deal. Poetry came, as Flecker remarked, 'Not to save souls but to make souls worth saving'. That was how they in England were accustomed to express this cardinal function of great poetry, but Americans naturally did so a little differently, which brought him to the subject of his address. A short time ago he received from America a book called *The Poetry Cure*, and described as a medicine chest of verses. In it the compounder prescribed a variety of mental cocktails by bards like Don Marquis, W.S. Gilbert, and Oliver Herford; or spiritual pick-me-ups by carbonated poets like Christopher Morley or John Masefield. They would find in this poetic pharmacy a shelf of anodyne for sorrow, another of poppy juice for insomnia, electric vibrators for a torpid imagination, massage appliances for a hide-bound spirit, accelerators for sluggish blood, a wide selection of pills to purge melancholy, sedatives for impatience, stimulants for a faint heart, etc. All this struck him (Mr Harvey) as a lot too good to keep to himself;

besides he wanted to experiment.

Proceeding, Mr. Harvey gave what he described as 'pills', 'potions', 'prescriptions' and 'remedies' for complaints like 'inflated ego', 'anaemic soul', 'hardening of the heart', 'insomnia', 'earnestness about nothing in particular', 'faint heart', and 'sluggish blood'; and antidotes for the strenuous life. Amongst the poems he recited or gave extracts from as bearing on the various complaints were: 'I'm Nobody' (Emily Dickinson), 'House of a Hundred Lights' (Ridgeley Torrence), 'The Bells of Heaven' (Ralph Hodgson), 'About Ben Adhem' (Leigh Hunt), 'God's Pity' (Louise Driscoll), 'To Sleep' (Wordsworth), 'The Lotus Eaters' (Tennyson), 'Ducks' (F.W. Harvey), 'The Rich Man' (Franklin P. Adams), 'The Celestial Surgeon' (R.L. Stevenson), 'Invictus' (William Ernest Henley, an old boy of the Crypt School), 'Solitude' (William Allingham), 'The Scythe Song' (Andrew Lang) and 'Leisure' (William S. Davis). Mr Harvey quoted the following excerpt from the work of Robert Graves, an English poet: 'Poetry is no more a narcotic than a stimulant; it is a universal bitter-sweet mixture for all possible household emergencies; a well-chosen anthology is a complete dispensary of medicine for the most common mental disorders, and may be used as much for prevention as cure.' (Applause)

Mr Harvey sang Leigh Hunt's 'Jenny Kissed Me' (music by Graham Peel), and was further assisted by Mr Percy Aas, who sang John Masefield's 'Trade Wind' (Fred Keel), Gerald H. Crow's 'O Lily, Lady of Loveliness' (Maurice Besly) and Tennyson's 'Now Sleeps the Crimson Petal' (Roger Quilter), while Mr W.H. Bell sang John Masefield's 'Sea Fever' (John Ireland). Mr D.S. Hole was the accompanist.

On the motion of the Chairman, Mr Harvey was cordially thanked for his address and the entertaining way in which he had presented it, a similar compliment being paid to Messrs Aas and Bell for the sympathetic manner in which they had by their singing illustrated the beauties of poetic work, and to Mr Hole for his accompaniments at the piano. . .

Subsequently the social was continued. Mr Harvey singing 'The Old Bold Mate' (Ivor Gurney) and Mr A.W. Bundy 'The Veterans' Song.'

. . . . .

Following his return from Germany in 1919, Will Harvey had no wish ever to leave Gloucestershire again, and indeed his journeys outside his own county were rare. However, when in February 1933 he was invited to speak to the Apollo Society, a literary club of St Catherine's College, Oxford, he readily agreed to go. It so happened that in that Hilary Term of 1933 the president of the Apollo Society was an undergraduate from the Forest of Dean, Ivon Adams. As president, Adams had the honour of choosing the speakers and, in his own words, 'as one Gloucestershire lad to another, I invited F.W. Harvey. (There was some collusion – it so happened also that my tutor, Chesney Horwood, later Dean of the college, was also a Gloucestershire lad.)' When Harvey and Adams met, another lifelong friendship began.

Harvey gave his talk on 20 February before 'a group of earnest, dreamy Oxford undergraduates' who were inclined to giggle as the 'thick-set, dark-haired, dreamy little man, uncouth to see' entered the room. But within moments of his beginning to speak he was addressing a rapt audience; an audience of young men who, a few years later, would be called upon to fight a second war.

During the four days that Harvey was in Oxford, a university concert was advertised in which the famous oboist Leon Goossens was to be the soloist. Harvey very much wanted to attend the concert, but unfortunately it was an 'all-gown' affair. Ivon Adams explained the dilemma to his tutor: since Harvey was not a graduate he had no gown. Chesney Horwood solved the problem by lending the visiting speaker a gown of his own, and Harvey entered the concert hall suitably dressed and with the dignity and pride of any don.

The next day Adams took Harvey for a walk around Oxford to

show him the colleges. When they came to the entrance of Brasenose, Eric Harvey's old college, Will fell silent for a while and then, turning to his guide, said quietly, 'They shot the wrong one'.[3]

. . . . .

From time to time Will travelled down to Dartford to visit his dear friend Ivor Gurney in the City of London Mental Hospital. He found a tortured soul pleading for liberty or death. 'Get me out of here, Willy!' he would say.[4] Will would promise to do his best, but knew that any idea of release for his friend was useless.

To Ivor Gurney

Now hawthorn hedges live again;
    And all along the banks below
Pale primrose fires have lit the lane
    Where oft we wandered long ago
    And saw the blossom blow.

And talked and walked till stars pricked out,
    And sang brave midnight snatches under
The moon, with never a dread nor doubt,
    Nor warning of that devil's wonder
    That tore our lives asunder.

And left behind a nightmare trail
    Of horrors scattered through the brain,
Of shattered hopes and memories frail
    That bloom like flowers in some old lane
    And tear the heart in twain.

This hawthorn hedge will bank its snow
    Spring after Spring, and never care

What song and dreams of long ago
    Within its shade were fashioned fair
    Of happy air.

But you within the madhouse wall,
    But you and I who went so free,
Never shall keep Spring's festival
    Again, though burgeon every tree
    With blossom joyously.

Not that I fear to keep the faith;
    Not that my heart goes cravenly;
But that some voice within me saith
    'The Spring is dead!' yea, dead, since he
    Will come no more to me.

It needeth but a tear to quench
    The primrose fires: to melt the snow
Of Spring-time hedges, and to drench
    With black the blue clear heavens show . . .
    And I have wept for you.

After 1926 Gurney composed no more music but continued to write poetry; hundreds of complete poems and verse-pieces, many of them masterpieces. On 26 December 1937, Ivor Gurney died from tuberculosis. He was forty-seven years old and had spent fifteen years within asylum walls.

Gurney's body was returned to his beloved Gloucestershire and buried in the little churchyard at Twigworth, just outside Gloucester. The service was conducted by Gurney's godfather, Canon Alfred Cheesman, and Herbert Howells played the organ. Will stood next to Brian Frith at the sad, winter graveside and, as the coffin was lowered down, he threw into the grave a tiny sprig of rosemary, plucked at Minsterworth that morning; to it was tied a small label bearing the words 'Rosemary for Remembrance'.[5]

. . . . .

Will Harvey, *c.* 1940.

During the Second World War, Harvey served in the Home Guard. Patrick joined the Glosters and was twice wounded on active service. Eileen left home to work in the Royal Air Force Records Office. For Will, the war was a betrayal by politicians of all he and his comrades had fought for between 1914 and 1918.

As the war ended, he suffered the greatest blow of all. His mother, for whom his childlike devotion never waned, died at Minsterworth. Twenty-five years earlier Tillie's life had been saved by major surgery, but Will, thinking that he would lose her then, and echoing *The Tempest* in his title, gave expression to the sorrow which was to become reality in 1945.

This Isle is Full of Noises

I

'What, closed to-day?' I asked. The inn seemed shut.
'Not likely, sir,' quoth he. I asked then, 'Why
Are your blinds drawn?' Then suddenly knew that I
Had been a fool, and stammered pardon. But
He answered coolly, 'Mother's dead'. He was
Thin, forty, pasty-faced, no whit the host
Of Christmas stories: spoke without a ghost
Of feeling in his tone. But 'twas because
Of these cold careless words of his my blood
Stopped running: of a sudden, shot was I
With this one bullet-thought, 'Yes, all will die –
All mothers. All men's mothers bad and good
Must die'. And that was twenty years ago.
Yet till to-day how, oh, how could I know?

II

How could I guess until this hour that she –
Whose influence more permanent had been

Than timeless things; than all that I had seen,
Or heard, or felt, since first I came to be:
She whom, if seeing not, I know was there,
Some miles or score of miles away at home –
Would find a dwelling where I might not come
To touch her hand even, or touch her hair:
Would me maroon upon this lonely isle,
The little barren most unhappy earth
Of my sole self, and things not brought to birth
By the sweet vital sun of her dear smile;
Condemned to stare upon and never pass
Those seas dividing all that is, and was?

III

Yet though my life is now a desert isle,
There springs a mercy out of common air:
This isle is full of noises, everywhere
Do ghostly sounds and sweet my heart beguile;
Songs of childhood faintly calling, calling;
Tender replies wise as the water falling
From clouds that feed and soothe a thirsty plain;
Love answering Grief; Grief answering Love again.

They cease not: all the haunted air is made
Wise with a beauty, veiled no longer, thrown
From world to world. That Love which was her own
Cries sweet the gospel of Beauty's permanence,
And Grief herself forgets to be afraid
Heeding that word as Spirit wooeth Sense.

. . . . .

Will Harvey was proud to be a member of the Royal British Legion, proud to be elected president of his local branch and proud to wear his poppy on Remembrance Day. Brian Waters captured the poignancy of one such day in the late 1940s:

November is the saddest of months in the forest, as the oaks cling reluctantly to their leaves of gold, and it was on a sodden Sunday that I climbed the hill and crawled over the forest rim. It was Remembrance Day and the foresters were trickling towards the war memorial, a simple cenotaph on the sward among the oaks. As I joined them the village band came marching up the hill from the opposite direction. A couple of pigs in the road barred its progress until a forester disturbed their undignified complacency. A little phalanx stood on the sward, young men and a shingling of older ones – the survivors of two wars. Seated apart from them with the poppy wreath of the British Legion in his hand sat the poet, not by right of poetry but because he is the leading fighting man of the village. I have always hitherto met him face to face in the brisk companionship of friendship, but to-day, sitting in his isolation, I view him with detachment for the first time. I see him in profile, and the silhouette of that sensitive, genial face is that of a fighter who won the DCM for a feat of bravery more in keeping with the spirit of the Homeric age than modern warfare . . .

To-day a small, elderly man, he sits thinking, I am sure, of those comrades of his youth, who have been spared the bitter knowledge of another war.

Then as the time comes for him to lay a wreath on the memorial he strides forwards with the measured step of a countryman. But above everything else in the fusion of his earthly existence this poet and fighter is a man of religion, and beside the little fence, that protects the memorial from the grazing sheep and routing pig, he drops to his knees in prayer. It is a moment personal and compelling, and those of us who have not prayed for weeks are drawn into the orbit of this devotion.

He returns to his place in the congregation, and as we sing

> Before the hills in order stood
> Or earth received her frame

Gallant Friends

from Isaac Watts's hymn, they seem to express the forest landscape. At the end of the service, as I walk with the poet across the green, we gaze into the unchanged and ever-changing landscape of the forest bowl. To-day the sepia and purple hills are half covered in mist. 'Wave upon misty wave,' murmurs the poet; it describes the scene as perfectly as a painting. The village band passes like the fragment of a lost army.[6]

With typical modesty, Harvey responded to Brian Waters' words by writing the following disclaimer to the editor of his local newspaper:

Sir, – Mr Brian Waters has written a fine book on *The Forest of Dean*.

It contains many kind references to myself which I am loath to discourage in an age more notable for spiteful exchanges between fellow authors.

But I cannot permit him to write that I laid the British Legion wreath upon the cenotaph because I was 'the best fighting man of the village'.

That honour was accorded me because I happened to be President of the local Legion Branch.

I hold that all soldiers who tried bravely to do their duty (whether decorated or not) are equal – there can be no 'best' among them.

Thanking you therefore, Brian, for your generous praise, but disclaiming this item.

Your sincere admirer and friend.

F.W. Harvey

PS   On review I find the word used was 'leading' not 'best' but the disclaimer still stands. F.W.H.

. . . . .

Harvey wrote a number of poems to mark the Armistice, but none of them finer than that inspired by the words of a tiny Brian Frith,

315

F. W. *Harvey* SOLDIER, POET

playing in the garden at The Redlands with his brother Geoffrey, one day shortly after the Great War.[7]

'Out of the Mouths of Babes –'

Two children in my garden playing, found
    A robin cruelly dead, in Summer hours.
I watched them get a trowel, and heap the mound,
    And bury him, and scatter over flowers.

And when their little friend was laid away,
    In lack of burial service over the dead
Before those two grave children turned to play:
    'I hope he'll have a happy *dead* life!' one said.

What more was there to say for bird or beast?
    What more for any man is there to say?
What can we wish *them* better, as with priest
    And choir we ring the cross on Armistice Day?

F.W. Harvey, Armistice Day, *c.* 1930.

XXX

Sporting Times and Radio Times

One of the earliest photographs of Will Harvey, taken in 1910, shows him sitting proudly in the captain's seat with the team of the Minsterworth Amateur Football Club.

Sport was important to Harvey, not only because he was a skilful

Minsterworth AFC.

F.W. *Harvey* SOLDIER, POET

all-rounder, nor simply for recreation and fitness. He was an active sportsman for the first forty years of his life and found in games a strenuous, head-clearing counterbalance to introspection. Equally, he enjoyed the companionship of fellow-sportsmen with whom he could relax as an admired team member.

Will had helped to form the Minsterworth AFC in 1906, the year after he left Rossall School. Of schooldays he once wrote of himself: 'Prizes came not his way, but he got honours for hockey, cricket and football, which included a mention in *The Sportsman* for the most wonderful fluke-goal ever notched in a public school match (a centre that went astray in the annual Rossall v Stonyhurst contest!).'[1] Back in Minsterworth he was soon sharing his footballing skill with the local farm boys.

In their first game, Minsterworth AFC played away against the nearby village of Huntley. Will took his protégés to the match in the horsedrawn wagon from The Redlands. Only he possessed proper football kit; the other boys were obliged to play in their

Gloucester Hockey Club, *c.* 1921. Will Harvey, seated on the extreme right. Seated centre is fellow poet and solicitor, John Haines, who was also president of the club.

everyday working boots and a mixture of shorts, shirts and pullovers. The match ended in a 5–1 defeat for Minsterworth, compensated for by Will who treated the whole team to high tea at the Red Lion in Huntley.[2]

The 1910 photograph shows Minsterworth AFC kitted-out in a smart football strip, and perhaps by then their prowess at the game was similarly improved.

Of Will's record with the Gloucester Hockey Club Thursday XI nothing remains except a photograph taken in the 1920s in which John Haines, the chairman of the club, sits surrounds by the team. Fortunately, a little more is known of Harvey the cricketer.

Leonard Clark recalled how in 1923, as a seventeen-year-old schoolboy, he first met Will Harvey.

> I had begun to write – and to have printed in the local paper – what John Emery called 'your little bits of verses'. One day someone told me that the author of 'Ducks', a poem I knew by heart, lived only a few miles away. I could hardly believe it. I had pictured the writer of that poem living in some remote poet's arcadia. I wrote to him, told him I wrote poetry, and asked if I could come and see him. By return came a creased postcard with a sepia picture of the Severn Bore on one side, and on the other, in jagged handwriting, the magic words 'Come next Saturday. Have just seen Parker take eight for forty.' Parker was one of my cricketing heroes, the Gloucestershire left-arm spin bowler, then at the height of his magnificent destructive powers. Saturday came. With my notebook of original poems tucked safely into my pocket I cycled, in a dream, all the way downhill to the charmed village of Minsterworth. I kept on reminding myself that I was going to see a real poet. I had once seen a real Field-Marshal and a real live Lord, and had not been disappointed. I got to Minsterworth half an hour too soon, wandered about a bit aimlessly and then knocked at the door of the Georgian house where Will Harvey lived with his newly-married wife, his mother and sister. The great man was not at home. 'Would I wait for him in the

parlour?' asked his sister. 'He's out playing cricket.'

'Oh, could I go and see him? I ventured, rising eagerly from my chair.

'Well, he's at Gloucester.'

I sat down again. Gloucester was three or four miles away and I feared that if I left the house I might miss him. Four o'clock came, and no poet. By five we had finished tea. At six, having nothing more to talk about, I thought it was time to go home. Mother would be wondering if I had been drowned in Severn. About a quarter past he arrived, still in his 'whites', and breathless with apologies. He had forgotten to tell me about the match. I later learned from a hypnotised eye-witness that he had scattered the spectators with some terrific off-drives, and almost maimed a fielder for life who had been so foolish as to get in the way of a wicked square cut. The truth is that, both as batsman and fielder, Will Harvey was near county class; his bowling, on the other hand, was poetical in the extreme – very slow and not very straight. Before I had left that welcoming household he had glanced at my notebook of poems, said a few kind words about them, toasted our muse in cider, and invited me to come again the following Sunday. 'And there'll be no cricket match this time, I promise you.'[3]

The cricketers of the Gloucester City Club still play on The Spa ground which they have used since 1863 and which until 1924 was also the home of the Gloucestershire CCC.

Will had played at The Spa before 1914, but the Great War meant the end of cricket for the City Club for four years, although a single game was played in 1915 between the 'Wounded' and the 'Old Crocks'. After the war, Will took up his bat once more.

Grahame Parker, who in 1932 scored 952 runs for the City Club, remembered the post-war years in Gloucester and at The Spa:

Those were the days when lamplighters toured the city streets at dusk lighting the lamps with their long poles, when trams rattled through the main streets out into the country,

and all Gloucester seemed to go to Barton Fair on the Ham
and stopped on Westgate Bridge, to watch the one-legged
diver, when the Wave and Lapwing made daily trips in
summer along the canal from Gloucester to Sharpness, and
when cheapjacks on Wildman's Ground had to shout above
the boxing booth caller to make themselves heard . . .

I may have forgotten the shots, but I will never forget the
scene (at The Spa). The wooden Pavilion, already in some
state of decay, with its spacious upper storey and below the
changing rooms, the cramped tea room, leading out on to
the field across a gravel path. Then the Pump Room beyond
the trees, spectators leaning over the railings on the Spa
Road side, shoppers going to town from across the girder
bridge over the railway with goods trains rattling on their
way to and from the Docks.[4]

In 1923 the captaincy of the Gloucester CC was taken over for a
single season by Ivor Gurney's brother, Ronald, 'a good all-
rounder. It was, however, an undistinguished season. The Club
played 28 games, won 10, lost 15 and drew 3; indeed the first eight
games were all lost. Hollingsworth scored 442 runs, including one
innings of 119, and Gurney did well with 68 wickets.'[5] Following
Ivor's committal to the City of London Mental Hospital, Will
maintained contact and friendship with Ronald Gurney. When the
cricketing days of both men were over, they continued to meet
occasionally.

In 1924, when he and Anne moved to Broadoak, Will resigned
from the Gloucester CC and was then selected to play for the
Lydney CC.

Harvey's first match for Lydney was at Cardiff, where he
held four catches, taking them 'unorthodoxly low down'. He
was as unorthodox in his cricket as in his general life.
Against Cinderford St John's he hit three sixes; at Weston-
super-Mare on 10th July, 1926, he hit three boundaries over
the heads of the slip fielders! Weston were beaten in the last
over.[6]

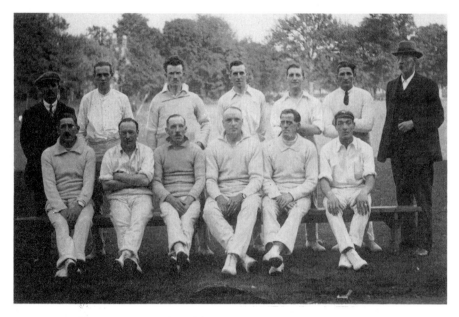

Gloucester City Cricket Club, 1923. Captain Ronald Gurney. F.W.
Harvey is second from left in the front row.

The 1925 cricket season at The Spa in Gloucester opened with a
match between the City Club and Lydney. The match, or mismatch,
was reported in *The Citizen* of Monday 4 May.

SATURDAY'S CRICKET.

Gloucester v. Lydney.

CITY OPEN WITH EASY VICTORY.

Gloucester, with the assistance of the two County players,
Hammond and Bloodworth, beat Lydney at The Spa on
Saturday by 105 runs. The team as a whole did not show very
convincing form; for while the two County men put on 100
runs for the first wicket, the rest of the team could only muster
50 between them, and when Lydney went in it was Hammond
who did all the damage, taking eight wickets for 17 runs. A.G.
Brett, the Rugby footballer, showed good form as a bowler for

Lydney, breaking up the home team's first wicket partnership in his first over by taking Bloodworth's wicket, getting Dr. Taylor two balls later, and Loveridge in his second over without a run being scored off him. His final analysis was six for 23. F.W. Harvey made top score for the visitors, and square cut in an attractive manner. Scores:–

Gloucester.

B.S. Bloodworth, c Fletcher, b Brett 50
W.R. Hammond, c Elliott, b Mills 51
Dr. G.C. Taylor, c Fletcher, b Brett 0
G.P. Hollingworth, b Brett 23
R.N. Loveridge, b Brett 0
P. Tilley, l-b-w, b Levison 13
C.A. Bretherton, b Brett 0
A.T. Voyce, b Levison 0
S.P. Ball, c M. Jarrett, b Levison 4
S.F. Taylor, not out 7
W. Cousins, b Brett, ... 3
    Extras 9

Total 160

Lydney

Capt. Cornock, b Hammond 0
P. Grey, b Hammond 4
A.G. Brett, b Hammond 1
P. Mills, c Bloodworth, b Hammond 10
G. Elliott, b Hammond 0
M. Jarrett, b Hammond 4
F.W. Harvey, l-b-w, b Hollingworth 18
C. Levison, run out 6
S. Jarrett, c Bloodworth, b Hammond 1
E. Fletcher, not out 0
A. Vanstone, b Hammond 0
    Extras 11

Total 55

Facing opposition from Bloodworth and the great Wally Hammond, Lydney could hardly be expected to win. In the circumstances, Will Harvey's top score was the more creditable.

In the 1925 season Lydney won 16 matches, lost 6 and drew 2. Harvey played 20 innings and scored 269 runs. In the following year Lydney had one of its most successful seasons, being undefeated on its own ground. The First XI played 18 matches, of which they won 13, drew 4 and lost one.[7] For Will Harvey, however, the season was less successful. He scored 82 runs in only 8 innings and dropped out of the team before the 1927 season began. His club cricket days were over, but his sportsmanship and the humour which he brought to the game were not forgotten. After Harvey's death, a contemporary wrote in a letter to *The Citizen*:

'The Little Man' peering through his glasses at his fellow men, laughed not at them, but with them.

Those who saw him fielding at 'silly point' for Lydney many years ago will know what I mean. Having mesmerised the batsman he would proceed to take a catch, practically off the face of the bat, and would hug the ball to his bosom with intense enjoyment before handing it back to the bowler.

Will Harvey's legacy to the game he loved was enshrined in a poem about another catch from an innocent, remembered time. It is the best known of all poems about cricket and was published in *A Gloucestershire Lad* and also in a book entitled *A Poetry of Cricket*.

Cricket: The Catch

Whizzing, fierce, it came
Down the summer air,
Burning like a flame
On my fingers bare,

And it brought to me
As swift – a memory

Happy days long dead
  Clear I saw once more.
Childhood that is fled: –
  Rossall on the shore,
Where the sea sobs wild
Like a homesick child.

Oh, the blue bird's fled!
  Never man can follow.
Yet at times instead
  Comes this scarlet swallow,
Bearing on its wings
  (Where it skims and dips,
  Gleaming through the slips)
Sweet Time-strangled things.

. . . . .

Harvey's co-operation with Dr Herbert Brewer in the 1925 Three Choirs Festival led to a meeting with the organist's son, Charles, who at that time was recovering from a serious wartime flying accident, and earning an uncertain living dealing in steam coal with a company in Newport. One year later, Charles Brewer had secured a position as assistant to the drama producer in the Cardiff station of an adolescent British Broadcasting Corporation. So began for Will Harvey a long association with the BBC.

In the years before and during the Second World War, Harvey made several broadcasts on the West of England Home Service, some from Cardiff and some from the Bristol studios. Many of his talks were about the Forest of Dean and his friends the Foresters. He was an expert in Gloucestershire dialects and much in demand by BBC programme producers to read his own, often hilarious, dialect poems over the air.

Why He Left

Overheard in the Country

Dussunt cum'ere a-courtin' moi darter:
  Ver a yappin' sawny vool thee bist!
A cyawllpin' fisslin' half-baked cratur
  Whose neck wer only fit to twist.
Thy mother never adn't arter
  Let thee a bin. Thee ze moi vist:
Go, 'vore I choke thee in her's garter.

. . . . .

Arter her's feythur spake thic to oi,
I took me 'at and went awoy.
  Ussunt thee?

The treasure of the English language was a frequent theme in his broadcasts. One of Harvey's greatest delights was to share the company of a friend of like mind and to say, 'Let you and I walk and talk about poetry.' Then the two would set off down forest paths for countless hours. Walking with Ivon Adams along the forest ridge one day, Will pointed to the William Tyndale monument which towers over the Gloucestershire landscape south of the River Severn. 'That is why we have our language,' he said. An enigmatic observation upon which he expanded in a 1935 radio programme, and in a letter to the *Daily Mail*:

The Forest of Dean is a stronghold of those forms of religion whose authority is purely Biblical. Every man being his own Pope, the natives are naturally well versed in the book which they must ponder and interpret for their daily guidance. Biblical language thus becomes familiar and natural.
  The Bible is written in old English, and the Forest of

Dean, being until recently practically cut off from the rest of the world, naturally retained the old forms of speech longer than less secluded places.

Tyndale, whose monument greets the gaze of every Forester looking across the Severn, was the earliest translator of the Bible, and a Gloucestershire man.

Not only in the Forest of Dean, but in other remote parts of this beautiful and unspoiled county, may be heard the speech of the Bible.

Perhaps Harvey would have guessed that within half a century of his broadcast there would be hardly any truly remote areas left in Gloucestershire, and that continuing shifts in population would have eroded Biblical speech. Equally, it is not difficult for us to guess what he might have thought about *some* modern translations of the Bible!

In a 1944 broadcast entitled 'Here Lies . . .' Harvey turned the thoughts of his listeners to epitaphs:

> Beneath this stone in hopes of Zion
> Lies the Landlord of the Lion,
> Resigned unto the heavenly will.
> His son keeps on the business still.

Epitaphs should, I take it, be first short, because carved on stone, and secondly, arresting, because no one picks up a stone to take home and read in bed. So much for the technique of the thing. But if that were the only criterion, I suppose the most successful epitaphs would be –

> John Ross
> Kicked by a hoss.

Or the epitaph on Richard Goombridge in Horsham churchyard, which reads simply:

> He was.

Wordsworth came to the conclusion that the shortest,
plainest, truest epitaphs are best, and it would be difficult to
better the moving tribute on the graves of the unknown
soldiers of the last war which are inscribed with the words

Known to God.

Sir Thomas Browne, on the other hand, believes that the
mighty benefactors of the world do not *need* epitaphs. This
is already done by their works. Their naked names are the
only fit tribute. I am reminded of Beethoven's stone, with its
one word, inscribed 'Beethoven'. Or of Sir Christopher
Wren's epitaph in St Paul's Cathedral, which translated
reads: 'Look around if you would see my monument.'

It takes a good poet to write a good epitaph. There's
probably more bad verse written on tombstones than on any
other page on earth. Not all have the fortune of the lady
who wrote so simply and movingly:

Love made me poet,
And this I writ,
My heart did do it
And not my wit.

Her heart was a surer guide than some, as a study of any
country churchyard will testify.

Here lies the body of Joan Carthew,
Born at St Columb, died at St Cue;
Children she had five,
Three are dead, and two alive,
Those that are dead choosing rather
To die with their mother
Than live with their father.

This may of course not be as unconscious as it sounds.

Sporting Times and Radio Times

Epitaphs are part of a desire to preserve, to salvage something from the wreck of time. We desire always to lend our lives significance, to perpetuate any strong emotions, be it love, or hate, or merely malice. Perhaps the fact that there were no women stonemasons may have had something to do with it.

> My wife is dead and here she lies,
> Nobody laughs and nobody cries;
> Where she is gone, and how she fares,
> Nobody knows, and nobody cares.

Or:-

> Here lies my wife; sad slattern and shrew,
> If I said I regretted her, I should lie too.

Though I don't know that I don't prefer that to the lame and probably unconscious indictment of Lady O'Looney which comes from Pewsey in Bedfordshire. It's written in prose and runs pompously as follows:

> Here lies the body of
> LADY O'LOONEY,
> Great niece of Burke,
> commonly called the sublime:
> She was bland, passionate, and deeply religious:
> Also she painted in water colours,
> And sent several pictures to the Exhibition.
> She was first cousin to Lady Jones.
> And of such is the kingdom of heaven.

For a heavier, countrified wit, here is one upon the death of a very fat woman:

F.W. *Harvey* SOLDIER, POET

All flesh is green, the Scriptures they do say,
And grass when dead is turned into hay,
Now when the reapers her away do take,
Lord, what a wopping haystack she will make.

But there is one kind of epitaph in which there is no
laughter, only faith and pathetic regret. The death which all
epitaphs take quite seriously is the death of a child. This is the
epitome of waste. Surely, they seem to say, the gods can't be
so stupid and so cruel as to let this be the end. And so
simplicity and pathos are the keynotes. There's one, for
example, by Walter de la Mare:

Here lies but seven years old, our little maid,
Once of the darkness, oh, so sore afraid.
Light of the world, remember that small fear,
And when no moon nor stars do shine, draw near.

I think it's Galsworthy who says that it's only recently
we've come to understand animals, and that in historic times
the cat was simply an animated mousetrap, the horse a slave,
and the dog a sheep-dog or a watch-dog. I do not think this
can be so, for was not Argus the only living creature to
recognise and welcome Ulysses on his return! And there is also
a Greek epitaph on a dog which, translated, means:

Here is a grave. It is mine.
I am only a dog, but tears fell for me.
My master erected this stone to mark my burial place.

Surely there must have been an understanding, not to say
affection, there?
Classical epitaphs, of course, present a tremendous field.
One of the best and most epigrammatic Latin ones is that
commemorating Alexander the Great:

Sporting Times and Radio Times

Cui non sufficeret orbis suffcit huic tumulus.

Here a mound suffices for one, for whom the
world was not large enough.

For a nice mumbo-jumbo compromise of classic
pretentiousness and native wit, how about this?

Here lies John Shorthouse,
Sine hat, sine coat, sine breeches.
Qui fuit dum vixit
Sine rank, sine land, sine riches.

Not many men write their own memorials, but some do. For
instance, I have. It's contained in five words, which you can
take any way you like. I should like to be buried in my own
parish church where my mother and father are lying, and
the bloom blows over the wall from a nearby orchard. And I
should like a granite tombstone – marble doesn't wear well
in this hostile climate of ours, and on that tombstone I
should like inscribed the five words

'And the same to you.'

Later in 1944 Harvey gave the last of his radio talks: 'From All
Over England'.

In the National Sound Archives and also at the BBC, only a little
under seven minutes of Harvey's voice remain on recordings. In
them he is reading five of his own poems, from a programme
broadcast in 1938: 'Willum Accounts for the Price of Lamprey',
'November', 'Out of the Mouths of Babes', 'Elvers', and 'Warning'.
When not assuming brilliantly a dialect not his own, we hear the
voice of a man of culture; confident, resonant, distinctive and with
'space' around the words. He was undoubtedly a natural broadcaster.

. . . . . .

In the spring of 1955 Charles Brewer telephoned the distinguished actor Stephen Jack and asked if he knew the poetry of F.W. Harvey. As it happened, Stephen Jack had been a friend of Roy Harvey and his wife Netta for nearly twenty-five years, but had known and enjoyed Will Harvey's poetry since 1925 when an aunt had given him a copy of *Poems of Today* (Second Series). He told Charles Brewer that he found Harvey's poetry particularly attractive. 'I am so glad to hear that,' said Brewer. 'I want you to come to Bristol and take part in a programme I am preparing. I can never understand why the BBC so often waits until a man is dead before his achievements are commemorated. I want to get Harvey himself along to the studio to compère a selection of his poems. Will you be one of my readers?'

On 5 May 1955 Will Harvey, far from well and wearing only his old overcoat over a pair of pyjamas, was taken by car to the Bristol studio.

Stephen Jack still cherishes the memory of that broadcast as an experience he will never forget. Amongst the poems to be read was, of course, 'Ducks'. Harvey told Stephen Jack how he would like it read: with a slight West Country accent and with extra emphasis on syllables that rhyme with 'quack', such as 'black' and 'stack'.

The title of the programme was 'Sing a Song of Gloucestershire'. It was introduced by Charles Brewer and produced by the writer and broadcaster Robert Waller.[8] Harvey told the story of his capture by the Germans, of his two years in captivity, and of his love for his own county:

Gloucestershire was in my mind most of the time I was a prisoner – its hills, its valleys, its woodlands, the music of its streams. Yes, and I think music was what I craved most in prison (books, thank God, can be carried in the pocket). I must say the Germans were very good – they let me send home a whole book of verse I'd written, and it was published while I was still a prisoner. And many of these poems sang themselves into being in my mind.

Sporting Times and Radio Times

On Dinny Hill the daffodil
Has crowned the year's returning.
The water cool in Placket Pool
Is ruffled up and burning
In little wings of fluttering fire:
And all the heart of my desire
Is now to be in Gloucestershire.

Stephen Jack and Patricia Watson read a selection of the poems.
Charles Brewer spoke of Harvey's humour and quoted the story in
verse about how to get a struggling pig across the Minsterworth
ferry in a shaky boat ('A River, a Pig and Brains').

'In this programme', said Brewer, 'we have meandered, like its
quiet rivers, through Gloucestershire; we have travelled to France,
to Germany and to war prisons – and now we close, once again in
the green meadows of the West Country bordered by river and
forests. We have sung of the wonder of daffodils and primroses –
even the wonder of ducks and pigs.'

'Yes', said Harvey, 'wonder is the root of wisdom and the root of
poetry. It is the root of everything!'

The programme ended with Stephen Jack reading –

Quietly I Will Bide Here

Revised – From Comrades in Captivity.

Quietly I will bide here in the place where I be
Which knew my father, and his grandfather, and my dead
  brothers, and me
And bred us and fed us, and gave us pride of yeoman
  ancestry.

Men with sap of earth in their blood, and the wisdom of
  weather and wind,

Who ploughed the land to leave it better than they did
  find,
And lie stretched out down Westbury way, where the
  blossom's so kind.

And lie covered with petals from orchards that do shed
Their blooms to be a light white coverlet over the dead
Who ploughed the land in the daytime, and went well
  pleased to bed.

'Sing a Song of Gloucestershire' was broadcast on Wednesday 18
January 1956.

XXXI

Lovers Goodbye

In 1947, under the title *Gloucestershire*, Oliver & Boyd published a collection of the poems of F.W. Harvey, the first to be presented to the public for twenty years. The book contained many poems from earlier editions and some not previously published. The initiative for it no doubt came from the publisher Oliver, himself a fellow prisoner of war with Harvey.

In the introduction to *Gloucestershire*, Will's good friend and fellow POW, Hugh Walker, wrote of Harvey, 'To the core he is Gloucestershire, the poet of its people, its farms, its churches, its pubs, the Severn, Cotswolds, the Forest of Dean, and to this piety Scots and Irish, Colonials and Allies warmed as to a voice from their own home.' Harvey dedicated the book to Hugh Walker in Byron's words of dedication to John Hobhouse in *Childe Harold's Pilgrimage*, Canto the Fourth:

To one whom I have known long and accompanied far, whom I have found watchful over my sickness and kind in my sorrow, glad in my prosperity and firm in my adversity, true in counsel and trusty in peril – to a friend often tried and never found wanting.

Much of the best of Harvey was gathered between the covers of *Gloucestershire*. Here was the poet of many styles, moods, even personalities. Harvey would say to his family, 'Why do I have to be so many different people?'[1] In his poems, those people sail by, one by one: the countryman with his love of natural things, the soldier and patriot, the bucolic humorist, the lover, the religious penitent, the angry fighter against injustice, and the childlike innocent; all afloat upon an everchanging sea of dreams.

Reviewing *Gloucestershire* for the *Dean Forest Mercury* in 1948, Leonard Clark wrote, 'Harvey is, of course, the greatest and most native of Gloucestershire poets ... Harvey's poems are the true mirror of the man. They are forthright, tender, and humorous. They spring from a kindly heart, and from a deeply religious mind which has never allowed itself to be seduced by the prevailing poetic fashion.'

In his own county, Harvey is still remembered as 'The Forest Poet' and 'The Laureate of Gloucestershire', but, kindly meant as those epithets are, to leave it there is to do him an injustice. At its finest, Harvey's verse has a timeless universality which distinguishes it from the work simply of a 'local' poet. It is both approachable and popular whilst sacrificing nothing of depth. It is the work of an important poet who, had he not chosen to retreat into his forest fastness, would undoubtedly have gained even wider recognition in his lifetime.

In his preface to *Gloucestershire*, T. Hannam-Clark, an old school-friend of Will's and a prominent figure in county civic, literary and musical circles wrote: 'Though his work may not follow the fashion of the moment, let us not wait for it to be re-discovered after his death. The movement and magic of poetry are often here. Perhaps Gloucestershire made them, and Harvey only listened and wrote them down.' In a letter to Hannam-Clark, Harvey commented, 'I think it may be said of many [poems] that Gloucestershire made them, and *he* only listened and wrote them down. But I suppose that may apply to all poetry, for we are but God's ends or "Pan's pipers".'[2] This surely is the point. Successful poetry is the product of an inexplicable and mystical chemistry in which 'place' is an essential catalyst.

Writing in 1948 in *Gloucestershire Countryside* magazine, Harvey gave his own views on poetry and the public, and who today would argue with him?

The trouble is that the poet is regarded, and has come to

regard himself, as something not normal. Thus in war many people were surprised to find that poets could fight. It did not help matters much, because war itself was then considered poetic. And afterwards, when it was proved to be nothing of the sort, they told themselves that fighting was an abnormal activity. So it never occurred to them that the poet fought for precisely the reasons of other men, including even that of conscription. Peace found that fraternity once more splendidly isolated.

Yet, Chaucer could serve the King, Milton the Parliament, Herrick and Donne the Church. Poetry did not cause Villon to be any less competent in thieving. Burns could plough. Shakespeare could act, or at least hold horses' heads. All could talk, drink, fight, make love – just as though they had been really practical men.

There is in truth no foundation for the extraordinary belief that poets are other than men susceptible of life's normal calls; save this, that 'in the town-writing of the eighteenth century, ordinary life was put into verse that was not poetry, and when poetry came back with Coleridge and Shelley, it went into verse that was not always human'. That is why it is not always the poor public's fault, but the fault of those critics who have called great men gods, and blindly followed them long after their great war had been victorious. Blindly, for in opening eyes to the particular and poetic virtues of the great Romantics they blinked upon the general and human virtues of the Elizabethans. Remembering the poet in Keats, they doubted the man in Shakespeare and forgot Chaucer altogether. This was more than strange in that the wand of Keats was borrowed from the Elizabethans – those great livers of life.

And so 'poet' came to mean something both more and less than man – a wanderer with Ancient Mariners, but never with the Wife of Bath; a friend of fairies and the elfin twilight, but not of Falstaff, or of country taverns.

Intent upon hitching their wagons to stars, writers forgot that there might be something poetic in hitching them to horses: and this bred in the great a splendid inhumanity and in the little ones a pose.

'Let the poet,' said they, 'don his mantle and clear his throat before singing, for no man might sing or even whistle in shirt-sleeves.' Poor Villon, poor Herrick. High spirits were anathema, and humanity tolerated only in its purple patches, those which in his egg the legendary curate would certainly have avoided.

To healthy people food and drink have always and will always be poetic things. These were scorned by enthusiasts intent only upon the milk of Paradise skimmed by Coleridge.

It is therefore fitting that an anthology need contain Herrick's rhyme upon a little jelly sent him by a friend, Dekker's round from *The Shoemaker's Holiday*, 'London Chanticleers' out of Lamb's invaluable *Specimens*, and Calverly's 'Ode to Tobacco'.

And since even love has become a matter to avoid (though sex has not) the songs of Campion, and those of many others of Elizabethan times (including Shakespeare) shall also be found there.

Somebody, this is the plain fact, must somehow or other convince the public that poetry can and does comprehend normal joys and normal beings. Then books of verse may again be among the best sellers, and why should they not be? Then their production will no longer be what it is to-day, a class – nay worse – a money privilege. Then also will poetry be what by right it is – the joy of common men, not the little superiority of cliques.

. . . . .

'Not a day passes,' wrote Brian Waters of Harvey, 'that he is not reading one of the poets who have gone before him, not always the great names, but such immortals as Cotton, Prior or Cowper. He loves his Chaucer, but with Shakespeare he is continually returning to *A Midsummer Night's Dream*, partly because it contains some of the finest of Shakespeare's young verse, and partly because the humour of the play is akin to his own. His favourite books are those richest in humour: Chaucer, Rabelais, and Handley Cross.'[3]

In 'To The Makers of Laughter', Harvey celebrated his humorous saviours, Chaucer, Rabelais and 'the renowned sporting Citizen of St Botolph Lane and Great Coram Street', John Jorrocks, whose hunting adventures were related by Robert Surtees in *Handley Cross*.

To the Makers of Laughter

Though life with sorrow's woven,
And Hope be liar proven,
   Yet Laughter shall remain,
And, deeper than man's reason,
Acquit the earth of treason;
   The heavens of disdain.

A toast to you, old Francis
Rabelais whose spirit dances
   Like light upon the wave
Of trouble tumbling round me:
For surely had it drowned me
   But for your jesting brave!

Dan Chaucer, hail! Your dirt is
Than our soap cleaner. Surtees,
   Your clumsy English jig
Is lighter than our dancing
And Merrier. Set them prancing –
   John Jorrocks, Huntsman Pigg!

You sit there broadly grinning,
And often maybe sinning;

Yet kings o'er all the rest,
Whose solemn looks of yearning
Disgust the saints; whose learning
Is lighter than a jest.

All praise, high-hearted shakers
Of hell! – Good laughter-makers,
Earth's salt you are, and were!
Who seeing, clear, life's sorrow,
Yet mock it down, and borrow
Strong courage of despair.

The list of poets read and loved by Harvey was great, but of them all one stands out with whom his character and beliefs were most in sympathy. However, unlike the fifteenth-century poet François Villon, whose ballades and rondeaux were early models for his own, Harvey was neither vagabond nor thief of necessity. Even so, towards the end of his life, he could certainly have said with Villon:[4]

His tents, pavilions all have flown
As legacies to friend and friend;
He's kept just coppers for his own,
Which won't take very long to spend.

And in Will Harvey's poetic tribute to Villon, the 'mist of mumbled prayer' to Our Lady could well have come from his own lips.

Francois Villon

Above the angels doth Our Lady sit.
A mist of mumbled prayer comes up from earth
Floating to shape itself at length to fit
The pattern of that wish which gave it birth:
Ugly or splendid, beautiful or base,
Each naked prayer comes up and shows its face.

. . . . .

And in his favourite tavern worlds away
   Sits poet Villon, vagabond and worse,
Whose head is aching sore: as well it may,
   Within whose pocket is an empty purse.
And to forget how worldly pleasure roves,
   For joy of lovely words, and for the sake
Of one old simple woman whom he loves,
   And to forget how much his head doth ache,
While that his fellows quarrel, game, and curse,
The poet Villon sits and scribbles verse.
Anon to where the ready angels wait
   There comes a winged sound, both strong and sweet,
Like hands of desperate music at the gate
   Of heaven beating to clutch the Saviour's feet:
'What voice is this of saint or holy maid?'
   Enquireth Peter, 'Who is this who prays
Possessed of holy love and unafraid
   To seek its Source?' Our Lady, answering, says:
   'Villon the poet in a tavern lays
His gift upon the whirring wing of love,
   And this (albeit his soul is stained with sin)
Hath power to bear it to my ear above.
   Open the door of heaven and let it in!'

     . . . . .

Within a shining opalescent mist
   Of prayer has formed a face
Aged and worn, oft-times of Sorrow kissed,
Yet somewhile too of Love (a vagrant son's).
   'God pity his old mother of His grace,
And pardon (e'en as she) such erring ones.'
   Softly Our Lady said.

     . . . . .

The poet Villon staggered home to bed.

F.W. *Harvey* SOLDIER, POET

. . . . .

In his letter to Hannam-Clark dated 1947, Harvey laments that many of his poems were unpublished and that *all* were out of print. He admits that, 'Living (a rather melancholy Jacques) in the Forest during 30 years of "Peace" ("a period of cheating between two periods of fighting" – Ambrose Bierce *The Devil's Dictionary*) has strained, but I hope *not* broken what Masefield wrote of my poem [sic] *Comrades in Captivity* in two words – "Courage and Gaiety".'

Leonard Clark described his last visit to Will Harvey during those thirty years of 'Peace'.

The last time I saw Will Harvey was on a serene autumn day in his village of Yorkley. We walked in the woods during the golden afternoon, taking with us his two young children, a sparkling, excited little boy and a shy, elfin girl. The acorns and beech nuts were strewn on the sun-patched turf. A few late foxgloves still flared in the browning bracken. One or two birds sang as if summer was still lingering. At every turn we saw the grey, forest sheep nibbling the grass. The two children ran on, and in and out of the undergrowth, Will and I walked and talked and sang. We sang some of the old folk songs and Irish melodies, he with his soft pleasant baritone and me with my uncertain tenor. The evening mists began to fall, so we went back through the ghostly trees to his home and ate a late tea by the light of a fire glowing with holly logs. He sat at table with his collar off and the light of the table lamp fell on his stubby fingers. Around us were his books, the remnants of what had been once a fine library. The children were put to bed and Will's Irish wife began to tidy up for the night. He got up and fetched a copy of Shakespeare's sonnets from the top of the dresser and began to read one of them out loud. 'He's got everything,' he said, 'and they'll never better him.'

Then he closed the smooth-covered book, which had been his companion in captivity, and gave it to me. I still have it, with all his comments, scribbled over its pages. Then he quietly bowed his head, looked at me over the top of his spectacles, and put his hand on my shoulder with the words, 'Well, after all, I did write *Ducks* and they can't take *that* from me.' I said goodnight to Mrs Harvey and then Will and I went out into the darkness. I do not think we said anything else except the usual goodbyes. I got the bus which was to take me back home, and looked through the back window to catch my last sight of him. There he was, smiling at me and waving his old trilby hat. Then he faded into the Forest night. I never saw Will Harvey again.[5]

. . . . .

In 1956 a Forest of Dean newspaper invited Harvey to attend a Three Choirs Festival performance of Elgar's *The Dream of Gerontius* in Gloucester Cathedral and to write a review. Over the years a number of his articles had been published in local papers; poems too, but many of these, although charming, are little more than space-fillers.

Harvey had music in his soul, and of all music none was dearer to him than the oratorio which, in 1906, had ignited a spiritual flame that was still alight forty-five years later.

He was taken to Gloucester by car and spent the night of the concert, Tuesday 4 September, with his old friends the Friths at their home in the city. The melancholy of years seemed to have fallen away from him as, time and again on the way to the cathedral, he repeated, 'This *is* nice. Oh, this *is* nice.'[6] In his pocket was a small, red-bound edition of Newman's poem and, by courtesy of the newspaper, a one-guinea ticket for a seat in the nave. Most of his thoughts on *The Dream* for his review had been written in advance, and he needed only to add the names of the soloists, Rowland Jones, Harvey Alan and Norma Proctor; to end it he wrote:

Let us all remember this: *Great spirits were in travail to produce this work.* The poetry was written by Cardinal Newman. Elgar brooded over it for ten years before he finally laid pen to paper. The theme is commonplace, and stupendous. You, reader, and I, are (or shall be) quite personally involved, for the theme is no less than Death and the Hereafter.

As it opens a man is dying. Words and music paint the passing of spirit from flesh, which makes Gerontius to cry:

> ''Tis this strange innermost abandonment,
> (Lover of souls! great God! I look to Thee,)
> This emptying out of each constituent
> And natural force, by which I came to be.'

And so comforted by Faith and the prayers of priest and friends (church plain-song theme) Gerontius dies, and there is achieved by Elgar a marvel. He presents in sound *utter silence!* Such is his orchestral mastery.

In Part II the soul in the charge of its guardian angel (whose farewell song can never be forgotten) is taken past mocking demons into the presence of God – and here in climax upon climax arise strains of Newman's great hymn 'Praise to the holiest in the height!' and the work closes down with a seven-fold Amen.

. . . . .

Will Harvey made no more excursions from his home. Shortly after that performance of *The Dream of Gerontius* he fell ill and was put to bed. Visiting friends found him weak, but still with the old humour dancing in his eyes. As Ivon Adams took his hand, he smiled and said, 'Don't shake too hard, I'll fall to bits.' His last words to Brian Frith were, 'I have burnt myself out for Gloucestershire.'

Will Harvey – the last photograph, *c.* 1950.

F.W. *Harvey* SOLDIER, POET

Harvey died on 13 February 1957. Left among his possessions was his pocket edition of *The Dream of Gerontius*, still with the cathedral ticket tucked inside it, along with the final page cut from a copy of Kipling's *Barrack Room Ballads*:

> And only the Master shall praise us, and only the Master shall blame;
> And no one shall work for money, and no one shall work for fame,
> But each for the joy of the working, and each, in his separate star,
> Shall draw the Thing as he sees It for the God of Things as They Are!

The underlining was Will Harvey's own.

. . . . .

In his happiest days before the Great War, Will Harvey had written of Minsterworth, 'This is home . . . This is where I shall come when I die – if I go to heaven . . . The orchards are so beautiful beneath the fog to me it is like music – white soft music playing to my spirit.'

True to his wishes, Harvey's funeral was at Minsterworth. Denomination lost relevance. The congregation sang 'Praise to the Holiest' and 'Praise the Lord, ye Heavens adore Him'. In the churchyard, he was buried under the shadow of an ancient yew tree; British Legion standards were slowly dipped in a last salute, and a wreath of Flanders poppies was laid on the grave.

. . . . .

After Will Harvey's death, Mr Frank Green, a Forest of Dean schoolmaster, printed privately a small collection of the poet's

Lovers Goodbye

unpublished poems under the title *Forest Offering*, and from this little book comes a final rondeau.

Lovers goodbye! I cannot stay
To linger out a dusty day,
There is soft sleep beneath the yew
Whose lamps burn red above my head.
I need no ray to light the way –
All ways are ended. I am dead.
'Tis from the grave I call to you,
    Lovers goodbye!

Notes

F.W. Harvey's own record of the two years which he spent in German prison camps, *Comrades in Captivity* (Sidgwick & Jackson, 1920), provides the chief source material for Chapters XII to XXII of this book.

It has been possible to reconstruct a fairly detailed account of Harvey's other war experiences through the information given on the 1/5th Battalion Glosters in *The Gloucestershire Regiment in the War 1914–1918* by Everard Wyrall (Methuen, 1931), and on the 2/5th Battalion Glosters in *The Story of the 2/5th Gloucestershire Regiment 1914–1918* edited by A.F. Barnes, MC (The Crypt House Press, Gloucester, 1930). In addition, the first-hand account by the late Mr W.J. Wood, *European War with the 5th Gloucesters (at Home and Overseas from 3rd August 1914 to 21st March 1918)*, as published in *The Back Badge* and also privately printed by Mr Wood's family, has been particularly valuable. In the following notes these three references are identified by 'Wyrall', 'Barnes' or 'Wood' as appropriate.

Those of Harvey's notes or letters which are held by the Gloucestershire Record Office are indicated by the abbreviation 'G.R.O.', and those held in the Local History Collection of the Gloucester City Library by 'G.C.L.'.

I

1. Eileen Griffiths reminiscences.
2. Clark, *A Fool in the Forest*, pp. 107–108.
3. Georgina Dye reminiscences.
4. Wickerwork funnels for trapping the fish.

Notes

II

1. Eileen Griffiths and Patrick Harvey reminiscences.
2. Hurd, *The Ordeal of Ivor Gurney*, p. 13. (Herbert Howells reminiscences).
3. Patrick Harvey reminiscences.
4. Eileen Griffiths and Georgina Dye reminiscences.
5. Rossall School Register.
6. Eileen Griffiths and Patrick Harvey reminiscences.
7. Eileen Griffiths reminiscences.

III

1. Patrick Harvey reminiscences.
2. Ian Parrott, *Elgar* (The Master Musicians series).
3. Quotation from *The Dream of Gerontius*.
4. Hurd, *The Ordeal of Ivor Gurney*, p. 24.
5. Robin Haines reminiscences.
6. ibid.

IV

1. Eileen Griffiths reminiscences.
2. Patrick Harvey reminiscences.
3. ibid.
4. G.R.O.
5. Patrick Harvey reminiscences.
6. G.R.O.
7. ibid.
8. Gurney Archive, G.C.L.
9. G.R.O.
10. Eileen Griffiths reminiscences.
11. G.R.O.
12. Gurney Archive, G.C.L.

V

1. Wyrall, p. 1.
2. Wood.
3. 5th Battalion Old Comrades Association Register.
4. Eileen Griffiths reminiscences.

VI

1. Eileen Griffiths reminiscences.
2. ibid.

VII

1. Wyrall, pp. 59–60.
2. Wood.
3. Records of the 5th Battalion Old Comrades Association.
4. G.R.O.
5. Boden, *Stars in a Dark Night*.
6. Records of the 5th Battalion Old Comrades Association.
7. Barnes, p. 22.
8. Wood.

VIII

1. Wood.
2. ibid.
3. Wyrall, p. 129.
4. Wood.
5. ibid.
6. ibid.
7. Wyrall, p. 131.

IX

1. Wood.
2. Wood and Records of 5th Battalion Old Comrades Association.
3. Wood.
4. Wyrall, p. 131, and Wood.
5. Wood.
6. G.R.O.
7. Boden, *Stars in a Dark Night*.
8. Gurney Archive, G.C.L.

X

1. Wood.
2. ibid.
3. ibid.
4. Robert Herrick (1591–1674):

> *Delight in Disorder*
> A sweet disorder in the dress
> Kindle in clothes a wantonness:
> A lawn about the shoulders thrown
> Into a fine distraction:
> An erring lace which here and there
> Enthralls the crimson stomacher:
> A cuff neglectful, and thereby

Ribbons to flow confusedly:
A winning wave, deserving note,
In the tempestuous petticoat:
A careless shoe-string, in whose tie
I see a wild civility:
Do more bewitch me than when art
Is too precise in every part.

5. Eileen Griffiths and Patrick Harvey reminiscences.
6. Harvey, *Comrades in Captivity*.

XI

1. Boden, *Stars in a Dark Night*.
2. Patrick Harvey reminiscences.
3. Barnes, pp. 29–30.
4. Wyrall, pp. 60–1.

XIII

1. Gurney Archive, G.C.L.

XIX

1. Barnes, pp. 53–4.
2. ibid., p. 56.
3. ibid., pp. 58–9.
4. Gurney Archive, G.C.L.
5. ibid.
6. Barnes, p. 68.
7. Gurney Archive, G.C.L.

XXII

1. Barnes, p. 136.

XXIII

1. Gurney Archive, G.C.L.
2. ibid.
3. ibid.
4. ibid.
5. ibid.
6. ibid.
7. ibid.

XXIV

1. Gurney Archive, G.C.L.
2. Letter in possession of Patrick Harvey.
3. G.R.O.
4. ibid.
5. ibid.
6. ibid.
7. ibid.
8. Georgina Dye reminiscences.
9. Gurney Archive, G.C.L.
10. Brian Frith reminiscences.
11. G.R.O.

XXV

1. G.R.O.
2. ibid.
3. Eileen Griffiths reminiscences.
4. Brian Frith reminiscences.
5. Hurd, *The Ordeal of Ivor Gurney*, Chapter XV.
6. Brian Frith reminiscences.
7. Eileen Griffiths reminiscences.

XXVI

1. Clark, *A Fool in the Forest*, pp. 102–103.
2. *A Sprig of Shamrock* was published by Novello & Co.
3. R. George Thomas, Introduction to *The Collected Poems of Edward Thomas*.

4.
The Wife of Usher's Well
There lived a wife at Usher's Well,
And a wealthy wife was she;
She had three stout and stalwart sons,
And sent them o'er the sea.

They had not been a week from her,
A week but barely one,
When word came to the mother herself
That her three sons were gone.

They had not been a week from her,
A week but barely three,
When word came to the mother herself
That her sons she'd never see.

'I wish the wind may never cease,
    Nor fishes in the flood,
Till my three sons come home to me
    In earthly flesh and blood!'

It fell about the Martinmas,
    When nights are long and dark,
The mother's three sons they all came home,
    And their hats were of birch bark.

It neither grew in marsh or trench
    Nor yet in any ditch;
But at the gates of Paradise
    That birch grew fair and rich.

'Blow up the fire, my maidens!
    Bring water from the well!
For all my house shall feast this night,
    Since my three sons are well.'

And she has made to them a bed,
    She's made it large and wide;
And she's taken her mantle her about,
    Sat down at the bed-side.

Up then crew the red, red cock,
    And up and crew the gray;
The eldest to the youngest said,
    ''Tis time we were away.'

The cock he had not crowed but once,
    And clapped his wings at dawn,
When the youngest to the eldest said,
    'Brother, we must be gone.

'The cock doth crow, the light doth grow,
    The channelling worm doth chide;
If we be missed out of our place,
    A sore pain we must abide.'

'Lie still, lie still, but a little wee while,
    Lie still but if we may,
If our mother should miss us when she wakes,
    She will go mad ere day.'

'Fare ye well, my mother dear!
Farewell to barn and byre!
And fare ye well, the bonny lass
That kindles my mother's fire.'

XXVII

1. G.R.O.

XXVIII

1. G.R.O.
2. ibid.
3. Obituary, Forest of Dean Newspaper.
4. Clark, *A Fool in the Forest*, pp. 108–109.
5. Ivon Adams reminiscences.
6. W.B. Cornock, letter (1957) to *The Citizen*.
7. From F.W. Harvey's poem 'A Song of Gloucestershire'.
8. Clark, *A Fool in the Forest*, p. 108.
9. Robin Haines reminiscences.
10. Brian Frith reminiscences.

XXIX

1. Waters, *The Forest of Dean*, pp. 107–108.
2. Ivon Adams reminiscences.
3. ibid.
4. Eileen Griffiths reminiscences.
5. Brian Frith reminiscences.
6. Waters, *The Forest of Dean*, pp. 159–61.
7. Brian Frith reminiscences.

XXX

1. G.R.O.
2. Arthur Rigsby reminiscences.
3. Clark, *A Fool in the Forest*, pp. 106–107.
4. Gloucester City Cricket Club 150th Anniversary Souvenir Book.
5. ibid.
6. Hart, *101 Not Out (The Story of Lydney Cricket Club 1862– 1963)*.
7. ibid.
8. Stephen Jack and Robert Waller reminiscences.

XXXI

1. Patrick Harvey reminiscences.
2. G.C.L.

Notes

3. Waters, *The Forest of Dean*, p. 108.
4. Villon, 'The Legacy (Le Lais)', last four lines of stanza 40.
5. Clark, *A Fool in the Forest*, pp. 110–11.
6. Brian Frith reminiscences.

Bibliography

Published works by F.W. Harvey

A Gloucestershire Lad at Home and Abroad (Sidgwick & Jackson, 1916; re-issued McLean, 1988).
Gloucestershire Friends (Sidgwick & Jackson, 1917).
Ducks and other Verses (Sidgwick & Jackson, 1919).
Comrades in Captivity (Sidgwick & Jackson, 1920).
Farewell (Sidgwick & Jackson, 1921).
September and other Poems (Sidgwick & Jackson, 1925).
In Pillowell Woods and other Poems (Frank Harris, 1926).
The Augustan Books of English Poetry – F.W. Harvey (Editor Humbert Wolfe, 1926).
Gloucestershire (Oliver & Boyd, 1947).
A Forest Offering (Frank Green).
F.W. Harvey, Collected Poems 1912–1957 (McLean, 1983)

Other Works

Boden, Anthony (Ed.), *Stars in a Dark Night; The Letters of Ivor Gurney to the Chapman Family* (Alan Sutton, 1986).
Brewer, Charles, *The Spice of Variety* (Muller, 1948).
Clark, Leonard, *A Fool in the Forest* (Dobson, 1965; paperback edition 1977). Extracts reproduced in *The Listener*.
Hurd, Michael, *The Ordeal of Ivor Gurney* (Oxford University Press, 1978; paperback edition 1984).
Kavanagh, P.J. (Ed.), *Collected Poems of Ivor Gurney* (Oxford

University Press, 1982; paperback edition (revised), 1984).

Thornton, R.K.R. (Ed.), *Ivor Gurney War: Letters* (Carcanet Press, 1983; paperback edition, Hogarth Press, 1984).

Thornton, R.K.R. (Ed.), *Ivor Gurney, Severn & Somme and War's Embers* (Carcanet Press, 1987).

Townsend, Frances, *The Laureate of Gloucestershire* (Radcliffe Press, 1988).

Waters, Brian, *The Forest of Dean* (J.M. Dent, 1951).

Acknowledgements

I am indebted to F.W. Harvey's daughter, Eileen Griffiths, for her advice, support and friendship; to his son, Patrick, for making available to me the poet's own copies of his published works, for granting permission to quote his father's poems and prose, for reading my typescript and making many valuable suggestions; and to Harvey's niece, Rosemary Passmore-Rowe, who not only typed out my manuscript but also provided encouragement, hospitality and many of the Harvey family photographs in this book. To these three, to the poet's cousin and close contemporary, Georgina Dye (née Harvey), and to Ivon Adams, Richard Carder, Brian Frith, Robin Haines, Phyllida Harris, Stephen Jack, John Marchant, Arthur Rigby, Robert Waller and David Wyatt, I am grateful for their time and reminiscences.

I would like to thank Mr R.A.J. Bell, Mr D.A.L. Thomas and Mr R.C. Aldridge for their memories of Lydney cricket, and Dr Cyril Hart for permission to quote from his history of the Lydney Cricket Club, *101 Not Out*; Mr Frank Hubber, secretary of the Gloucester County Hockey Association; and Mr Terry Smith, secretary of the Gloucester City Cricket Club.

I must also thank Lt.-Col. H.L.T. Radice, archivist of the Gloucestershire Regimental Museum; Mrs Jill Voyce, Mrs Barbara Griffith and the staff of the Local History Dept., Gloucester City Library; Mr D.J.H. Smith, the County Archivist, and the staff of the Gloucestershire Record Office; Mrs Ann Smith for giving me access to her late father Mr Walter Deavin's records of the 5th Battalion Glosters Old Comrades Association; and Mrs Monica

Acknowledgements

Adams for allowing me to borrow her late father Mr W.J. Wood's personal account of his service with the 5th Battalion Glosters between 1914 and 1918.

I am grateful to the headmaster of King's School, Gloucester, The Revd Alan Charters, and the Vicemaster of Rossall School, Mr Peter Bennett, for details from old school registers, and to Mr and Mrs F.S. Stait for allowing me the opportunity to visit their home, The Redlands, Minsterworth.

The photograph on page 16 is published by courtesy of Gloucester City Library; those on pages 69, 70, 94, 100, 116, 160, 200, 203 and 206, The Imperial War Museum; that on page 301, *The Citizen*, Gloucester; and that on page 117, Camera Press, London. The drawing on page 270 is by L. Schiele.

The extracts from Leonard Clark's *A Fool in the Forest* and Brian Waters's *The Forest of Dean* are reproduced by courtesy of Dobson Books Ltd. and J.M. Dent & Sons Ltd. respectively. Quotations from the letters and poems of Ivor Gurney are published with the kind permission of the Trustee of the Ivor Gurney Estate, Mr Robin Haines.

A.N.B.
January 1988